Michael Roberts is Robert Rich Professor of Latin, Wesleyan University.

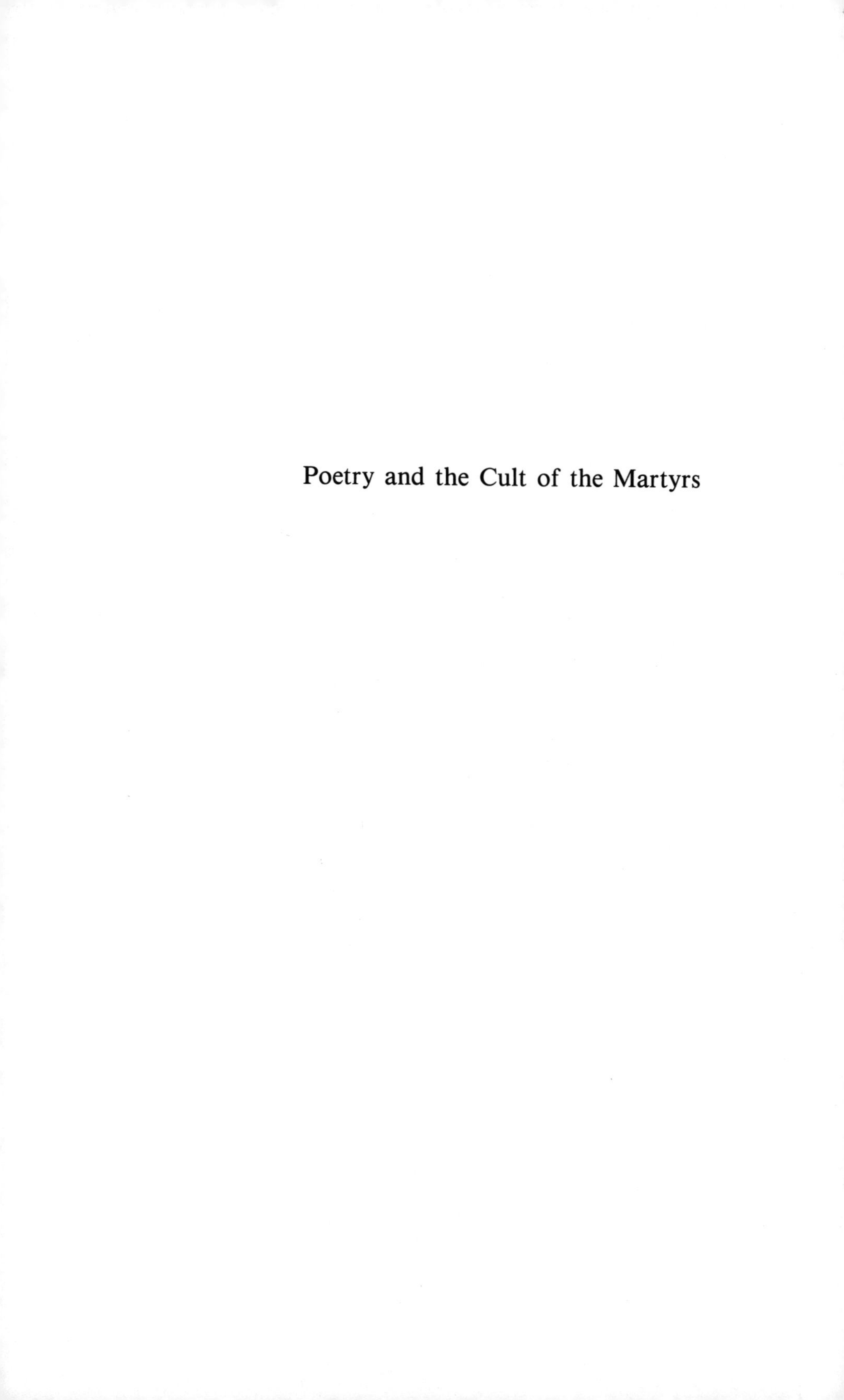

Poetry and the Cult of the Martyrs

RECENTIORES: LATER LATIN TEXTS AND CONTEXTS

Poetry and the Cult of the Martyrs: The Liber Peristephanon *of Prudentius*
by Michael Roberts

Poetry and the Cult of the Martyrs

The *Liber Peristephanon* of Prudentius

Michael Roberts

Ann Arbor

The University of Michigan Press

Published in the United States of America by
The University of Michigan Press
Manufactured in the United States of America

1996 1995 1994 1993 4 3 2 1

A CIP catalogue record for this book is available from the British Library.

Library of Congress Cataloging-in-Publication Data

Roberts, Michael John, 1947–
Poetry and the cult of the martyrs : the Liber peristephanon of Prudentius / Michael Roberts.
p. cm. — (Recentiores : Later Latin Texts and Contexts)
Includes bibliographical references and index.
ISBN 0-472-10449-7 (alk. paper)
1. Prudentius, b. 348. Peristephanon. 2. Christian poetry, Latin—History and criticism. 3. Christian martyrs in literature. 4. Rome in literature. I. Title. II. Series.
PA6648.P6P477 1993
272′.1′0922—dc20 93-31245
CIP

The Latin text of Prudentius' *Peristephanon* may be consulted and downloaded free of charge from the Center for Computer Analysis of Texts of the University of Pennsylvania. To obtain text, you may reach the server ccat.sas.upenn.edu through either the anonymous ftp or gopher programs: change to the directory /pub/recentiores. In case of difficulty, consult jod@ccat.sas.upenn.edu. Because of copyright restrictions the text posted is an older, out-of-copyright edition with a few corrections and does not match at all points the critical editions quoted in Professor Roberts' study. While this access cannot be guaranteed for the life of acid-free paper, it is our intention to make these texts available indefinitely.

Acknowledgments

Most of the research for this book and a good deal of the writing was done during 1987 when I held a Fellowship from the American Council of Learned Societies. I am grateful to that body for its financial support, without which this book would still be some way from completion. Portions of the text have been delivered as papers at the 23d International Congress on Medieval Studies, Kalamazoo, Michigan, May 5–8, 1988, at the Annual Meeting of the American Philological Association, San Francisco, California, December 27–30, 1990, to the literary seminar of the Cambridge University Faculty of Classics, and at the Universities of Sheffield and Nottingham. I am grateful, too, to Professor John Petruccione of the Catholic University of America, who read and provided helpful commentary on chapters three and four of this book, and to my former colleagues at Wesleyan University, Professors Stephen Dyson and David Konstan, who have been generous with advice and encouragement. I owe a debt to Professor Eleanor Leach of Indiana University, whose NEH Summer Seminar at the American Academy in Rome in 1986 encouraged me to think about the relations among literature, art, architecture, and urban space. Chapter five of this book is a first small payback on the perspectives developed in that seminar. Thanks are due as well to two Wesleyan students, Sarah (Holly) Campbell Ambler and Andrew Goldman, who worked with me on topics related to the subject of the book, and who helped me refine my own thinking on martyrs and the martyr cult; to the staff of the Olin Library at Wesleyan University, especially of the Inter-Library Loan Department, who kept me amply supplied with the books and articles I needed for my research; and to the editor of this series, Professor James J. O'Donnell, and the staff of the University of Michigan Press, especially Ellen Bauerle, for the care they took in bringing this book to publication. Most of all, though, my loving gratitude to my family, Linda and Christopher, and my parents, Betty and Harry Roberts, to whom this book is dedicated (to my father *in memoriam*).

Contents

Abbreviations

Journal abbreviations follow the usage of *L'année philologique*. In addition to the journal abbreviations, the following abbreviations are used for reference works and text series and collections.

CCL — *Corpus Christianorum, Series Latina.*

CSEL — *Corpus Scriptorum Ecclesiasticorum Latinorum.*

Daremberg-Saglio — Ch. Daremberg and Edm. Saglio, eds., *Dictionnaire des antiquités grecques et romaines d'après les textes et les monuments.* 5 vols. in 9 (Paris, 1877–1919).

DThC — *Dictionnaire de théologie catholique,* eds. A. Vacant and E. Mangenot. 15 vols. (Paris, 1924–50).

Halm — Karl von Halm, *Rhetores Latini Minores* (Leipzig, 1863).

ICUR — *Inscriptiones Christianae Urbis Romae, Nova Series,* eds. A. Silvagni, A. Ferrua, and D. Mazzoleni. Vols. 1– (Rome, 1922–).

ILCV — *Inscriptiones Latinae Christianae Veteres,* ed. E. Diehl. 3 vols. (Berlin, 1925–31).

MA 1 — *Miscellanea Agostiniana: Testi e studi, pubblicati a cura dell'ordine eremitano di S. Agostino.* Vol. 1 *Sancti Augusti Sermones post Maurinos Reperti,* ed. G. Morin (Rome, 1930).

Mai — *Novae Patrum Bibliothecae Tomus Primus, Continens Novos ex Codicibus Vaticanis Sermones,* ed. A. Mai (Rome, 1852).

OLD — *Oxford Latin Dictionary.*

PG — *Patrologia Graeca,* ed. J.P. Migne.

PL	*Patrologia Latina,* ed. J.P. Migne.
RlAC	*Reallexikon für Antike und Christentum.*
ThLL	*Thesaurus Linguae Latinae.*

The poems of Prudentius are abbreviated as follows:

A.	*Apotheosis*
C.	*Cathemerinon*
C. Symm.	*Contra Symmachum*
D.	*Dittochaeon*
H.	*Hamartigenia*
Pe.	*Peristephanon*
Pr.	*Praefatio*
Ps.	*Psychomachia*

Unless otherwise indicated, I cite the poems of Prudentius in the most recent edition, of Maurice P. Cunningham (see Text Editions Used), though with some changes in punctuation. The translations contained in the text are my own unless otherwise indicated, and they are intended to represent accurately the sense of the Latin without aspiring to any literary finish. In translating Prudentius I have regularly consulted the versions of Lavarenne and Thomson.

Introduction

In the late fourth century the cult of the martyrs, along with the growth of asceticism and monasticism, was transforming the intellectual and spiritual horizons of the Christian world. Paulinus of Nola, looking out at the Roman Empire from the shrine of Felix, saw a world throughout which God "had dispersed the memorials of the holy like the lights of stars in the night sky."[1] While Paulinus himself composed in his *Natalicia* poems for the annual festival of the local Campanian saint, St. Felix, the Spanish poet Prudentius ranged more widely over the Roman Christian world. His martyr poems, collected in the *Peristephanon,* embrace a variety of saints and locations. Their subjects extend from the major figures of the Roman church, Saints Peter, Paul, and Lawrence, to the local saints of the Spanish city of Calahorra, Emeterius and Chelidonius. They include deacons and bishops, soldiers and teachers, Christian virgins and a reformed schismatic. The legends Prudentius recounts and his manner of telling vary a great deal, but he always brings to his poems the perspective of a sophisticated devotee of the late fourth century. From the *Peristephanon* a reader can understand something of what the cult of the martyrs meant to a Christian of late antiquity.

Little is known of Prudentius as a historical figure. Like Theodosius, the emperor he served as a high official of the imperial bureaucracy, he was from Spain, born in 348, almost certainly in Calahorra in the province of Tarraconensis.[2] The main source for his biography is the

1. Paulinus, *C.* 19.18–19: *sic sacra disposuit terris monumenta piorum, / sparsit ut astrorum nocturno lumina caelo.*

2. Italo Lana, *Due capitoli Prudenziani: la biografia, la cronologia delle opere, la poetica,* Verba Seniorum, Collana di testi e studi patristici n.s. 2 (Rome, 1962), 1–43, is fundamental for Prudentius' biography; for Prudentius' birthplace see also José Madoz, "Valerian, Bishop of Calahorra," in Joseph M.F. Marique, ed., *Leaders of Iberean Chris-*

Praefatio he wrote to introduce a collected edition of his poetry. In it Prudentius speaks of turning from a flourishing secular career to one given over to the service and celebration of God.[3] In so doing he followed the same course as his slightly younger contemporary, Paulinus of Nola, who had similarly withdrawn from public life to devote himself to a form of Christian asceticism, initially on his estates in Spain in 389, but finally settling at the shrine of Felix of Nola in 396.[4] Prudentius lacks the close personal identification with a particular saint that Paulinus enjoyed at Nola. It is more likely, as Fontaine suggests,[5] that he withdrew to his own estate and there devoted himself to the life of the *conversus*, the lay convert to an ascetic way of life, as Paulinus' correspondent, Sulpicius Severus, did at Primuliacum or others were later to do in the disturbed conditions of early fifth-century Gaul.[6] In Prudentius' case his new life took the form of composing poetry, in the meters of classical Latin, to the greater glory of God.[7] We know next to nothing of

---

tianity, 50–650 A.D. (Boston, 1962), 157–63. Anne-Marie Palmer, *Prudentius on the Martyrs* (Oxford, 1989), 23–24, 29–30, building on Jill Harries, "Prudentius and Theodosius," *Latomus* 43 (1984): 69–73, has recently challenged some of Lana's chronology. Jacques Fontaine, "Société et culture chrétiennes sur l'aire circumpyrénéene au siècle de Théodose," *Bulletin de littérature ecclésiastique de Toulouse* (1974): 241–82 (= *Études sur la poésie latine tardive d'Ausone à Prudence* [Paris, 1980], 267–308), and *Naissance de la poésie dans l'occident chrétien: Esquisse d'une histoire de la poésie latine chrétienne du IIIe au VIe siècle* (Paris, 1981), 143–60, is especially useful for the Spanish cultural milieu in which Prudentius was writing and the similarities between the manners of life and poetic projects of Paulinus and Prudentius.

3. The *Praefatio* has been the subject of much critical attention and presents real difficulties of interpretation. Palmer, *Prudentius on the Martyrs,* 6–20 has a valuable discussion; for a literary treatment, see also Charles Witke, *Numen Litterarum: The Old and the New in Latin Poetry from Constantine to Gregory the Great,* Mittellateinische Studien und Texte 5 (Leiden,1971), 106–13.

4. For a chronology of Paulinus' career see Pierre Fabre, *Essai sur la chronologie de l'oeuvre de Saint Paulin de Nole,* Publications de la Faculté des lettres de l'Université de Strasbourg 109 (Paris, 1948), 137.

5. Fontaine, *Naissance de la poésie,* 145–47.

6. For the life of the *conversus* see Élie Griffe, *La Gaule chrétienne à l'époque romaine,* vol. 3 (Paris, 1965),128–48—other examples of *conversi* include Paulinus of Pella and the anonymous author of the *Carmen Ad Uxorem,* attributed to Prosper of Aquitaine. Villas of the Hispano-Roman aristocracy have been discovered in some numbers in the province of Tarraconensis (S.J. Keay, *Roman Spain* [Berkeley, 1988] 191–96).

7. It is a matter of debate whether all Prudentius' surviving poetry was written after his withdrawal from public life, which must have taken place some time in the 390s. Palmer, *Prudentius on the Martyrs,* 23–31, believes, for instance, that some of the poems of the *Peristephanon* were written for Spanish patrons before Prudentius left the imperial court. The more traditional view, which relies on a literal reading of *Praefatio* 31–42, imagines that all Prudentius' major works (i.e., possibly excluding the *Dittochaeon*) were

Prudentius' life after his withdrawal to Spain, though it is possible that the journey to Rome described in *Pe.* 9, 11, and 12 was taken during this period.[8] His writings make up an ambitious corpus of didactic (the *Apotheosis, Hamartigenia,* and *Contra Symmachum*), epic (the *Psychomachia*), and lyric poetry (the *Cathemerinon* and *Peristephanon*).[9] Prudentius' aspirations were high: nothing less than to give expression in his poetry to the mental, spiritual, and material world of the late fourth-century Roman Christian.[10]

The *Peristephanon* occupies a special place in this poetic project because of the central importance of the cult of the martyrs in late antique Christianity.[11] But, despite the importance of the *Peristephanon,* few scholars have studied the collection until the last few years, when this situation has changed.[12] Two books have appeared. In the first, *Prudentius*

---

produced in a burst of creative activity in the years after his withdrawal from public life and before 404/405 (the date of the *Praefatio*), though Danuta Shanzer, "Allegory and Reality: Spes, Victoria and the Date of Prudentius' *Psychomachia,*" *ICS* 14 (1989): 347–63, has recently argued for a later date for the *Psychomachia,* a poem that is not unambiguously referred to in the *Praefatio.* The analogy with Paulinus, whose surviving Christian poetry was all written after his conversion to asceticism, gives some support to the traditional position. If Prudentius wrote poetry before his withdrawal, which is very likely, it may well have been secular in content, as Paulinus' was.

8. Lana, *Due capitoli Prudenziani,* 23–24, who dates the journey to 401. But not all scholars accept this date; see Harries, "Prudentius and Theodosius," 71–73, with the counterarguments of Danuta Shanzer, "The Date and Composition of Prudentius' *Contra Orationem Symmachi Libri,*" *RFIC* 117 (1989): 461, n.1, Palmer, *Prudentius on the Martyrs,* 29–31, and my chapter 5.

9. The *Apotheosis* and *Hamartigenia* are antiheretical in content, the *Contra Symmachum* antipagan apologetic. For uncertainty about the date of the *Psychomachia* see above, n.7. The *Dittochaeon,* a sequence of epigrams on biblical themes perhaps to accompany paintings, is not mentioned in the *Praefatio.*

10. See Wolfgang Kirsch, *Die lateinische Versepik des 4. Jahrhunderts,* Schriften zur Geschichte und Kultur der Antike 28, (Berlin, 1989), 238–44.

11. Robert Markus, *The End of Ancient Christianity* (Cambridge, 1990) emphasizes the key role of the cult of the martyrs in the growth of asceticism and beginnings of monasticism, the organization of the liturgy, and the sacralization of place and time: "The image of the martyr . . . came to stand for the epitome of all the aspirations of fourth-century Christians. The central importance of the martyr in the Christian cult as it took shape in the post-Constantinian world was one of the most powerful of pressures behind the wide appeal of asceticism and monasticism" (72); "At mass he [the individual Christian] was united with them [the martyrs], caught up in the perpetual legacy which embraced him within the society of the angels and saints" (99); "The cement that most potently aggregated the community of the saints straddling heaven and earth was the martyrs' relics" (146).

12. In her review (at *CR* 34 [1984]: 327) of Henke's monograph on *Peristephanon* 10, *Studien zum Romanushymnus des Prudentius,* Europäische Hochschulschriften, Reihe 15, Klassische Sprachen und Literaturen 27 (Frankfurt am Main, 1983) Palmer wrote "the

on the Martyrs, Anne-Marie Palmer offers a thorough introduction to the *Peristephanon,* discussing the form and purpose of the martyr poems, their sources and their imitation of pagan poets. Within traditional categories of philological research, she has written a book that lays the groundwork for appreciation of the poetic achievement of the *Peristephanon.* A second book, by Martha Malamud, *A Poetics of Transformation: Prudentius and Classical Mythology,* begins the project left largely untouched by Palmer, the literary interpretation of the *Peristephanon.* She discusses three poems, those on Saints Hippolytus, Cyprian, and Agnes (*Pe.* 11, 13, and 14). Although I share a few common perceptions with Malamud, otherwise our approaches and results are significantly different. She raises important questions, especially in her discussion of *Pe.* 14, but her interpretations, I believe, are often open to question because of insufficient concern for context, both cultural—i.e., the social, religious, and intellectual climate of late antiquity—and textual—i.e., the thematic structures of the specific poems under discussion and of the collection as a whole. I read Prudentius' poetry as an expression of devotion to the martyrs, while Malamud is inclined to see evidence, especially in the use of classical allusion, of an attitude critical toward that devotion.[13]

Peristephanon Liber in general has been neglected as the subject of detailed consideration." English-speaking scholars have preferred to write about the *Psychomachia*: Macklin Smith, *Prudentius' Psychomachia: A Reexamination* (Princeton, 1976), Kenneth R. Haworth, *Deified Virtues, Demonic Vices and Descriptive Allegory in Prudentius' Psychomachia* (Amsterdam, 1980), S. Georgia Nugent, *Allegory and Poetics: The Structure and Imagery of Prudentius' Psychomachia,* Studien zur klassischen Philologie 14 (Frankfurt am Main, 1985); on the continent of Europe the *Cathemerinon* has been most studied: Marion M. van Assendelft, *Sol Ecce Surgit Igneus: A Commentary on the Morning and Evening Hymns of Prudentius (Cathemerinon 1,2,5, and 6)* (Groningen, 1976), Willy Evenepoel, *Zakelijke en literaire Onderzoekingen betreffende het Liber Cathemerinon van Aurelius Prudentius Clemens,* Verhandelingen van de k. Academie voor Wetenschappen, Letteren en schone Kunsten van België, Klasse der Letteren, Jaarg. 41, 1979, nr. 91 (Brussels, 1979), Jean-Louis Charlet, *La création poétique dans le Cathemerinon de Prudence* (Paris, 1982).

13. In a review of Palmer's book (*CPh* 86 [1991]: 266) Malamud criticizes Palmer's view that "the 'complete cultural context' of the fourth century is readily available to us" on the grounds that "our conception of the fourth-century culture may be inadequate and shaped by scholarly and cultural bias." Though I would question Palmer's use of the word "complete," and while I share some of Malamud's reservations about the conservative, nontheoretical basis of Palmer's work, Malamud is too sweeping in her dismissal of the possibility of reading Prudentius against the fourth-century cultural context. The poems can be read with understanding only in the context of late antique culture, particularly of the cult of the martyrs. We must beware of modern cultural presuppositions, or for

Prudentius' poetry is a product of its time. By the end of the fourth century neither the classical nor the Christian is an unproblematic category, to be directly identified with the values of Augustan poetry or the early Church, as they are understood by modern scholars.[14] Roman secular tradition and the evolving teaching and institutional forms of the newly victorious Church interact in a variety of social, architectural, and literary expressions. As the conversion of Roman aristocrats gained momentum toward the end of the fourth century, new cultural forms emerged that combined Roman and Christian elements in a stable synthesis. Prudentius' poetry shares these qualities. As an educated Roman he was entirely familiar with the pagan authors[15] and by his secular career he was fully imbued with the ideology of the Roman Empire. At the same time, he showed himself devoted to the ideals of ascetic Christianity by adopting the life of a *conversus,* while his relations with Bishop Valerian of Calahorra[16] demonstrate that he remained in touch with the episcopal hierarchy of his native Spain.

The *Peristephanon* presents a double challenge to the reader. Firstly, it is a collection of hagiographical texts, from a single hand and from a period that is pivotal in the growth and institutionalization of the cult of the martyrs. The poems must be set in the context of late antique spirituality and especially of the special sanctity of a martyr's shrine. Worshippers at such shrines felt themselves removed from normal everyday circumstances of time and place. In a city like Rome, whose ceremonies are described by Prudentius in *Pe.* 11 and 12, civic institutions, the organization of the liturgy, and architectural forms reinforce the worshipper's sense of the sacred. The emphasis on liturgy, ceremony,

that matter of privileging classical literature and the discourse of classical texts, but that does not mean we have any alternative to approaching these poems in terms of their own and other contemporary discursive patterns and practices, however flawed our understanding of these may be.

Specific points of disgreement between Malamud's book and mine relate mainly to *Pe.* 13 (see chap. 4 of my study). Otherwise there is very little overlap. Both of us treat *Pe.* 11, but from different perspectives: Malamud is interested in Prudentius' attitude to the classical myth of Hippolytus, I in the experience of the poet/devotee (and implicitly reader), as described in that poem. (*Pe.* 14 does not play a large role in my study.)

14. See Michael Roberts, *The Jeweled Style: Poetry and Poetics in Late Antiquity* (Ithaca, N.Y.,1989), 3–5.

15. Among the pagan authors the poets Virgil, Horace, Ovid, Lucan, and Seneca are most important for the *Peristephanon.* See Palmer, *Prudentius on the Martyrs,* 98–204, and ch.1, n.60.

16. *Pe.* 11. 1–2, 231–46.

and the organization of space is prominent in the *Peristephanon,* accurately reflecting the spatio-temporal environment of late fourth-century Christianity.[17]

But the reader must also take into account its qualities as poetry; Prudentius' narratives cannot simply be treated as just one more, if usually the first surviving, version of a saint's legend. In the collection form and content—poetry and the martyrs—are thoroughly interconnected. Prudentius is a gifted poet; his poems are self-conscious attempts to give appropriate expression to the new conceptual world of the martyrs. Poetry offers special advantages for such a project. Even though prose and poetry were less clearly distinguished in late antiquity than in the classical period, the poet still enjoyed significantly greater freedom in his choice of vocabulary and intertextual allusion.[18] Prudentius makes good use of this freedom. In particular, he is sensitive to the consequences

17. Peter Brown, *The Cult of the Saints: Its Rise and Function in Latin Christianity,* Haskell Lectures on History of Religions n.s. 2 (Chicago,1981), explores the social organization and systems of belief that inform the cult of the saints. I have used Brown's characterization of the cult and of the special sanctity accorded to a saint's shrine in my reading of the *Peristephanon.* Jean-Louis Charlet, "Prière et poésie: La sanctification du temps dans le *Cathemerinon* de Prudence," in *Le temps chrétien de la fin de l'antiquité au moyen âge, IIIe-XIIIe siècles,* Colloques internationaux du Centre National de la Recherche Scientifique 604 (Paris, 1984), 391–97, has applied successfully the concepts of sacred space and time to the *Cathemerinon*; Pietri's monumental study of Christian Rome, *Roma Christiana: Recherches sur l'Église de Rome, son organisation, sa politique, son idéologie, de Miltiade à Sixte III (331–440),* Bibliothèque des écoles françaises d'Athènes et de Rome 224, 2 vols. (Rome, 1976), 1: 575–624, pursues the same concepts in an urban setting; see also "Les origines du culte des martyrs (d'après un ouvrage récent)," *RAC* 60 (1984): 300–304. For a recent treatment of sacred space in late antique Christianity and its relation to pagan and Jewish traditions see Sabine MacCormack, "Loca Sancta: The Organization of Sacred Topography in Late Antiquity," in Robert Ousterhout, ed., *The Blessings of Pilgrimage* (Urbana, Ill., 1990), 7–40.

18. Poetic license, according to ancient theory, involved a wider choice of vocabulary and greater freedom in the use of tropes and figures, especially figures of diction, than was normal in prose (Michael Roberts, "The Prologue to Avitus' *De Spiritalis Historiae Gestis*: Christian Poetry and Poetic License," *Traditio* 36 [1980]: 400–402). Modern theoreticians also speak of the poetic as constituted by the formal properties of language, for instance Roman Jakobson, "Closing Statement: Linguistics and Poetics," in Thomas A. Seboek, ed., *Style in Language* (New York, 1960), 356–59 (= *Language in Literature,* edd. Krystyna Pomorska and Stephen Rudy [Cambridge, Mass., 1987], 69–72), who defines the poetic function of language as involving "a set toward the message," that is, it is characterized by the reiteration of equivalent compositional units that draws attention to the form of the message rather than its referential content. For some criticisms of the limitations of Jakobson's approach, especially as a critical tool, see Jonathan Culler, *Structuralist Poetics: Structuralism, Linguistics, and the Study of Literature* (Ithaca, N.Y., 1975), 55–74.

of word selection. Tropes, particularly allegory, metaphor, metonymy, and synecdoche, play a key role in the *Peristephanon.*[19] They provide the equivalent in language to the blurring of categories experienced by a devotee at a martyr's shrine and thereby render Prudentius' account of Church history and cult practice sacred.

In what follows, then, I have set myself a number of questions to answer: preeminently, what is the relation between martyr text and martyr cult in the *Peristephanon*? how are the beliefs about and the practice of the martyr cult embodied in the text? what is Prudentius' poetics of the martyr text? In a first chapter I relate the poems to the growth and practice of the cult of the martyrs in the fourth century, taking as the starting point the work of Peter Brown. How does Prudentius himself present the history and theology of the cult of the martyrs, especially with regard to the coordinates of time and place? From there I propose, in the second chapter, a simple typology of the Prudentian martyr text: the basic martyr narrative in the *Peristephanon* has a three-part structure, characterized by a contest-victory sequence, which is capable of repetition at various levels of integration. I have tried to be systematic and show how this simple narrative skeleton can be fleshed out, paying special attention to the choice of language as an expression of the poetic in Prudentius' martyr texts and of his spiritual vision. From this elaboration on the three basic stages of passion, subsequent chapters focus in more detail on specific poems, exploring how controlling figures (the metaphors of prison and the road to heaven) and thematic concerns (the episcopal martyr) shape the basic martyr narrative as a vehicle for theological and ideological speculation, and for reflection on the nature of the martyr text. This process culminates in the three pilgrimage poems discussed in chapter five. In them Prudentius maps out a synoptic view of the cult of the martyrs, taking Rome as the model for the entire Christian Roman world. The three poems cover many dimensions of the cult of the martyrs: the sacralization of place and time; the experience of individual and communal veneration; the place of text, image, and architecture in the cult of the saints; and the relationship between the cult of the martyrs and the ideology of Christian Rome. In adopting this cumulative sequence I intend to do justice to the two inseparable aspects of the *Peristephanon,*

19. For the importance of allegory in Prudentius see Reinhart Herzog, *Die allegorische Dichtkunst des Prudentius,* Zetemata 42 (Munich, 1966), 13–41. It is a limitation of both recent studies of the *Peristephanon* in English that the allegorical and figurative dimensions of Prudentius' martyr poetry receive relatively little attention.

as poetry and as a document of the cult of the martyrs, and thereby to begin to plot the poetics of the Prudentian martyr text. Though chapters will in the main be organized thematically, the book is also a series of readings of the individual poems—or most of them—that make up the *Peristephanon.*

Finally, Prudentius, in his attitude to the martyrs and his high level of literary education, is a product of his class and time. But he is also an individual and a creative poet. Although the poems are probably intended for a readership of highly educated Christian aristocrats and church-people,[20] they share a large element of personal meditation and speculation on the meaning of the cult of the martyrs to the individual and to Roman society as a whole. Despite their similar hagiographic subject matter, Paulinus of Nola's poems for the annual festival of Felix are far more public and performance-oriented in tone. Moreover, the *Peristephanon* is the product of a very specific period in late Roman history, that is, the decade or so of Christian Roman triumphalism that extends between the anti-pagan legislation and military victories of Theodosius and the tremendous shocks administered to the Roman world by the Germanic invasion of Gaul on the last day of 406, and by the subsequent fall of Rome to Alaric's Visigoths in 410. It is a measure of Prudentius' achievement that the poems of the *Peristephanon* continued to be valued as an expression of devotion to the martyrs long after the collapse of the imperial structure that provides the informing context for his view of the martyrs.[21]

---

20. See Palmer, *Prudentius on the Martyrs,* 86–97.

21. For instance, with some modifications, in the Mozarabic hymnal (Palmer, *Prudentius on the Martyrs,* 67–68, 85–86). Venantius Fortunatus, in the sixth century, selects Prudentius' martyr poems for special mention: *martyribusque piis sacra haec donaria mittens / prudens prudenter Prudentius immolat actus* (*V. Mart.* 1.18–19). Prudentius' poetry was known to Anglo-Latin authors and in the Carolingian period (Eugene Bartlett Vest, *Prudentius in the Middle Ages* [Ph.D. diss., Harvard University, 1932], 78–110). From the ninth century on manuscripts or references in manuscript catalogs become frequent (Bergman, edition of Prudentius, 19–20, Max and Karl Manitius, *Antiker Autoren in mittelalterlichen Bibliothekskatalogen,* Beiheft zum Zentralblatt für Bibliothekswesen 67 [Leipzig, 1935], 213–20).

CHAPTER 1

The Martyr in Time and Place

The *Peristephanon* contains fourteen poems, varying in length from a brief eighteen-line epigram (*Pe.* 8) to the 1140 iambic trimeters of *Pe.* 10. This last poem is anomalous in the collection, both in its length and because it is the only one dedicated to an Eastern saint, Romanus of Antioch. It is not included among the poems of the *Peristephanon* in the manuscripts and stands apart from the rest of the collection in containing a large element of antipagan apologetic.[1] *Pe.* 2 and 5, both in iambic dimeters and both dedicated to martyr-deacons, Lawrence of Rome and Vincent of Saragossa and Valencia, are the longest of the poems securely attributed to the *Peristephanon* (584 and 576 lines respectively), but most of the poems are substantially shorter: *Pe.* 11 is the next longest (246 lines). Martyrs from Spain and Rome figure most prominently in the collection: from Spain, Emeterius and Chelidonius (*Pe.* 1 and 8), Eulalia of Mérida (*Pe.* 3), the eighteen martyrs of Saragossa (*Pe.* 4), and Fructuosus of Tarragona (*Pe.* 6); from Rome, Lawrence (*Pe.* 2), Hippolytus (*Pe.* 11), Peter and Paul (*Pe.* 12), and Agnes (*Pe.* 14). (Cassian of Imola, an Italian saint, is the subject of *Pe.* 9; Quirinus [*Pe.* 7] suffered martyrdom in Siscia, Cyprian [*Pe.* 13] in Carthage.) The choice of subjects reflects Prudentius' Hispano-Roman perspective; but despite common threads running through the collection and some thematic asso-

1. *Pe.* 10 is always placed before or after, never among, the other poems of the *Peristephanon,* and is given the title *Romanus, Contra Gentiles* in the manuscripts. Anne-Marie Palmer, *Prudentius on the Martyrs* (Oxford, 1989), 87–88, argues that the poems of the *Peristephanon* were not collected by Prudentius, but compiled, in varying orders, by subsequent editors and copyists. She is, therefore, reluctant to see *Pe.* 10 as exceptional.

ciation of individual poems, no overall structuring principle is detectable. In the choice and treatment of saints' legends, in form and especially meter, Prudentius strives for variety.[2]

The majority of the poems in the *Peristephanon* display a tripartite structure, with a central narrative framed by introductory and concluding passages that give details of the location of the martyr's passion, the nature of his cult, and, especially in the conclusion, an exhortation to sing the praises of the saint and a prayer for his or her favor, either to the community as a whole or the poet in particular.[3] In the case of *Peristephanon* 1, the introduction, and especially the first 21 verses (22–24 are transitional), establish a series of oppositions that are significant not just for this poem but for the collection as a whole. They set the terms for Prudentius' and the reader's understanding of the cult of the martyrs, and make *Peristephanon* 1 an appropriate introduction to the collection.[4]

Scripta sunt caelo duorum martyrum vocabula,
aureis quae Christus illic adnotavit litteris;
sanguinis notis eadem scripta terris tradidit.

2. Only two meters are repeated in the collection, iambic dimeters (*Pe.* 2 and 5) and elegiac couplets (*Pe.* 8 and 11). Prudentius has close affinities with Ausonius in his metrical versatility (Jean-Louis Charlet, *L'influence d'Ausone sur la poésie de Prudence* [Aix en Provence, 1980], 85–119). On the heterogeneity of the *Peristephanon* see Palmer, *Prudentius on the Martyrs,* 75–87. For common threads and the grouping of individual poems see chapter 5, *init.*; for attempts to detect a structure to the collection as a whole, note 4 in this chapter.

3. For the tripartite structure of all but *Pe.* 4, 7, 8, 11, and 12, see Jean-Louis Charlet, *La création poétique dans le Cathemerinon de Prudence* (Paris, 1982), 63. Willy Schetter, "Prudentius, *Peristephanon* 8," *Hermes* 110 (1982): 110–17, detects a three-part structure in *Pe.* 8, but according to different criteria from those observed in the majority of the poems in the collection.

4. Cunningham, in his edition of Prudentius, xxvi, attributes no authority to the *ordo communis* of the *Peristephanon,* which goes back (with the exception of the position of *Pe.* 10) to the Aldine edition of 1501 and to the family of manuscripts designated by Bergman (xxix–xxx of his edition) as Aa. On the other hand, the sequence 1–9, 11–14 is not without manuscript support, and seemed persuasive to Ludwig in his thematic and metrical study of the structure of the collection, with the minor exception of his proposed transposition of *Pe.* 4 after *Pe.* 7 (Walther Ludwig, "Die christliche Dichtung des Prudentius und die Transformation der klassischen Gattung," in *Christianisme et formes littéraires de l'antiquité tardive en occident,* Fondation Hardt, Entretiens 23 [Vandoeuvres, 1977], 321–39). See also Italo Lana, *Due capitoli Prudenziani: la biografia, la cronologia delle opere, la poetica,* Verba Seniorum, Collana di testi e studi patristici, n.s. 2 (Rome, 1962), 24, n. 101. Certainly *Pe.* 1 is not out of place at the head of the collection.

Pollet hoc felix per orbem terra Hibera stemmate;
hic locus dignus tenendis ossibus visus deo,
qui beatorum pudicus esset hospes corporum.

Hic calentes hausit undas caede tinctus duplici;
inlitas cruore sancto nunc harenas incolae
confrequentant obsecrantes voce, votis, munere.

Exteri nec non et orbis huc colonus advenit,
fama nam terras in omnes percucurrit proditrix
hic patronos esse mundi quos precantes ambiant.

Nemo puras hic rogando frustra congessit preces;
laetus hinc tersis revertit supplicator fletibus
omne quod iustum poposcit inpetratum sentiens.

Tanta pro nostris periclis cura suffragantium est;
non sinunt inane ut ullus voce murmur fuderit;
audiunt statimque ad aurem regis aeterni ferunt.

Inde larga fonte ab ipso dona terris influunt,
supplicum causas petitis quae medellis inrigant,
nil suis bonus negavit Christus umquam testibus.

(*Pe.* 1.1–21)

[Two martyrs' names are enrolled in heaven; there Christ registered them in golden letters, but on earth he recorded the names in figures of blood. With this glory the happy land of Spain wins renown throughout the world; this spot seemed worthy to God to hold their bones, and be the chaste host of their blessed bodies. This place, wet with double bloodshed, drank in the warm flood, where now the inhabitants throng to the sands, dyed with holy blood, to worship with voice, vows, and offerings. Here too has come the dweller in the outside world, for fame has crossed to every land to tell the tale that here are universal patrons to be beseeched in prayer. No one here, if his requests are honorable, has prayed in vain, but the suppliant returns joyfully from here, his tears wiped away, in the knowledge that every proper request he made has been fulfilled. Such is the concern for our perils of these protectors; they allow no whisper to be uttered idly but no sooner is it heard than carried to the hearing

> of the Eternal King. From these, gifts flow in abundance over the earth from the true source, and bathe suppliants' sufferings in the healing they sought for; Christ in his mercy has never denied anything to his martyrs.]

The two martyrs mentioned in the first line of the poem are identified in manuscript superscriptions as Saints Emeterius and Chelidonius, of Prudentius' native Calahorra. Their cult is localized at a particular place on earth, *hic locus* (5)—a formula common in inscriptions from martyrs' shrines and repeated elsewhere in the *Peristephanon*.[5] The importance of physical location is emphasized in stanzas 2 through 5 by the repetition *hic* (5) . . . *hic* (7) . . . *huc* (10) . . . *hic* (13) . . . *hinc* (14). Beyond this, Prudentius situates the martyrs' shrine in space and time by a series of oppositions between the past of the historical passions and the present cult of the martyrs, between the immediate location of the shrine and the larger world outside (4–5, 10–12) and between the realms of heaven and earth (1–3, 18–19). Although the *locus* of worship is terrestrial, here and now (7–8), the cult of the martyrs has the power to subvert and briefly to abolish the distinctions that define it.

"The graves of the saints," in Peter Brown's words, "were privileged places, where the contrasted poles of Heaven and Earth met."[6] The intercession of the saints carried petitioners' prayers from earth to heaven, to "the hearing of the Eternal King" (18), from whom all blessings flowed; the role of the martyrs was to activate the flood by the special force of their advocacy. While the tomb is a single *locus,* the gifts to be derived from prayer there are universal (*terris,* 19). Geographically distinct lands are united by the universality of the saints' reputation (11), and by the diverse peoples' presence in pilgrimage at their shrine (10). Time is spanned by the survival of the record of the martyrdom, in the "figures of blood" (3), a text that supplies the absence of a formal written Passion

5. See Peter Brown, *The Cult of the Saints: Its Rise and Function in Latin Christianity,* Haskell Lectures on History of Religions, n.s. 2 (Chicago, 1981), 86 and Yvette Duval, *Loca Sanctorum Africae: Le culte des martyrs en Afrique du IVe au VIIe siècle,* Collection de l'école française de Rome 58 (Rome, 1982), 2: 468 on the frequency of this formula in North African inscriptions. For variations on the formula in Prudentius, see *Pe.* 8.1 and 15, and 11.175. For the authority of the manuscript *inscriptiones* to the *Peristephanon* see Maurice Cunningham, "The Nature and Purpose of the *Peristephanon* of Prudentius," *Sacris Erudiri* 14 (1963): 40 and Palmer, *Prudentius on the Martyrs,* 75–83. They are already present in the earliest (sixth century) manuscripts of Prudentius.

6. Brown, *Cult of the Saints,* 3.

as a representation of the act of sacrifice from which the power of the martyr derives. The ambiguity of the phrase *inlitas cruore sancto . . . harenas* in line 8 is no accident. Does it mean "sands were dyed with holy blood" in the past, or "still dyed with holy blood," i.e., the stain remains? In practice both. At the grave of the martyr the temporal distinction of then, the time of the passion, and now is abolished. The remarkable preservation of the blood of the martyrs can be paralleled by Ambrose's account of the discovery of the bodies of Saints Gervasius and Protasius. "Their tomb," he tells us, "was wet with blood, the characters of their triumphant blood were visible"—*cruoris triumphalis notae,* a striking parallel with *sanguinis notis* of *Pe.* 1.3—"their relics were found inviolate in their due place and order, the head torn from the shoulders."[7] The still-wet blood is the text of the passion and embodies its continuity in the present. The written text of a martyrdom, whether in Prudentius' poems or in a prose narrative, inherits this capacity to make present events from the past. At a martyr's shrine worshippers find themselves freed from the normal constraints of time and place, at a spot where heaven and earth meet, in the presence of a throng of fellow worshippers, native and foreign, and surrounded by evidence of a past event continually called up afresh by the proximity of the saints' physical remains and the indelible stain of blood that constitutes the minimal Passion text.

This sense of the graves of the saints as beyond time still presupposes and coexists with the historical sense of time as a process of change. The fullest treatment of the origins of a martyr's cult in Prudentius is in *Pe.* 5, devoted to the Spanish saint, Vincent. There Vincent is briefly released from prison after terrible tortures in order that, as his persecutor says, "he should be renewed and provide fresh nourishment for his punishments" (*ut pastum novum / poenis refectus praebeat,* 5.331–32). In fact, nothing of the sort happens. Vincent dies before the torturers can get at him again. But in the narrative space thus created Prudentius gives an account of the attentions the martyr receives from the Christian community (*turba fidelis,* 334) as he lies at the threshold between life and death, heaven and earth.

Coire toto ex oppido
turbam fidelem cerneres,

7. *Sanguine tumulus madet, apparent cruoris triumphalis notae, inviolatae reliquiae loco suo et ordine repertae, avulsum humeris caput, Ep.* 77 (22). 12 (*CSEL* 82.134.124–26). See also Paulinus, *V. Ambrosii* 32 (*PL* 14.40D), on the invention of Nazarius.

mollire praefultum torum,
siccare cruda vulnera.

Ille ungularum duplices
sulcos pererrat osculis,
hic purpurantem corporis
gaudet cruorem lambere.

Plerique vestem linteam
stillante tingunt sanguine,
tutamen ut sacrum suis
domi reservent posteris.

(5.333–44)

[You could see the throng of the faithful come together from the whole city, set up a soft bed, and dry his raw wounds. One ranges with kisses over the double furrows left by the claws, another rejoices to lick the red blood from his body. Many dip linen garments in the drops of blood so as to preserve in their homes a sacred source of protection for their descendants.]

In this passage prostration over Vincent's body prefigures the veneration that the martyr will receive at his grave from his posthumous devotees.[8] As the martyr's followers collect *linteamina* dipped in the saint's blood to serve as domestic tokens of his protection, so it was the custom of Prudentius' day to create "contact relics" by letting down pieces of cloth, *brandea,* through holes in the top of a martyr's tomb in order to impregnate them with the holy power present there.[9] Prudentius' account of Vincent's death bed anticipates and legitimizes this practice.

The first critical point in the establishment of a martyr's cult comes with the disposal of his or her mortal remains. It is vital that the Christian community keep those remains in its control. The persecuting magistrate,

8. Kissing the threshold of Lawrence's basilica/Hippolytus' tomb: 2.520 and 11.193; prostration at the tomb: 2.533–35, 5.563–64, 9.5, 9.99–100, 11.178.

9. For arrangements made for such *brandea* at the basilicas of Lawrence and the Apostles at Rome, see Charles Pietri, *Roma Christiana: Recherches sur l'Église de Rome, son organisation, sa politique, son idéologie, de Miltiade à Sixte III (331–440),* Bibliothèque des Écoles françaises d'Athènes et de Rome 224 (Rome, 1976), 1:39, 67, and 518.

Datian in Vincent's case, intervenes himself in an attempt to prevent the *plebs gregalis* (5.391—the pagan equivalent of *turba fidelis*) from collecting the martyr's bones and setting up a monument to the martyr (*titulum martyris,* 5.392). He first exposes the body so that it will be eaten by wild animals and birds of prey; then, when this is unsuccessful, he attempts to sink the body at sea. Again he fails. In the case of the martyrdom of Bishop Fructuosus and his deacons Augurius and Eulogius at Saragossa, the devotion of the Christians themselves presents a greater threat to the integrity of a martyr's remains. Christian piety (*fratrum tantus amor*) impels individuals to carry home portions of the bones and ashes of the saints (6.133–35).[10] Only the intervention of the saints themselves, a vision of three men clothed in snow-white garments, secures the restoration of the relics and their common burial, "enclosed in a hollow marble tomb" (*cavoque claudi / . . . marmore,* 6.140–41).

The distinction between contact relics (which might legitimately provide protection to the individual household) and bodily parts or their metonymic equivalents, bones and ashes, is present once more in the account of Hippolytus' martyrdom. The saint's dismembered corpse is recovered in its entirety and a place (*locus*) laid out for his tomb (11.147–51).[11] But the *palliola* and *spongia* that individuals have soaked in the martyr's blood (11.141–44) have no role to play in restoring the saint's corporal integrity, and are therefore available to individual devotees.[12]

Prudentius' attitude to relics reflects issues surrounding the cult of the martyrs in his own day. When he insists that the remains of a saint be available to the community as a whole, rather than distributed among individuals, he is following the practice of Ambrose, who built the Basilica Ambrosiana to house the newly discovered relics of Gervasius and Protasius.[13] Fear of what Brown calls "the privatization of the holy,"

10. *Fratrum tantus amor domum referre / sanctorum cinerum dicata dona / aut gestare sinu fidele pignus.* For the same episode in the pre-Prudentian prose Passion, see Hippolyte Delehaye, *Les origines du culte des martyrs,* Subsidia hagiographica 20 (Brussels, 1933), 66–67.

11. *Cumque recensetis constaret partibus ille / corporis integri qui fuerat numerus, / nec purgata aliquid deberent avia toto / ex homine extersis frondibus et scopulis, / metando eligitur tumulo locus.*

12. Contrast the emphasis on the corporality of Hippolytus' physical remains (*sacro quidquam de corpore,* 145; *corporis integri numerus,* 148; *toto / ex homine,* 149–50) with the more insubstantial nature of the rain of bloody dew, which has to be absorbed from the earth on which it has fallen.

13. Ambrose, *Ep.* 77 (22); Ernst Dassmann, "Ambrosius und die Märtyrer," *JbAC* 18 (1975): 49–68, especially 52–57; Brown, *Cult of the Saints,* 36–37.

that is, the appropriation of holy relics and of preferred access to the saint by persons of special distinction, exercised Augustine in his *De cura pro mortuis gerenda.*[14] By keeping all the bodily remains of a saint under the control of the whole Christian community of a town or city, as represented by its bishop, and by making them available to all through the building of a public basilica, episcopal and ecclesiastical authority was strengthened and the private appropriation of relics avoided.

Where the practice of Rome and that of Ambrose in Milan differ, however, Prudentius accords with the Roman example. Ambrose's attitude to the translation and distribution of relics was more liberal than that of the Roman church; in this respect he was closer to the eastern pattern. Not only was he involved in the translation of relics (Gervasius and Protasius in Milan, Vitalis and Agricola in Bologna) but he also freely distributed the relics of these saints among Western churches, thus creating a network of relationships throughout the world of Western Christendom, with Milan at its center.[15] Rome, on the other hand, refused to circulate *reliquiae* of its own martyrs, permitting only the creation of contact relics for distribution to other churches. The Basilica Romana in Milan may have been founded to contain such objects, contact relics probably of the Apostles.[16] Prudentius carefully distinguishes in the Vincent and Hippolytus poems between the bodily remains of the martyr and the private acquisition of materials soaked in his blood, and insists that the integrity of the former be maintained. In this it looks as though he is inspired by Roman practice. If so, these two martyr accounts serve to legitimate later fourth-century Roman practice by reading it back into the founding legends of the martyr cult. Given the important, even exemplary, role that Roman martyrs play in the *Peristephanon,* it is not surprising that in the question of relics, too, Prudentius follows Roman practice.

The development of the martyr cult in the fourth century can be

14. Brown, *Cult of the Saints,* 34.

15. For Ambrose's more liberal attitude to relics, see Delehaye, *Les origines du culte,* 65–66 and Dassmann, "Ambrosius," 54. Recipients included Victricius of Rouen, Gaudentius of Brescia, and Paulinus of Nola (Nikolaus Gussone, "Adventus-Zeremoniell und Translation von Reliquien: Victricius von Rouen, De laude sanctorum," *Frühmittelalterliche Studien* 10[1976]: 126–27). In some cases, these may have been contact relics, or other noncorporeal remains, but if Paulinus of Nola's language is to be pressed (*Ep.* 32.17; 292.21 *ossa piorum*) physical remains also may have been sent.

16. For the Roman refusal to circulate bodily relics, see Pietri, *Roma Christiana,* 606–7; the Roman attitude is in accordance with imperial legislation (*CTh* 9.17.6 and 7). For the Basilica Romana at Milan, see Dassmann, "Ambrosius," 53.

traced in its architecture, from unassuming memoria to lavish basilica. Prudentius' poem on the Spanish martyr Vincent records a critical stage in this development; the end of the persecutions and the new favor Christianity enjoyed in the Roman empire (*subactis hostibus / iam pace iustis reddita,* 5.513–14) meant a new era in Christian architecture. A simple *tumulus* no longer suffices for the saint; an altar is set up over the blessed remains (5.514–15). Synonymic repetition emphasizes the importance of this act for the cult of the martyrs. Three words are used for altar (*altar, sacrarium, ara,* 515, 517–18), and we are told three times that the bones are situated below the altar (*subiecta . . . sacrario, / imamque ad aram condita / . . . subter hauriunt,* 517–20). In other poems, too, though not as emphatically, burial beneath the altar is described.[17] Devotion at the saint's tomb is simultaneously worship at the "altar dedicated to God" (*ara dicata Deo,* 11.170; cf. 9.99–100 *conplector tumulum . . . / altar tepescit ore*). In the act of worship and veneration, Christ, martyrs, and supplicant join together in a single devotional act. The privilege of burial under the altar is granted to the martyrs because of the similarity between their passions and the Passion of Christ.[18] Their presence at the eucharistic table incorporates them into liturgical ritual and makes their presence available to all.[19] Their position below the altar—whence, according to Prudentius, "they drink in the breath of heavenly bounty" (*caelestis auram muneris,* 5.519), i.e., at one level, the offerings of the mass[20]—is a visual reminder in the layout of the church of the privileged access that the saints enjoy to God, access that devotees, in their prayers, hope will be turned to their own or their community's interests.

Prudentius' poem about the Roman martyr Hippolytus (*Pe.* 11) illus-

---

17. 3.212, 4.189, 9.100, 11.170 and 175.

18. So Ambrose, *Ep.* 77 (22). 13 (*CSEL* 82.3; 134.132–35): *Succedant victimae triumphales in locum ubi Christus est hostia. Sed ille super altare qui pro omnibus passus est, isti sub altari qui illius redempti sunt passione*; also Simone Deléani-Nigoul, "L'utilisation des modèles bibliques du martyre par les écrivains du IIIe siècle," in Jacques Fontaine and Charles Pietri, edd., *Le monde latin antique et la Bible,* Bible de tous les temps 2 (Paris, 1985), 334–36. The association of martyr's bones and altar was not original to Ambrose, though the incorporation of the cult of the martyrs into the sacramental and liturgical life of the community was more of an innovation; see F. Homes Dudden, *The Life and Times of Ambrose* (Oxford, 1935), 302, and Dassmann, "Ambrosius," 54–55, who corrects Dudden in some respects.

19. Dassmann, "Ambrosius," 55.

20. Lavarenne, in his edition and commentary (90), interprets this phrase as a periphrasis for the mass (but see my discussion in the Conclusion).

trates a further stage in the development of the martyr cult. The crowds flocking to the festival of Hippolytus become too large to be accommodated in the original crypt, and a lavish new basilica must be built adjacent to his underground resting place (11.211–18).[21] Although Prudentius attributes the increased popularity of the saints to Christian piety, he has in mind also the role of Damasus (bishop of Rome, 366–84) as promoter of the martyrs. During his papacy Damasus set up epigrams around Rome where Christian martyrs were buried, thereby providing a circuit and centers of devotion for pilgrims to Rome. Hippolytus was among the saints commemorated by the pope. Prudentius' poem begins with a reference to the many sepulchral inscriptions in the city and contains a number of textual parallels with Damasus' own epigrams, in particular with that to Hippolytus.[22] The pope's activities will have popularized Hippolytus and other Roman martyrs.

Parallels to Prudentius' accounts of the cult of Vincent and Hippolytus can be traced in the history of the shrine of St. Felix at Nola. Like Vincent, Felix first receives a simple tomb (*pauper tumulus, C.* 18.169) during the time of the persecutions; as with Hippolytus the spectacular growth of Felix' cult is promoted by an influential member of the elite (Paulinus of Nola, settled at Nola 395) and necessitates the building of a new, much larger basilica near the saint's tomb. There are, it is true, differences. Felix' body is not buried under the altar of the pre-Paulinian basilica, although when Paulinus erects his new structure (completed by January 404) he follows the Ambrosian model by dedicating it with relics of apostles and martyrs.[23] But the pattern of devel-

21. For the actual description of basilicas in *Pe.* 11 and 12, see chapter 5.

22. Damasus, *Epigrams* 16 and 35; *Pe.* 11.11–12, 19–20, 28–30. There is perhaps an implied model in Damasus' activities for Valerian, bishop of Calahorra, the addressee of the poem. For Damasus' involvement with the *memoria* of Hippolytus, see Pietri, *Roma Christiana,* 545–46.

23. Paulinus, *C.* 27.403–39; *Ep.* 32.17; 292.21–293.4. The list consists of John the Baptist, the saints Andrew, Thomas, and Luke, and the martyrs Vitalis, Agricola, Proculus, Euphemia, and Nazarius. The relics of Nazarius were supplied to Paulinus by Ambrose (*C.* 27.436–37). The pre-Paulinian so-called Basilica Vetus at Cimitile is dated by Pasquale Testini, "Note per servire allo studio del complesso paleocristiano di S. Felice a Cimitile (Nola)," *MEFR(A)* 97 (1985): 349, in his survey of the archaeological evidence for the site to within a decade or so of the middle of the fourth century (i.e., pre-Ambrosian). Victor Saxer, *Morts, martyrs, reliques en Afrique chrétienne aux premiers siècles: Les témoignages de Tertullien, Cyprien, et Augustin à la lumière de l'archéologie africaine,* Théologie historique 55 (Paris, 1980), 301–2, quotes the cases of Tebessa and Tipasa in North Africa as examples of the monumentalization of the cult of the martyrs in the Theodosian period, i.e., the replacement of small *memoriae* by large-scale basilicas.

opment is sufficiently close to suggest that the picture derived from *Pe.* 5 and 11 has a certain general validity.

Most of the evidence for the growth of the cult of the martyrs is set in past time in the narrative sections of the poems. But we have seen how past event and present worship are frequently blended so that the narrative shares the ability of the devotional moment itself to transcend temporal distinctions. In the following chapter I shall discuss the narrative sections of the *Peristephanon,* and in particular the central accounts of the martyrdoms, from this perspective. But in the cult of the martyrs spatial distinctions, too, failed to hold; worshippers experienced the martyr's grave as meeting place of heaven and earth, and looked to the martyr as a powerful intermediary between the two realms. How does Prudentius understand the martyr's role as intermediary? The evidence is largely in the introductory and concluding passages to the poems, describing contemporary worship at the martyrs' shrines.

Pe. 1, the text with which this chapter began, lays out the basic syntax of a petition at a martyr's grave, from prayers (9, 12–13) to fulfillment of those prayers (15, 19–21). No prayer, if it is pure (*puras,* 13; cf. *iustum,* 15), goes unanswered—the principle is repeated three times for emphasis (15, 17, 21). Prayer may be accompanied by a vow or offering (*votis, munere,* 9), but only the prayer is indispensable to the act of communication.[24] Prayer, however, is offered in a particular state of emotional excitement: *Pe.* 1 refers to the tears of the suppliant (14); often worshippers prostrate themselves at the tomb to express their complete dependency on the power of the martyr.[25] And when the petitioner realizes that his wish has been achieved (*inpetratum sentiens,* 15) his tears turn to joy (*laetus . . . tersis . . . fletibus,* 14). The movement from grief to joy is a common one in Christian poetry.[26] In *Pe.* 1 the joy of the individual suppliant in the achievement of his petition finds an echo at the end of the poem in the joyful chorus of wives and mothers celebrating the saints' festival (*sit dies haec festa nobis, sit sacratum*

24. For the role of prayer, see 2.536 (accompanied by tears and prostration) and 565–67, 5.546 and 557 (prostration), 9.97, 11.175 and 178 (prostration). *Pe.* 14.6 stresses the importance of the spirit in which a request is made (*puro ac fideli pectore*), 9.95 that a prayer be *iustum vel amabile.*

25. For the prostration, see nn. 6 and 22. Prudentius describes most fully the poet's own response to martyrs' graves: 9.5–8, 9.99–102, 11.178–82.

26. Michael Roberts, *Biblical Epic and Rhetorical Paraphrase in Late Antiquity,* ARCA. Classical and Medieval Texts, Papers and Monographs 16 (Liverpool, 1985), 170, 176–77, 220, 226.

gaudium, 120). The communal thanksgiving of that day reenacts and expresses gratitude for the joyful experiences of individual petitioners throughout the year.[27]

The martyr is able to mediate the act of communication between heaven and earth because of his or her ability to move rapidly between the two realms, if not to be in two places at once. In *Pe.* 1 (18) the martyrs hear a petition and immediately carry it to the ear of God. Their *praesentia* is sought on earth to hear prayers (*adesto nunc,* 5.545; cf. *ceu praesto semper adsies,* 2.569), but they are expected to plead for suppliants before God the Father's throne (*orator ad thronum patris,* 5.548). Burial of the martyr's bones under the altar expresses this special status for Prudentius; the poet moves easily between Eulalia's bones under the altar and the martyr herself "at the feet of God" (*ossibus altar et inpositum, / illa dei sita sub pedibus,* 3.212–13). Although it is possible to assimilate the heaven : earth opposition to that between body and spirit, as Prudentius does in *Pe.* 2.551–52 (*est aula nam duplex tibi, / hic corporis, mentis polo*), this is another distinction liable to be subverted by the language of the martyr cult. Thus, as Lavarenne points out,[28] when the martyrs of Saragossa are described (*Pe.* 4.189) as "buried under the eternal altar" (*sub altari sita sempiterno*), the phrase refers simultaneously to their mortal remains, situated under the altar, and to the place the saints occupy in heaven, an allusion to Rev. 6:9.

In his theology of the martyrs Prudentius is always careful to emphasize that Christ is the source of the blessings that the martyrs secure for their devotees (1.19 and 21; cf. 6.114 and 161). The martyr's role is to secure a gift (*munus, donum*) from Christ for the individual or community. Ultimately the benefits that derive from this relationship are God's doing (*opus*)—the martyrs are only the intermediaries who bring petitions before him.[29] While God may employ the martyrs to distribute his gifts, their role in this part of the transaction is less firmly established. Augustine hesitates, attributing the communication of benefits to the martyrs or the angels, or to both. But on the role of the martyr as go-between, representing human devotees in heaven, he has no reservations. Even if the angels are responsible for bringing the gifts thus acquired

27. For the association of *gaudium* and the festivals of the martyrs, see *Pe.* 11.211 and 12.1–3.

28. Lavarenne (edition of *Peristephanon*) 221.

29. Ambrose, *Ep.* 77 (22). 18: *Unius etiam potentiam laudamus auctoris nec interest utrum opus sit an munus, cum et muneretur in opere et operetur in munere* (*CSEL* 82.3; 137.185–87).

to earth, the role of the martyrs is secure in their "prayers (advocacy) and requests, if not by their personal agency" (*orantibus tantum et inpetrantibus non etiam operantibus*).[30] The language used of gifts (*dona*) and of making and securing requests (*inpetro*) finds an echo in Prudentius. In *Pe.* 1, for instance, the devotee realizes his request has been granted (*inpetratum,* 15); because of the martyr's intercession, gifts (*dona,* 19) flow over the earth.[31]

Prudentius, like Augustine, insists upon the martyrs' role as transmitters of petitioners' requests from earth to heaven. In late antiquity this transaction was viewed in terms of the relationship between patron and client, a relationship deeply rooted in Roman society.[32] Prudentius describes Saints Emeterius and Chelidonius, in *Pe.* 1, as *patroni* (12), and uses the word (of the martyrs) in three other passages (2.579, 6.145, 13.106). The usage was comparatively recent. It is first found in Ambrose's *Homilies on Luke* (A.D. 378) and subsequently in his letter to his sister Marcellina on the discovery of the relics of Gervasius and Protasius, and it receives a full elaboration only in the writings of Prudentius' contemporary, Paulinus of Nola,[33] who began writing his *Natalicia* in 395 and may have had some influence on the Spanish poet.[34] The literary texts undoubtedly represent a widespread perception of the role of the saint in the Christian community as a whole.[35]

Beyond the word *patronus* Prudentius' language reflects how fully he

30. *De Civ. Dei* 22.9 (*CSEL* 40.2; 613.13–14).

31. See also 2.566 (*inpetratum*), 9.98 (*ratas*), 13.106 (*dona*).

32. Alba Maria Orselli, *L'idea e il culto del santo patrono cittadino nella letteratura latina cristiana,* Università degli studi di Bologna, Facoltà di lettere e filosofia, Studi e ricerche, n.s. 12 (Bologna, 1965); Brown, *Cult of the Saints,* 38–41, 45–47, 60–68.

33. Ambrose, *Expos. Evang. Luc. 10.12* (*CSEL* 32.4; 460.6 *patroni*) and *Ep.* 77 (22). 10 (*CSEL* 82.3; 132.101 *patrocinia*), and 11 (133.119–20 *patroni*); for these passages and a pair of other references in Ambrose, see Jean Doignon, "Perspectives ambrosiennes: SS. Gervais et Protais, génies de Milan," *REAug* 2 (1956): 325–27, Orselli, *L'idea e il culto del santo patrono,* 39–45. Paulinus, *C.* 13.27; 14.105; 18.5, 111, 269; 19.296, 371; 20.11, 17, 254, 278; 21.6, 27, 186, 344, 754, 756, 793; 23.99, 202, 214, 318; 26.64, 211, 232; 27.136, 147, 198, 502; 29.8, 23; *Ep.* 5.15 (34.21), 12.11 (83.9), cf. Orselli 46–51 and 75–77. The word is applied to nonmartyred saints once each by Gaudentius of Brescia (*Sermo* 21; *PL* 20. 1002A) and Sulpicius Severus (*Ep.* 2.8), Orselli 45–46.

34. For the influence of Paulinus on Prudentius, see Salvatore Costanza, "Rapporti letterari tra Paolino e Prudenzio," *Atti del Convegno XXXI Cinquantenario della morte di S. Paolino di Nola (431–1981),* Nola 20–21 March 1982 (Rome, 1983), 25–65, and Jean-Louis Charlet, "Prudence et la Bible," *RecAug* 18 (1983): 121–25.

35. Augustine's reference to the popular expectation that Saints Peter, Paul, and Lawrence would protect Rome against the Visigoths (*Sermo* 296.5.6; *PL* 38.1355) is revealing in this respect.

viewed the role of the martyr in terms of the patron-client relationship. Orselli has identified two distinguishable, though complementary and overlapping, functions of the patron, as *advocatus* and *defensor.*[36] When Augustus describes the martyrs as *orantes et inpetrantes* he has the former function in mind. The martyr is an *orator,* in the Christian sense, who repeats the suppliants' prayers before God; but he is also an orator in the traditional Roman sense, representing a client's interest in the courts. Roman social institutions are replicated in heaven, but in such a way that heaven and earth are united in a single social fabric through the mediation of the martyrs. The court at which the orator speaks is both the court of a supreme ruler and a court of law; God or Christ, before whom he speaks, combines the roles of *aeternus rex* (*Pe.* 1.18) and *sempiternus iudex* (*Pe.* 10.1133). The martyr's advocacy of a suppliant's case before Christ the Judge prefigures the ability to intervene in the individual Christian's interests even after death—hence the popularity of burial *ad sanctos*—and ultimately to speak for that devotee before the divine *iudex* at the Last Judgment.[37] When Prudentius addresses St. Vincent as "effective spokesman for our crimes before the throne of the Father" (*nostri reatus efficax / orator ad thronum patris,* 5.547–48), the context is of a wish that the saint be present here and now to hear our prayers (*adesto nunc et percipe / voces precantum supplices,* 5.545–46). But the language calls to mind the Last Judgment and evokes the transtemporal patronage of the martyr, before a court that is both a court of law (*reatus*) and of a ruler (*thronum*). Once more in the act of devotion temporal distinctions are collapsed, and the eschatological future is present in the here and now.[38]

The noun *praesidium* (6.146), and the verbs *sospitant* (1.117), *servat* (4.2), and *protegit* (14.5) evoke the martyrs as defenders of a larger community, the role that receives most emphasis in Ambrose's letter to Marcellina. The verb *fovet* is a functional synonym for other verbs of "protection," but it is also used appropriately of the patron-client rela-

36. Orselli, *L'idea e il culto del santo patrono,* 43.

37. Cf. *Pe.* 10.1136–40, *Vellem sinister inter haedorum greges / ut sum futurus, eminus dinoscerer / atque hoc precante diceret rex optimus: / "Romanus orat transfer hunc haedum mihi, / sit dexter agnus, induatur vellere."*

38. This collapsing of time distinctions in a single sacred event finds its equivalent in the polysemy of Prudentius' language. Josef Engemann, "Zu den Apsis-Tituli des Paulinus von Nola," *JbAC* 17 (1974): 31–34, analyzes a *titulus* written by Paulinus of Nola for the apse of his basilica at Fundi, in which linguistic multivocality corresponds to the multiplicity of reference of the apse mosaic it describes.

tionship.[39] Properly it speaks of warmth, especially of a warm maternal or nurturing embrace. In a passage in *Pe.* 2, to Lawrence, Prudentius presents the martyr's protection in terms of a fostering embrace.

ceu praesto semper adsies
tuosque alumnos urbicos
lactante conplexus sinu
paterno amore nutrias.

(2.569–72)

[As if you were always present, and held your city foster-children in the embrace of your milky bosom and fed them with your father's love.]

Although the verb *foveo* is not present, the image in verse 271 is similar and conveys the special emotional force associated with a martyr's protection. The word *alumnus,* "foster-child," carries many of the same connotations as *foveo.* According to a recent study of the word in legal texts and inscriptions, "family-like bonds of warmth and affection were fundamental characteristics of the relation between fosterers and *alumni.*"[40] Although the Latin word most commonly used of the fosterer is *patronus* (*-a*), the fosterer's relationship with the foster-child has more in common with the parent-child than the patron-client relationship.[41] In choosing this vocabulary to describe the martyr's relationship to a city and its community, Prudentius invests that relationship with the warmth of parental affection. In the figure of the patron saint, the nurturing powers of the mother are combined with paternal protection. Moreover, the affection is mutual: the city of Siscia "warms its martyr, Quirinus, in its paternal (civic) embrace" (*conplexu patrio fovent,* 7.5; cf. 4.94–96),[42] and, by a process of metonymy, the saint's embrace of

39. Orselli, *L'idea e il culto del santo patrono,* 22, citing *CIL* 10.478. For relatively neutral uses of the verb *foveo* in the *Pe.*, see 3.215, 6.146, and 13.103. The word is already used by Damasus of the martyrs (*Epigr.* 21.11, 31.5, and 73.5). For the sense of physical embrace, see *ThLL* 6.1219.31–80.

40. Hanne Sigismund Nielsen, "*Alumnus*: A Term of Relation Denoting Quasi-Adoption," *C&M* 38 (1987): 150 (and 145). For other examples of the use of *alumnus* (*-a*) for the relation of saint and devotee see Paulinus of Nola, *C.* 21.356 and 793, and *ICUR* 17192.

41. Nielsen, "*Alumnus,*" 148, 184–85.

42. *Patrio* may be the adjective from *pater* or *patria.* For the confusion of paternal and maternal affection in the relationship between martyr and city, see *Pe.* 2.571–72 (quoted in the text above).

his community can be extended to the church where that saint is worshipped: Hippolytus' basilica is described as "opening wide its maternal breast to receive and warm its children, with its embrace laden with offspring" (*maternum pandens gremium quo condat alumnos / ac foveat fetos adcumulata sinus,* 11.229–30).

Finally, because of their special status in heaven the martyrs can be described as friends of Christ. In *Pe.* 11.16 the anonymous martyrs buried in Rome enjoy Christ's friendship (*utpote quos propriae iunxit amicitiae,* sc. *Christus*). The language is echoed in a sermon of Augustine where the martyrs are described as *Christi amici.*[43] Evidently those horizontal bonds of *amicitia* that maintained class solidarity between a late Roman aristocrat and his peers are not in question here. More relevant is the use of *amicus* as a polite euphemism for *cliens,* expressing a relation of subordination. But a closer equivalent is the institution of *amici principis,* familiar in the early Empire, which involves close confidants of the emperor who enjoy special access to him and are able to use their influence to direct the distribution of his largesse to those whom they favor.[44] The parallel with the patron-martyr is close. In particular, the imperial model of patronage stresses the majesty of the source from whom blessings flow and accounts for the role of martyr as intermediary, an aspect not emphasized in Republican forms of patronage. Divine worship and ceremony are commonly assimilated to imperial forms in fourth-century Christianity. Christian authors frequently describe the realm of heaven in terms of Roman political institutions, speaking of the "senate of heaven" with the martyrs as its "consuls."[45] In general,

43. Augustine, *Serm.* 332.1 and 3 (*PL* 38.1461–62); cf. Paulinus, *C.* 14.92, who calls Felix a *divinus amicus.*

44. For patronage under the emperor and the role of *amici principis,* see Richard P. Saller, *Personal Patronage under the Early Empire* (Cambridge, 1982), 41–78. For the word *suffragantes* used of such "brokers" of imperial favor, see G.E.M. de Ste. Croix, "Suffragium: From Vote to Patronage," *British Journal of Sociology* 5 (1954): 38–47—the word is used by Prudentius of the martyrs (*Pe.* 1.16). Fergus Millar, *The Emperor in the Roman World (31 B.C. to A.D. 337)* (London, 1977), 110–16, stresses the instability of such imperial "friendships"; see also Augustine, *Conf.* 8.6.15. (I am indebted to Professor James O'Donnell for these references.) A martyr, of course, would feel no such insecurity as a "friend of Christ."

45. Prudentius speaks of Lawrence as heaven's *perennis consul* (*Pe.* 2.560) and of the dwellers in heaven as a *senatus* (*Pe.* 4.147). The former passage elaborates on the theme of heaven as *Roma caelestis,* on which see V. Buchheit, "Christliche Romideologie im Laurentiushymnus des Prudentius," in Peter Wirth, ed., *Polychronion: Festschrift Franz Dölger zum 75. Geburtstag* (Heidelberg, 1966), 121–44, with the reservations of Klaus Thraede, "Rom und der Märtyrer in Prudentius, Peristephanon 2, 1–20," in *Romanitas*

the application of the terminology of patronage to the cult of the martyrs breaks down the distinction between heaven and earth by suggesting that every Christian enjoys membership in a single society, hierarchically organized to be sure, but one that takes in both the terrestrial and celestial. This transference from the spatial to the social is a common feature of the cult of the martyrs, as it was promoted by the western social and ecclesiastical elite. And even the hierarchical organization of Christian society was vulnerable to the martyr's capacity to be simultaneously present in heaven and earth, to be both at the feet of God and beneath the altar. The meeting of heaven and earth was experienced by the individual in the act of devotion; the dissolution of social divisions at the annual festival of the saint, when patrician and plebeian joined together in an undifferentiated throng of the faithful (*Pe.* 11.199–202).

With the crowds flocking to the martyr's shrine we move from the vertical dimension of space to the horizontal. Worshippers come not just from the martyr's "native" region, but from all around; both Latins and foreign pilgrims gather at Hippolytus' tomb (*Latios simul ac peregrinos,* 11.191). The antithesis between citizens and outsiders is already present in the introductory verses of *Pe.* 1 (*incolae,* 8; *exteri nec non et orbis . . . colonus,* 10). The shrine of the martyr has a specific geographic location, insisted on by the refrain *hic . . . hic . . . huc . . . hic . . . hic . . . hinc,* but it is also a place where all the world comes to pray and that diffuses its *dona* universally. In the conclusion to the poem Prudentius describes the martyrs' limbs as consecrated by Christ to "our city" (1.116). But he goes on to say "they now protect the settlers whom the Ebro washes," and early in the poem the saints are described as *patroni mundi* (1.12). Power emanates from the location of the martyrs' tomb in ever-widening circles until it embraces the whole world. The point of transmission, though, is a single *locus,* the destination of pilgrims from every land. This "tension between distance and proximity,"[46] between the individual martyr's shrine and the Christian community at large, provides the final subject for this chapter.

---

et Christianitas: Studia Iano Henrico Waszink . . . Oblata (Amsterdam, 1973), 317–27. Prudentius also describes the martyrs as *proceres purpurei* (*Pe.* 4.191–92)—for the application of the word *proceres* to martyrs, originally to the Apostles Peter and Paul, see Jean Doignon, "'Procer,' titre donné à Saint Martin dans une inscription Gallo-Romaine de Vienne," in *Saint Martin et son temps: Mémorial du XVIe centenaire des débuts du monachisme en Gaule, 361–1961,* Studia Anselmiana 46 (1961), 151–58—and *togata nobilitas* (4.75–76).

46. The phrase is Brown's, *Cult of the Saints,* 88.

The saint's protection of his or her native community is a recurrent theme in the *Peristephanon,* though it is not evenly distributed throughout the collection. It is, in fact, most common in the poems about the Spanish martyrs. The main exception is the poem dedicated to the Dalmatian city of Siscia and its somewhat obscure saint, Quirinus—incidentally, a saint who had established some kind of presence at Rome.[47] Agnes, it is true, "preserves the safety/salvation [*salutem*] of the Quirites," but her protection extends equally to foreigners (14.4–5), and her special patronage of Rome is not emphasized. Of the Roman saints only Lawrence is described as a patron martyr (2.561–72), and that in a poem that is written from Spain (537–40) and stresses the special status of Rome as a city that stands for the whole Roman world (417–32). For the fullest accounts of the martyr as patron of his or her "native" city we must turn instead to the Spanish poems *Pe.* 1, 3, 4, and 6, dedicated to the two military martyrs of Calahorra, to Eulalia of Mérida, to the eighteen martyrs of Saragossa, and to Fructuosus and his deacons, Augurius and Eulogius of Tarragona.

The affectionate regard between patron saint and community is mutual. As already noted, the verb *foveo* is used of both participants in the relationship. Similarly, *servare* can be used of the martyr's protection of a city, but also of the protection provided by the city (and by metonymic extension by its people, basilica, or earth) to the martyr buried there.[48] The language conveys the reciprocal obligations of patronage relationships, but invested with a new warmth of emotion. Eulalia, for instance, returns the protection Mérida gives her remains (*reliquias cineresque sacros / servat humus veneranda sinu,* 3.194–95) with loving concern (*amore colit,* 3.5).[49] Beyond this, though, cities derive real prestige and power from the patronage of a saint, a prestige that is comparable to and even transcends more traditional secular sources of status. Eulalia's grave at Mérida is described as follows:

Proximus occiduo locus est
qui tulit hoc decus egregium,[50]

47. *Pe.* 7.3–5, *urbis moenia Sisciae / concessum sibi martyrem / conplexu patrio fovent.* For Quirinus at Rome, see Lavarenne, in his edition, 101, and Pietri, *Roma Christiana,* 619.

48. Cf. *Pe.* 3.195 (quoted below), 4.1–2, 14.4.

49. Prudentius avoids the verb *colere* when speaking of the cult of the saints, preferring to use the verb *venerari* (*Pe.* 3.211, 4.32, 5.562, 11.235). In that way he avoids attributing worship to the saints in a way that would be theologically objectionable, and would imply a cult like that of the pagan gods, of whom *colere* is used.

50. The phrase is Virgilian (*Aen.* 7.473).

urbe potens, populis locuples,
sed mage sanguine martyrii
virgineoque potens titulo.

(3.6–10)

[Close to the setting sun is a spot that received this distinguished honor, a place powerful in its city and wealthy in its people, but all the more powerful because of the blood of its martyr and a virgin's tomb.]

From the normal perspective of the *laus urbis* Prudentius seems to be saying things backwards here. We would expect the city to derive power from Eulalia's grave (e.g., *urbs tumulo potens*), not vice versa. Rather than the tomb being outside the walls of the city and in some sense dependent on it, it is the city that is in a subordinate relationship to the shrine, the new source of power. Secular social institutions (*urbs, populi*) play a secondary role when compared with "the blood of a martyr and a virgin's tomb."[51]

The passage begins with a phrase reminiscent of the formula for introducing ecphrases, *est locus.* The geographical reference *proximus occiduo* reinforces this impression. But the text soon digresses from the descriptive to the more broadly epideictic. The locus of the martyr's grave is translated from landscape to location of civic power, a source of *potentia* on which city and people depend. The paronomasia of *locus* and *locuples,* as though the latter is etymologically derived from *locus* and *populis,* clinches by rhetorical means the association of the grave of a martyr (for which *locus* is regularly used in inscriptions) with temporal power. The emphasis on the word *locus* serves the same function as repetition of forms of the demonstrative *hic* in *Pe.* 1. The grave of the martyr becomes a source of what Peter Brown calls "clean power,"[52] a power laundered of the sometimes brutal associations of secular authority in late antiquity and deriving ultimately, through the saint, from God himself.[53] Though that power operates in the world, it unites terrestrial

51. I translate *titulus* "tomb" here, but it conveys a variety of other meanings present to some degree in Prudentius' text: inscription, martyr's church, and, abstractly, glory.

52. Brown, *Cult of the Saints,* 101–5.

53. The communication of *potentia* from the divine through the martyrs to a terrestrial community is encapsulated in *Pe.* 6.5–6, *arcem quandoquidem potens Hiberam / trino martyre Trinitas coronat.*

communities under God in a single Christian community, whose point of access on earth is at the tomb of the martyr.

The possession of martyrs' bones was soon to become a standard topos in the *laus urbis.*[54] Already in *Pe.* 6 thc narrative ends abruptly with an exclamation of joy at the prestige the martyrs bestow on their native city, "O threefold glory, O triple honor, by which the head of our city is exalted" (6.142–43). But the fullest assimilation of martyr text to *laus urbis* is *Pe.* 4. The poem is unusual as the only one in the collection that owes its structure to the enumerative principles of epideictic rather than to the temporal and spatial criteria of narration and description. Although it contains narrative elements, notably in the accounts of saints Vincent and Encratis (4.77–140), even there details of their sufferings are subordinated to the epideictic point that their names redound to the praise of "our city."[55]

As a *laus urbis Pe.* 4 takes untypical form. The geographical situation of Saragossa is entirely omitted. All that counts is proximity to the tomb of the martyrs (4.1–2), who become its new rulers by right of burial (*urbis unius regimen tenentes / iure sepulchri,* 4.175–76—praise of rulers and the honors bestowed by them on a city is also an element in the *laus urbis*).[56] Instead of situating Saragossa geographically with regard to the sea, mountains, plains, other countries, and climate, Prudentius places the city spiritually on the map of late antique devotion (at least as practiced in the western empire), by his catalog of cities and their martyrs (17–52). This Christianization of the topoi of the *laus urbis* extends also the praise of a city's buildings.[57] In the new order of things, a monument outside the city walls, the tomb of the martyrs, takes pride of place. Little is heard of the space within the walls, and when it is described (4.65–72) it is as a spiritual landscape, secure in the omnipresence of Christ, with the blood of the martyrs standing sentry at the gates.

54. See Ernst Robert Curtius, *European Literature and the Latin Middle Ages,* trans. Willard R. Trask (New York, 1953; reprint, 1963), 157–58.

55. Both passages end with emphatic assertions that the glory of the two saints belongs to Saragossa. See too the repetition of *noster est* and *noster et nostra . . . in palaestra* (97 and 101) and the phrase *hunc novum nostrae titulum fruendum / Caesaraugustae dedit ipse Christus,* 141–42.

56. Menander Rhetor 1 (365.10–13). The treatises attributed to Menander give valuable insights into epideictic rhetoric of the empire. I use the translations of Russell and Wilson for technical terms throughout my discussion of Menander Rhetor (D.A. Russell and N.G. Wilson, *Menander Rhetor* [Oxford, 1981]).

57. Menander Rhetor 2.3 (382.15–18 and 386.21–29).

This Christianization of the *laus urbis* is seen in miniature in the stanza of the catalog Prudentius devotes to Tingis and its martyr, Cassian. He first describes Tingis, in a phrase derived from the traditional topoi of the praise of a city, as "celebrated burial place of Massylian kings" (*festa Massylum monumenta regum,* 4.46). But Cassian's ashes have, paradoxically, "subdued the tribes and brought them under the yoke of Christ" (*Cassianum . . . / qui cinis gentes domitas coegit / ad iuga Christi,* 4.45 and 47–48). *Gentes,* of course, can mean "pagans." It is translated in this way by Lavarenne and Thomson. But it is also the natural word to use of the native African tribes. In the context, where we have just heard of the "burial places of Massylian kings," we are reminded that "subduing native tribes" (*gentes*) would be a praiseworthy achievement of an African king. Cassian, however, goes one better by subduing the *gentes* (i.e., in his case, pagans) not by military force but by his mere ashes. The stanza traces not only the conversion of pagans to Christians in North Africa, but also the literary Christianization of the *laus urbis* from secular to spiritual, from *reges* to martyr.

Comparisons are typical of epideictic, and of the praise of a city in particular. In the second treatise attributed to Menander Rhetor, the author recommends that under every division of the praise of a country or city a comparison should be adduced.[58] In *Pe.* 4 the catalog of martyrs and their native cities plays this role to some degree, as is evident in the concluding stanzas of the passage (49–64). The last of these stanzas combines a comparison with the panegyric topos of "surpassing" or "outdoing" (cf. the verb *superare*):[59] in the martyrs' tombs Saragossa well-nigh surpasses two great centers of secular and ecclesiastical power in the West, Carthage and Rome. There is an element of hyperbole, but underlying that is the suggestion that the cult of the saints does have the potential to reorganize or at least prompt a reassessment of longstanding power relationships in the western Mediterranean.

One heading of the *laus urbis* has special relevance to Prudentius' poem. In the first Menandrian treatise, one of the major divisions of such a speech is the actions (πράξεις) of a city, which are to be categorized by the four cardinal virtues: courage, justice, temperance, and prudence. Under justice a large section is devoted to piety (εὐσέβεια),

58. Menander Rhetor 2.3 (383.18–19).

59. Curtius, *European Literature,* 162–65; Klaus Thraede, "Untersuchungen zum Ursprung und zur Geschichte der christlichen Poesie II," *JbAC* 5 (1962): 155.

i.e., good relations between gods and men. Here the author makes a distinction that is of special interest to the martyr text, between "god-loved" (θεοφιλότης) and "god-loving" (φιλοθεότης).[60] Both are appropriate to the *laus urbis*. The former concerns the protection and blessings the gods bestow on a city, the latter private and public devotion to the gods. This double perspective is familiar in the relationships of cities and martyrs, but with a difference. In Menander's examples there is no suggestion of correspondence between love shown to and shown by the gods. The examples under each heading are discrete; particular instances of love for the gods do not correspond with examples of love from the gods. By comparison, this mutuality of exchange is stressed in the cult of the martyrs. We have already observed that language can be used indifferently of the attitude of martyrs to city or city to martyrs: cities and their people preserve martyrs' tombs (4.1–2), martyrs preserve cities and their people (14.5). Late antique *amicitia* relationships were similarly sustained by the exchange of functionally equivalent tokens of friendship, especially letters and gifts. Identity of objects given and received was such that, in the case of exchange of correspondence, the transaction could be compared to an echo.[61] And this identity of objects exchanged was a measure of identity of feeling (*unanimitas*). By representing the association between martyr and community in terms of such mutuality of services, Prudentius invests that relationship with the affectionate warmth of late antique *amicitia* relationships. Here again the hierarchical model of martyr-devotee ties is qualified by a horizontal model of social relationships between peers, though only as a member of the larger *populus* of a city can the individual worshipper participate in this relationship.

Much in *Pe.* 4 responds to analysis as a *laus urbis,* though the traditional topoi are thoroughly Christianized. In structure, however, the Christian component is determinative. The poem's introductory (1–64) and concluding (145–200) sections both center on liturgical acts.[62] In the former case this act is set in the future, at the Last Judgment, when the cities will present the bones of their patron martyrs to Christ. In the latter the context is the contemporary celebration of the eighteen martyrs of Saragossa, though the final stanza explicitly makes the connection

60. Menander Rhetor 1 (361.11–362.29).

61. Ausonius, *Ep.* 26.9–10 (Prete) = 21.9–10 (Green).

62. In the concluding section, in particular, references to the city : martyr relationship play only a minor role (175–76, 191–92, 196–200).

between the city's present devotion at the tomb of the saints and the future resurrection of those saints in the flesh with their devotees in their train (4.197–200).

After an introductory stanza, Prudentius sets out his eschatological vision in language intended to evoke as countertype the classical world and its pagan gods.

Plena magnorum domus angelorum
non timet mundi fragilis ruinam
tot sinu gestans simul offerenda
  munera Christo.
Cum deus dextram quatiens coruscam
nube subnixus veniet rubente
gentibus iustam positurus aequo
  pondere libram,
orbe de magno caput excitata
obviam Christo properanter ibit
civitas quaeque pretiosa portans
  dona canistris.

(*Pe.* 4.5–16)

[A house filled with glorious saints, bearing in its embrace so many gifts to offer all together to Christ, has no fear of the destruction of this transitory world. When God comes, brandishing his brilliant right hand and resting on a red-colored cloud, to establish for the peoples of the world the scales of justice, fairly balanced, each city from the great circle of the globe will hasten to meet Christ, head held high and carrying in baskets precious gifts.]

God's brilliant right hand (*dextra corusca*) is described in terms identical with Jupiter's hand, wielding the thunderbolt. But while the indiscriminate exercise of Jupiter's power is often criticized—his thunderbolt falls on just and unjust alike—God's fairness at the Last Judgment is exemplary (*iustam . . . aequo,* 11).[63] There is an element of contrast imi-

63. Cf. Virgil, *G.* 1.328–29, Seneca, *Ph.* 156 and *Oed.* 1029. Parallels are listed most fully in Bergman's edition. The standard treatments of Virgilian imitation in Prudentius are Albertus Mahoney, *Vergil in the Works of Prudentius,* Catholic University of America, Patristic Studies 39 (Washington, D.C., 1934) and Christian Schwen, *Vergil bei Prudentius* (Leipzig, 1937); imitation of Seneca is treated by G. Sixt, "Des Prudentius' Abhängigkeit

tation here, as there is in the phrase *dona canistris* (16), which recalls the food and drink presented by Aeneas to Evander at the annual festival of Heracles on the future site of Rome.[64] The pagan rituals yield place in the poet's eschatological vision to a ceremony of salvation in which the whole Roman world participates.

This evocation of myth and Roman history is reinforced by another reference to classical literature, to the beginning of Horace's third Roman Ode.

> Iustum et tenacem propositi virum
> non civium ardor prava iubentium
> non vultus instantis tyranni
> mente quatit solida neque Auster,
> dux inquieti turbidus Hadriae,
> nec fulminantis magna manus Iovis:
> si fractus illabatur orbis,
> impavidum ferient ruinae.
>
> (*C.* 3.3.1–8)

[Neither the fury of citizens with their corrupt commands nor the face of the threatening tyrant shakes in his firmness of mind the man who is just and stable of purpose, nor does the south wind, boisterous ruler of the troubled Adriatic, nor the powerful hand of Jove with his lightning: let the world break and fall, he will have no fear as the fabric collapses upon him.]

In Prudentius and Horace the situation is the same: the collapse (*ruina*) of the world, which is described as *fractus* (7) in Horace, *fragilis* (6) in Prudentius; yet this collapse can be viewed without fear (*impavidum/ non timet*) by the just man in Horace, and by the cities blessed with martyrs in Prudentius. As we have seen, Prudentius' reference to the "brilliant hand of God" provokes comparison with the thunder and lightning of Zeus, a force of terror in the Roman Ode (6). Here, too,

---

von Seneca und Lucan," *Philologus* 51 (1892): 501–6. The parallel with Horace's third Roman Ode, discussed below, is noted by Filippo Ermini, *Peristephanon: Studi Prudenziani* (Rome, 1914), 147. Unless otherwise indicated, parallels to these authors derive from these collections. For the indiscriminate use of Jupiter's thunderbolt, see, for instance, Aristophanes, *Clouds* 398–402 and Lucretius 6.390–95.

64. Cf. Virgil, *Aen.* 8.180–81, *onerantque canistris / dona laboratae Cereris, Bacchumque ministrant.*

however, the contrast between the classical and Christian contexts is most revealing. In Horace only a few individuals, in their philosophical ability to transcend their circumstances, achieve that security of mind the poet praises, and, as the poem continues, achieve apotheosis in heaven. In the *Peristephanon* such ascents to heaven are the province of the martyrs. But freedom from fear in the contemplation of cosmic catastrophe is not reserved for a privileged few, but communicated to all members of the Christian *civitas* through the special protection of the patron martyrs. The martyrs play a critical role in allaying the eschatological fears, so pervasive in the world of late antiquity,[65] that find a forerunner in the intimations of a return to primal chaos in Horace's ode. The fearful prospect of the Last Judgment is relieved by calling upon the familiar immediacy of a city's relationship with its martyrs.

Stanza 4 of the poem (13–16) describes a procession of cities, each presenting to Christ at the end of the world its own particular gift, the bones of its martyr or martyrs. This dramatic situation is maintained in the catalog that follows, especially in the choice of verbs.[66] In this respect Prudentius differs from the only earlier enumeration of cities and their patron saints in Christian Latin poetry, contained in poem 19 of Paulinus of Nola (76–84 and 141–54). While Paulinus presents a purely static catalog, Prudentius translates his material into the language of late antique ceremony.[67] The parallels with later dome and nave mosaics from the churches of Ravenna are striking. The dome mosaic of the Orthodox Baptistery (mid-fifth century) is made up of two concentric rings, encircling a central medallion representing the baptism of Christ in the Jordan. The inner of the two rings contains two processions of cross-bearing apostles, led by Peter and Paul. The later Arian baptistery (ca. A.D. 500) has the same arrangement, apostles with crowns, but this time the two files converge on an enthroned crown, which represents Christ in triumph, and which is certainly capable of referring to the

65. For this eschatological dread, see Brown, *Cult of the Saints,* 70–72. Such fears seem to have played a role in Paulinus of Nola's conversion to ascetic Christianity (*C.* 10.293–329).

66. *Promet* (17), *offeres* (22), *exhibebit* (29), *gestabit* (31), *habebit* (35), *porriget* (40), *ferre . . . iuvabit* (43), *ingeret* (45), *revehes* (53).

67. For the importance of ceremony in late antiquity, see Ramsay MacMullen, "Some Pictures in Ammianus Marcellinus," *ABull* 46 (1964): 435–55, and Sabine MacCormack, *Art and Ceremony in Late Antiquity,* The Transformation of the Classical Heritage 1 (Berkeley, 1981), 6–14, who coins the phrase (9) "the vast ceremoniousness of late Roman life."

eschatological future.[68] As in Prudentius, the mosaic shows a procession of figures carrying crowns, in a setting that evokes the Second Coming. (By a process of metonymic slippage the cities in Prudentius may be represented as carrying the martyrs themselves [31, 35, 45, 53], the bones, ashes, blood, and limbs of the martyrs [17, 38, 41, 44], or crowns representing their martyrdoms [20, 21].) The processions of crown-bearing male and female saints and martyrs in the nave mosaic of S. Apollinare Nuovo (ca. A.D. 560) furnish a still closer parallel. Here, on one wall of the nave, a procession of women bears crowns, while on the other wall the male saints converge on a seated figure of Christ, flanked by angels.[69] Prudentius' procession combines the two, with female figures presenting crowns of martyrdom to Christ. Although in Prudentius the participants are cities, not martyrs, the two are readily assimilated in the cult of the saints. Though late, the mosaics in S. Apollinare Nuovo still breathe the world of late antique ceremonial, a world that finds earlier expression in Prudentius' catalog of cities and their martyrs in *Pe.* 4.

As the poem begins, so it ends—with a catalog. Prudentius urges a choir (*chorus,* 153) to sing the names of the eighteen martyrs of Saragossa, along with those of the martyr Vincent, born in the city (though martyred elsewhere) the virgin Encratis, and the confessors Gaius and Crementius. The parallels with the earlier catalog are close. In both cases cities are imagined celebrating their saints. In the first catalog the cities are personified as female figures; in the second the city of Saragossa is first addressed (145–48), and associated with its Christian community joined together in a *chorus* to perform a song of praise (*vivax laus,* 159–60). Even in length the two catalogs are almost identical: there is a stanza difference.[70] The liturgical act performed by the community of believers

68. On the significance of the enthroned cross, see Engemann, "Zu den Apsis-Tituli," 33. For the two dome mosaics, see Ernst Kitzinger, *Byzantine Art in the Making: Main Lines of Stylistic Development in Mediterranean Art, 3rd to 7th Century* (Cambridge, Mass., 1977), 58–62. The comparison with the mosaics of Christian basilicas was already made in the nineteenth century by Allard, cited by Aimé Puech, *Prudence: Étude sur la poésie latine chrétienne au IVe siècle* (Paris, 1888), 139, but not developed.

69. The mosaics replaced scenes from the court of the Ostrogothic king Theoderic; see Kitzinger, *Byzantine Art,* 62–64.

70. The first occupies lines 17–64, the second 145–88, but it would be possible to end the first catalog at 56. The situation is further complicated by the fact that the stanzas on Gaius and Crementius (181–88) are omitted from *Parisinus Lat.* 8084, our earliest (sixth century) witness to the text. The stanzas are bracketed by Bergman and Lavarenne, while Cunningham, though including them in his text, concedes in his apparatus that Bergman may be right to exclude them.

in the here and now finds its counterpart in the future eschatological ceremony of salvation with which the poem begins; indeed, the latter is already implicitly present in the former. Once more in the celebration of the martyrs distinctions of time lose their meaning. While at the Last Judgment individual cities participate in a celebration that unites them into a larger Christian community through the martyrs, so in the occasion with which the poem ends individual members of the community unite as a single Christian *civitas* in a chorus of praise to the martyrs. The homology suggests that even here, in the work that is most thoroughly dedicated to the martyr as patron of a particular city, Prudentius does not lose sight of the ability of the martyr cult to break down divisions not only within but also between communities. The cities of Spain, Gaul, and North Africa that parade with their martyrs in the first catalog present a spiritual itinerary of the Christian world of the western Mediterranean.[71] Only Rome and Italy are omitted from the catalog proper, though Prudentius later compares Saragossa with "Rome enthroned" (*Roma in solio locata,* 62). Cities come together here not in veneration of a single, common saint, but in their shared devotion to the cult of the martyrs. Geographical unity is removed to a celestial, atemporal dimension, but the individual city replicates that ideal unity in the here and now of the Mediterranean world, and acts it out in miniature in its communal celebration of its patron saint or saints. Prudentius' poem gives expression to the Christian project described by Markus of "appropriating the space of the Roman Empire by taking imaginative possession of it." Prudentius maps out the new Christian world in the west by the "spatial projection of . . . sacred history" (i.e., primarily the sites of martyrs' burials) onto the map of the western empire, thereby creating "a sacred topography, a network of holy places."[72]

The omission of Roman and Italian saints from the catalog need occasion no surprise. In the *Peristephanon* as a whole, of which the passage in *Pe.* 4 is a small-scale version,[73] Roman and Italian martyrs

71. Fontaine, "Société et culture chrétiennes sur l'aire circumpyrénéene au siècle de Théodose," *Bulletin de littérature ecclésiastique de Toulouse* (1974): 249 (= *Études sur la poésie latine tardive d'Ausone à Prudence* [Paris, 1980], 275), makes the attractive suggestion that the "circumpyrenean" cities enumerated in the catalog trace the stages of Prudentius' pilgrimage to Italy along the *via Domitia.* See also Lana, *Due capitoli Prudenziani,* 4–5.

72. Robert Markus, *The End of Ancient Christianity* (Cambridge, 1990), 142.

73. *Pe.* 4 contains references to all the Spanish martyrs celebrated in the collection as a whole, as well as to Cyprian (*Pe.* 13). It is perhaps relevant that a Cassian is also

receive distinct treatments. There is, for instance, less emphasis on their role as patrons of a community. On the other hand, the conjunction of native and foreigner at the shrine of Roman saints is particularly prominent. (The introduction to *Pe.* 1 also contains this theme, but because that passage serves as an introduction to the collection as a whole, it accommodates elements that have a broader relevance than the immediate circumstances of the Spanish martyrs.)[74] The special treatment of the Roman martyrs reflects the special status of that church in the western Christian community and the vigorous efforts made to promote the cult of the martyrs in that city. But it also provides a standard to which the Spanish martyrs can be compared—this is the role of Rome in *Pe.* 4 (62)—and a model to which Spanish communities can aspire. We have already seen Prudentius make a distinction between contact and fragmentary relics inspired by the practice of the Roman church. In *Pe.* 11 he recommends for veneration in Spain a Roman saint, Hippolytus, who is to join the native martyrs Chelidonius and Eulalia and the African bishop Cyprian (11.237–38; all three are mentioned in *Pe.* 4). If part of his motive for writing the *Peristephanon* was to promote the cult of the martyrs in Spain, he probably emphasizes the role of martyrs as patrons of individual communities more in the Spanish poems because of the appeal this had to potential devotees.[75]

Peristephanon 4 and the introductory section to *Peristephanon* 1 provide complementary perspectives on the cult of the martyrs. While one emphasizes the capacity of the martyr to abolish distinctions of time and place, the other associates patron saints closely with particular communities. There is no contradiction here. The two aspects coexist in the veneration of the martyrs, as they do to a greater or lesser degree in the two poems. Social distinctions, too, can be abolished at the graveside, in the shared experience of proximity to heaven. The individual's experience of devotion is continuous with the celebration of the martyrs by

---

mentioned, though he is not identical with the martyr of *Pe.* 9. See Ludwig, "Die christliche Dichtung," 329, whose arguments for the transposition of *Pe.* 4 after *Pe.* 7 strike me as unconvincing. There is a thematic parallelism between the sequences 1, 2, 3 and 4, 5, 6 that should be maintained.

74. The same point is made by Palmer, *Prudentius on the Martyrs,* 143–44 and 152–53.

75. On the Spanish context of the *Peristephanon,* see especially Jacques Fontaine, "Romanité et hispanité dans la littérature hispano-romaine des IVe et Ve siècles," *Travaux du VIe Congrès international d'études classiques* (Bucharest and Paris, 1976), 310–18 (= *Études,* 318–26). For the archaeology of martyr shrines in Spain see Palmer, *Prudentius on the Martyrs,* 268–73.

the community as a whole, and, it might be added, with the composition of a poem on the martyrs by a Christian poet, itself a devotional act.[76] In the liturgical year the annual festival of a community's martyrs re-enacts the joyful granting of a request of a single petitioner, and the annual festival, in turn, prefigures the scene of salvation set in the eschatological future. Time and place are concertinaed, to use Peter Brown's phrase,[77] in the individual act of worship on a particular privileged *locus,* at a particular instance in time. The whole Christian community, in heaven and earth, is present in that instant and location, as well as the plenitude of time from the biblical martyrs and the Passion of Christ to the Second Coming. The martyrs' reenactment of Christ's Passion in their own suffering makes their tombs "a very special place."[78] In the next chapter, I shall investigate the accounts of martyrdom in the *Peristephanon* with these qualities of the cult of the saints in mind.

76. This aspect of Prudentius' poetic project is especially evident in *Pe.* 4. He represents himself instructing the community to sing the praises of its saints (so the imperatives in 147 and 149 are most naturally taken); i.e., the act of devotion operates at two levels, those of the poet and of the community. The reference to *carminis leges* (165) shows him self-consciously drawing attention to his own role as master of ceremonies. In the final stanzas of the poem, Prudentius will associate himself with the worshippers by using the first person plural (190 and 193), but will also speak of himself alone as hoping to benefit by an act of contrition (195–96). In the final stanza this ambiguous situation culminates in an instruction to the whole community to prostrate itself with him at the tomb (*sterne te totam generosa sanctis / civitas mecum tumulis,* 197–98). The poet is both of and not of the community; he shares in the communal devotion, yet is apart from it and directs it. In his own person he experiences that paradoxical coexistence of two states of being that characterizes the cult of the martyrs as a whole.

77. Brown, *Cult of the Saints,* 81.

78. I have concertinaed two of Brown's chapter headings, "A Fine and Private Place" (*Cult of the Saints,* chap. 2) and "The Very Special Dead" (ibid., chap. 4).

CHAPTER 2

The Martyr Narrative: Between Heaven and Earth

When Quintilian discusses *enargeia,* which is the characteristic quality of the rhetorical ecphrasis, he summarizes his method for achieving such descriptive vividness as the opening out of what is contained in a single word.[1] His example is the capture of a city (*eversio* [*urbis*]). Although the single word embraces all the individual events that make up the fall of a city, to achieve emotional force and visual immediacy the orator will enumerate all the actions that the more general wording contains—the collapse of buildings, reactions of the inhabitants, and taking of prisoners and booty. Something similar may be said of the Prudentian martyr narrative. For all that is contained in the martyr account is already implicit in the single word *passio,* or its metonymical (concrete for abstract) equivalent *sanguis.* Both words put special emphasis on the death of the martyr, the moment that distinguishes him or her from the confessor saint or holy man or woman. But the sense of both words extends beyond that specific moment to the sanguinary sufferings that precede death as preliminary engagements before the decisive battle.

Prudentius uses the word *passio* in its more restrictive sense, of the

1. *aperias haec, quae verbo uno inclusa erant,* 8.3.63. See Michael Roberts, *The Jeweled Style: Poetry and Poetics in Late Antiquity* (Ithaca, N.Y., 1989), 38–44. Roland Barthes, "Introduction to the Structural Analysis of Narrative," in *Image—Music—Text,* trans. Stephen Heath (London, 1977), 120 makes the same point as Quintilian from the reverse perspective when he speaks of the "elliptic power" of narrative. The basic narrative units can be ordered in a hierarchy of terms of ever greater generality, each level of which subsumes the terms below it. In this way "narrative lends itself to summary," a summary that in the case of martyr texts at the highest level of generality can take the form of the single word *passio.*

actual death (e.g., *Pe.* 6.113) but also in its broader sense, of the whole course of the martyrdom.

decursa iam satis tibi
poenae minacis munia
pulchroque mortis exitu
omnis peracta est passio.

(5.289–92)

[For you now the duties of menacing punishment have sufficiently run their course, and with the glorious release of death your whole passion is complete.]

With these words an angel announces to Vincent his imminent death. The word *omnis* (292) leaves no doubt that *passio* here is to be associated not just with death (*mortis exitu*), but also with the entire sequence of punishments that precedes that moment (289–90).[2]

Bloodshed, too, is essential to a passion. Augustine can describe martyrdom interchangeably as "a fight to the death" (*usque ad mortem certamen*) or "to the blood" (*usque ad sanguinem*).[3] Even martyrdom by drowning can be assimilated to a bloody death: both involve being drenched in a flood of liquid (*Pe.* 7.16–20).[4] All the earlier bloody *poenae* the martyr must endure can be seen as *species futuri,*[5] as prefigurations of the final fatal bloodletting. As observed in the previous chapter, the blood shed at the martyr's execution forms a text (*sanguinis notae, Pe.* 1.3), in which the whole course of the passion may be read: blood as the element indispensable to the historical act of martyrdom; blood as the text of the passion, by which the historical event is transmitted to

2. Compare the third-century use of *passio* and *passiones*: H.A.M. Hoppenbrouwers, *Recherches sur la terminologie du martyre de Tertullien à Lactance,* Latinitas Christianorum Primaeva 15 (Nijmegen, 1961), 155–57. The use of *pati* to express the idea of sufferings, including death, is specifically Christian (Hoppenbrouwers, 190); i.e., *pati* = *mori cum poenis.*

3. Aug., *Serm.* 284.5 (*PL* 38.129.1), *usque ad sanguinem certamen*; *Serm.* 286.1.1–2.1 (*PL* 38.1297) *usque ad mortem* and *usque ad sanguinem* used interchangeably.

4. *Nil refert, vitreo aequore / an de flumine sanguinis / tinguat passio martyrem, / aeque gloria provenit / fluctu quolibet uvida.*

5. The phrase *speciem futuri* is used of Vincent's preliminary loss of blood at Saragossa, before his martyrdom at Valentia (4.91). There is, however, no necessary suggestion in Vincent's case that he was the victim of persecution in his native land; Eugenius of Toledo (*PL* 87.361) speaks of a nosebleed.

and available for reenactment by subsequent generations; and blood as relic, metonymic equivalent of *ossa* or *cineres,*[6] and carrier of the martyr's *praesentia* and *potentia.* In the blood of that historical event is implicit not just the whole sequence of the martyrdom, but the capacity of the cult of the martyrs to transcend temporal differences; the blood of the martyrs, as Ambrose found out when he discovered the relics of Gervasius and Protasius, runs ever fresh.

From the single word *passio* or *sanguis* the account of a martyrdom can be generated by the lexical resources of metaphor, metonymy, and periphrastic elaboration on the themes of suffering and death, by the incorporation of topoi, derived often from the rhetorical tradition of resistance to tyrants,[7] and by the process of narrative doubling to produce episodes that repeat in basic structure the final confrontation between martyr and persecutor. Viewed synchronically this would seem to be a sufficient description of the late fourth-century *Passiones,* termed by Delehaye epic passions. Viewed diachronically, metaphorical elaboration of lexical resources and some formation of common narrative elements (i.e., topoi) represented a first stage towards the epic passion, evident already in some third-century accounts, assigned by Delehaye to the category of historical passions.[8] When the persecutions came to an end, martyrs enjoyed new status in a now-secure Christian community. The age of the martyrs increasingly became a heroic age, of figures larger than life, as the Homeric hero was to the people of post-heroic times.[9]

6. In the procession of cities carrying the relics of their patron saints in *Pe.* 4 (17–52) these offerings are referred to as: *ossa* (17), *cineres* (38), and *sanguinem* (41), as well as *coronas* (20), and *gemmis* (21), by the names of individual martyrs (19, 35, 45) or by the periphrasis *quos veneramur* (32). The range of expressions used illustrates the synecdochical equivalence of relics and martyr, and the potential for metaphorical extension of the poetic lexicon.

7. On this, see Ilona Opelt, "Der Christenverfolger bei Prudentius," *Philologus* 111 (1967): 252–57. Maccabees 4 and the fourth-century Greek martyr panegyrics will have played a role in transmitting or validating rhetorical topoi in the western hagiographical tradition.

8. Hippolyte Delehaye, *Les passions des martyrs et les genres littéraires,* Subsidia Hagiographica 13B, 2d ed. (Brussels, 1966), 171–73, for the distinction between historical and epic passions. Delehaye's low estimation of the latter depends on a somewhat restricted historical viewpoint; see Peter Brown, *The Cult of the Saints: Its Rise and Function in Latin Christianity,* Haskell Lectures on Religion, n.s. 2 (Chicago, 1981) 80–81.

9. See Simone Deléani-Nigoul, "L'utilisation des modèles bibliques du martyre par les écrivains du IIIe siècle," in Jacques Fontaine and Charles Pietri, edd., *Le monde latin antique et la Bible,* Bible de tous les temps 2 (Paris, 1985), 337–38. For what follows, see also Alison Goddard Elliott, *Roads to Paradise: Reading the Lives of the Early Saints* (Hanover, N.H., 1987) 8-9, and Anne-Marie Palmer, *Prudentius on the Martyrs* (Oxford,

At the same time, devotion at the martyrs' graves was no longer restricted. Under these circumstances martyr literature flourished. There was an immediate demand for commemorative inscriptions to publish the presencc of a martyr's grave. By the second half of the century, with the promotion of the cult of the martyrs by influential bishops like Damasus and Ambrose, new passions were being written to meet the needs of individual communities, devoted to their local saints. Not only was such literature increasing in volume, it was also changing in kind, to reflect the new attitudes to the martyrs of the "post-heroic" age. Prudentius' achievements must be seen in this context. He is not only one of the earliest exponents of the epic passion in the West, but also one whose aspirations to produce a work of literary excellence exceed the normal achievements in this genre.

The development of martyr literature can be traced in its use of language and in its narrative structure. From texts of the third to those of the fourth century and later, episodes are increasingly standardized, while background detail and the realistic impression of historical continuity are diminished. In the later texts individual episodes often repeat on a small scale the pattern of combat and victory, that is, the movement of the *Passio* as a whole. In the third century military and agonistic metaphors, i.e., martyrdom as warfare and martyrdom as athletic contest, are most widely used to expand the lexicon of martyrdom. Tertullian uses both metaphors, which have biblical antecedents.[10] The crown (*corona*) or palm (*palma*) awarded for victory in battle or in an athletic contest become standard expressions for the heavenly glory won by martyrdom. By Prudentius' time this metaphorical language has been absorbed into the lexicon of martyrdom and the sense of its figurative connotations has faded, especially in the use of the verb *vincere,* the noun *triumphus,* and their cognates. Only in *Pe.* 1, in the special case of martyrs who are former soldiers, and in the fourth and fifth stanzas of *Pe.* 2, does Prudentius strive to reactivate this metaphor.

1989), 227–34. At the end of the century Sulpicius Severus refers to a number of surviving Passions describing events of the Diocletianic persecutions (*Chron.* 2.32.6).

10. See 1 Cor. 9.24–25 for *agon, Ephes.* 6.10–17 for *militia*; for the metaphors in Tertullian, see Hoppenbrouwers, *Recherches sur la terminologie du martyre,* 71–73, for those in Cyprian, Edelhard L. Hummel, *The Concept of Martyrdom According to St. Cyprian of Carthage,* Catholic University of America, Studies in Christian Antiquity 9 (Washington, D.C., 1946), 56–90, and in martyr literature generally John Francis Petruccione, "Prudentius' Use of Martyrological Topoi in Peristephanon," (Ph.D. diss., University of Michigan, 1985), 25–33.

Duval's study of the inscriptional evidence from martyrs' tombs in North Africa helps to clarify developments in the fourth century. She speaks of an "explosion of the martyr cult"[11] after the Peace of the Church, which finds its reflection in the language of inscriptions. Epitaphs from the first decades of the fourth century employ brief, quasi-objective formulas in an exclusively factual notice. But after the fourth decade of the century, and especially toward the end of the century when literary passions are beginning to be written, "the formulary is enriched by poetic images and symbols . . . , common topoi of the literary texts."[12] In the last decades of the century periphrases emerge for the martyrs' combats with diabolical powers, for death and for victory, that put the emphasis on the spiritual content of the martyr narrative rather than on evoking the reality of literal persecution. Damasus' efforts in Rome in the 370s to promote the cult of the martyrs may have been influential in this development, according to Duval.[13]

Delehaye criticizes the epic passion as a historical record of the time of the persecutions.[14] But as documents of a changed attitude to the martyrs, the narratives reflect the new emphasis on the larger significance of martyrdom in the fourth century. The events of the individual passion transcend the historical moment, reenact a conflict between good and evil that has immediate relevance to every Christian's daily experience, and link, through repetition of the passion/judgment and victory themes, the biblical past, the time of the martyrs, and the eschatological future in a single text that moves easily between heaven and earth, the past, present, and future. The inscriptions from North Africa illustrate this new emphasis on the atemporal significance of martyrdom. For Prudentius the expanded connotative range of the *Passio* calls forth virtuoso movements on the metonymic and metaphoric registers of the martyr text.

A typology of the martyr narrative will facilitate analysis of these qualities in the *Peristephanon*. Quintilian recommends "opening out the single word," in this case *passio* (*sanguis*); that is, analyzing it into its constituent parts. The first division is between the two stages of the

11. Yvette Duval, *Loca Sanctorum Africae: Le culte des martyrs en Afrique du IVe au VIIe siècle,* Collection de l'École française de Rome 58 (Rome, 1982), 2: 755.

12. Duval, *Loca Sanctorum Africae,* 2: 471. Combat: *arma maligna, caecata saeculi nequitia*; death: *crudeli caede peremptum, purpureo vestitus sanguine*; victory: *victores Christi meruere coronam* (ibid., 2: 471–73).

13. Ibid., 2: 474.

14. See above, n. 8.

martyr's engagement with his persecutor: combat and victory; that is, in literal terms, examination (verbally or by torture) and death. Of these the first can be subdivided between the verbal and the physical, a division already made by Cyprian (*De dominica oratione* 15, *CSEL* 3.1.278.4–5). The martyr is to exhibit: *in sermone constantiam qua confitemur, in quaestione fiduciam qua congredimur, in morte patientiam qua coronamur* ("in speech the steadfastness with which we confess Christ, in examination [i.e., by torture][15] the faith with which we engage in combat, in death the endurance by which we are crowned"). Cyprian's analysis also establishes the spiritual equivalence of the three stages of martyrdom. The virtues assigned to each stage, *constantia, fiducia,* and *patientia,* have no unique attachment to the particular section to which they are allocated. Constancy inspired by faith is a quality of the martyr in all his actions, demonstrated in the passion as a whole, as in each of its separate parts.

The threefold scheme thus established for the epic passion has something in common with Delehaye's typology. He treats under separate heads "cross-examination and speeches" and "punishments," though he makes no distinct category for the death itself.[16] Although, of course, the death/victory category, by its very nature, can only occur once in a martyr narrative (unless more than one martyr is involved) and must always come at the end; by comparison, verbal and physical examination (i.e., torture) can be repeated. The more elaborate accounts, e.g., *Pe.* 10, often alternate description of tortures and speeches, though such speeches are sometimes imagined as being delivered while under torture. The alternation is in text sequence, not necessarily in the "real" circumstances that are being reported.

In some cases the martyr text describes events that precede the final judicial confrontation between persecutor and saint.[17] When events before the martyrdom are elaborated, most evidently in the *Peristephanon* the demand that Lawrence produce the Church's treasure (*Pe.* 2.37–312), they typically reproduce the movement of the martyrdom as a whole

15. A standard meaning of *quaestio,* which is required by the antithesis with *sermone*; Hummel, *The Concept of Martyrdom,* 80–81.

16. Delehaye, *Les passions des martyrs,* 173–218. His other two categories, "the characters" and "miracles," are arrived at by other classificatory criteria.

17. Opelt, "Der Christenverfolger," 243, proposes a typology that emphasizes the role of the persecutor and elaborates in greater detail the early stages of the duel between persecutor and martyr.

from conflict to victory. The principle of narrative duplication and the synecdochical relationship of part to whole still holds good.

Before investigating in more detail Prudentius' martyr narrative under these three heads, I should like to turn to a particular case, *Pe.* 1. The memory of a pair of martyrs is preserved by oral tradition, but there are no reliable written records; they were destroyed at the time of the persecution. Although this is a topos, found in other martyr texts,[18] the emphasis it receives suggests that we are to view this poem as an exercise in the construction of a martyr account from the most minimal of resources. The authenticating detail, it seems, is indispensable, in this case the vision of a ring and handkerchief ascending to heaven (85–88), visible manifestations of the martyrs' spirits. The repetition of forms of *videre,* four times in three lines (89–91), and the reference to bystanders (*conventus adstans,* 91) guarantee that this detail depends on eyewitness accounts. From this detail, confirming the status of the martyrs, and the additional datum that they were former soldiers, Prudentius is able to open out an account that occupies fifty-four lines (40–93).[19]

Of the three sections of the martyr text the verbal cross-examination is most immediately identifiable, though in this case it is reduced to a twelve-line speech of the martyrs. The two ex-soldiers speak the standard language of martyr texts: they express their devotion to Christ rather than to the world (58–60) and denounce idolatry (68–69); but

18. The persecutor is unable to suppress accounts of the martyrdom. The theme thereby replicates the conflict-victory movement of the Passion as a whole. Such attempts at supression are functionally equivalent to attempts to deny the Christian community the martyr's body (see Hippolyte Delehaye, *Les origines du culte des martyrs,* Subsidia Hagiographica 20, [Brussels, 1933], 39). Petruccione, "Prudentius' Use of Martyrological Topoi," 11–12, and "The Persecutor's Envy and the Rise of the Martyr Cult: *Peristephanon* Hymns 1 and 4," *VChr* 45 (1991): 327–36, treats such suppression as an example of the persecutor's *invidia.*

19. Fifty-four lines at a minimum. The phrase *forte tunc* introduces the narrative, but the three preceding stanzas (31–39), devoted to the conversion of soldiers, evidently have immediate relevance to the particular case of Emeterius and Chelidonius, and the three stanzas before that (22–30) describe martyrdom in general terms. In "opening out" his narrative the hagiographer finds himself in the position of an ancient historian working with a scanty historical record. The author will elaborate his account by recourse to "whatever is accustomed to happen" in such circumstances (*licebit etiam falso* **adfingere quicquid fieri solet**, Quintilian 8.3.70, on the rhetorical description); see also T.P. Wiseman, "Practice and Theory in Roman Historiography," *History* 66 (1981): 388–90, and A.J. Woodman, *Rhetoric in Classical Historiography: Four Studies* (London, 1988), 70–116, especially 88–94. For the freedom of treatment Prudentius enjoys in *Pe.* 1, compare Palmer, *Prudentius on the Martyrs,* 152–53.

the contamination of language derived from Roman military service with biblical reminiscence lends their speech an individual cast.[20] Although no words are attributed to the prosecutor or his representatives—the speech begins abruptly—some verbal expression of resistance by a martyr is a necessary part of a martyr text, implied by the simple fact of martyrdom.

Corporal punishments are treated more obliquely.

> Haec loquentes obruuntur mille poenis martyres;
> nexibus manus utrasque flexus involvit rigor
> et chalybs attrita colla gravibus ambit circulis.
>
> (70–72)

> [While they were saying these words the martyrs were subjected to a thousand punishments; the harshness of curved bands encircled both their hands and iron in heavy chains surrounded and chafed their necks.]

"A thousand punishments" is evidently hyperbole, but the narrative sequence requires some sort of punishment. Commonly in martyr accounts punishments are inflicted to silence a martyr.[21] Prudentius can infer from the martyr's speech of resistance the certainty of *poenae,* as a necessary consequence.

The only specific punishment mentioned is throwing the victims in chains. Singling out this *poena* suggests a special status for enchainment and imprisonment in a passion; they are punishments that cannot be dispensed with, even in a minimal martyr narrative like that of *Pe.* 1. The antithesis between *loquentes* on the one hand, and *manus* and *colla* on the other, plays on the body : spirit opposition that figures largely in some of the other poems. (The voice is the special organ of the spirit.)[22] In the present instance the opposition is merely hinted at. Quite typical of Prudentius is the metonymic shift involved in lines 71–72: abstract for concrete, *rigor* for *catenae,* and material for manufactured object, *chalybs* for *catenae.* The first of these permutations generalizes the mar-

---

20. Reinhart Herzog, *Die allegorische Dichtkunst des Prudentius,* Zetemata 42 (Munich, 1966), 20–21.

21. *Pe.* 10.450, 548–55, 891–92, 1104–5.

22. *Pe.* 1.48 *vox fidelis plectitur*; cf. 10.6–10.

tyrs' sufferings; both imply personification of the instruments of punishment. A martyr struggles not just with the persecutor, but with the abstract qualities of cruelty and harshness implied in that and every persecution, and against the physical instruments of persecution, that take on some of the active force of the persecutor himself.[23]

Far from being embarrassed by the absence of specific detail about the martyrs' sufferings, Prudentius draws attention to that gap in his information. The persecutor was able to suppress only two pieces of information: whether the prisoners' hair grew long in prison (80), a topos of the martyr narrative,[24] and "with what suffering, or rather splendor, the torturer regaled the saints" (*quo viros dolore tortor quave pompa ornaverit,* 81). The former is a correlative to the martyrs' pain: the longer the hair, the longer the stay in prison, and therefore the greater the suffering. Its place is supplied by the *rigor* of the martyrs' bonds and their "chafed necks" (*attrita colla*). These details of imprisonment—also by the synecdochical principle of part for whole—can stand for the whole course of punishments that the martyrs are presumed to have undergone (so *catenae* in 1.22). Prudentius, however, has other means to insinuate the kind of tortures the saints would have endured.

He can speculate about their likely sufferings, without committing himself to any specific punishment. The martyrs were ready to face whatever their final moments might bring, whether death by beheading or by exposure to wild beasts (55, 57), after a violent beating and torture on a bed of fire (*verberum post vim crepantum, post catastas igneas,* 56). Willingness to suffer and even to die for the faith is ultimately what counts. At a certain level of abstraction the particular punishments suffered are immaterial. Thus, in setting the scene for the death of the two soldier-martyrs, Prudentius can alternately enumerate specific punishments and describe persecution in abstract terms.

Liberam succincta ferro pestis urgebat fidem;
illa virgas et secures et bisulcas ungulas
ultro fortis expetebat Christi amore interrita.

23. The verbs *involvo* and *ambio* are sufficiently common with an impersonal subject that it would be wrong to insist too strongly on their metaphorical sense here. Nonetheless, the metonymic expressions that form their subjects may be sufficient to defamiliarize common usage and reactivate the metaphors (cf. *carcer . . . inpedit,* 1.46).

24. Cf. Prudentius, *Pe.* 11.53.

Carcer inligata duris colla bacis inpedit,
barbaras forum per omne tortor exercet manus;
veritas crimen putatur, vox fidelis plectitur.

Tunc et ense caesa virtus percussit solum
et rogis ingesta maestis ore flammas sorbuit;
dulce tunc iustis cremari, dulce ferrum perpeti.

(43–51)

[The plague of persecution, sword at its side, was suppressing the freedom of faith, while she of her own accord bravely confronted the rods and axes and two-forked claws, fearless in the love of Christ. Prison constrains necks in the grip of cruel chains, the torturer practices through every square his barbaric arts, and truth is counted a crime, the voice of faith punished. Then too virtue, cut down by the sword, falls to the earth, and heaped on gloomy pyres drinks down the flames, then it is sweet for the just to be burnt to death, and sweet to suffer execution.]

The passage describes the setting in which the particular martyrdom of Emeterius and Chelidonius took place. Time is defined not in a historically specific manner, but as a generalized backdrop of persecution. This introductory passage, beginning with the demand that the Christians sacrifice to idols (40–42), replicates the sequence of the particular martyrdom, but in more abstract terms: *fides* is put to the torture, *veritas* prosecuted, *virtus* executed.[25] But references to specific punishments are set in this generalized framework: beating, axes and two-forked claws, and imprisonment, *carcer,* the last described in a way that anticipates the chaining of Emeterius and Chelidonius (*inligata duris colla bacis,* 46; *attrita colla gravibus . . . circulis,* 72). In this way Prudentius has compensated for the near absence of details of punishment in the primary narrative by incorporating them in the more general, preliminary description of persecution.

Prudentius' introductory passage concludes with the third canonical element of the martyr narrative, the death (49–51). Two methods of death are enumerated, execution by the sword (49 and 51) and by fire

25. For *fides* and *virtus* as preeminent qualities of the martyr, see Cyprian, *Ep.* 60.1 *fidei ac virtutis vestrae testimonia gloriosa* (*CSEL* 3.2; 691.8–9); cf. Aug., *Serm.* 276.1 (*PL* 38.1256) and 283.1.1 (*PL* 38.1286).

(50–51).[26] In this case, however, the primary narrative does retain the method of execution (92–93), but subordinated to the authenticating vision of the martyrs' ring and handkerchief ascending to heaven, tokens of the release of the saints' spirits before the fact. (Compare the death of Eulalia, where ascent of dove and spirit are simultaneous and inseparable, *Pe.* 3.161–70.) The displacement of the death scene performs a number of functions; the vision is, after all, the single detail unambiguously vouched for by oral tradition. The content of the vision establishes what is the most important element of martyrs' deaths, the immediate translation of their souls to heaven. Even before the executioner's stroke the saint, through suffering, is brought close to God. As the ring and handkerchief are metonymic equivalents of the two martyrs' spirits, to that degree anticipating the role of relics at a martyr's shrine after death, so they also metaphorically embody the abstract qualities exemplified in this and every martyrdom: *fides* (*fidem figurans,* 85) and *virtus,* for the *textilis candor* (89) of the handkerchief is most naturally understood of the purity of the saint's life, which receives its ultimate test and vindication in martyrdom.[27]

The martyr's death is *dulce* (51). It has already been described as *decorum*: *hoc genus mortis decorum, hoc probis dignum viris* ("this style of death is glorious, and worthy of honest men," 25). The lines in question are some distance apart, but Palmer is surely right to see here an evocation of Horace's *dulce et decorum est pro patria mori* (*C.* 3.2.13). She persuasively argues that allusions to the second Roman Ode run through *Pe.* 1 and throw into relief Prudentius' account of Christian *militia.* Both Horace and Prudentius are talking of military virtue, though Prudentius contrasts literal with spiritual warfare, and both speak of *virtus* as opening the way to heaven.[28] As was the case with the

26. For the language used of burning alive (*ore flammas sorbuit,* 50), see also *Pe.* 2.343 and 3.160. Martial, *Epigr.* 1.42.5, uses similar language of the death of Brutus' wife Porcia: *dixit et ardentis avido bibit ore favillas.* Peter Howell, *A Commentary on Book One of the Epigrams of Martial* (London, 1980), ad loc., cites a number of other examples of death by "swallowing fire." See especially Seneca, fr. 124 (Haase) *sive flamma ore rapienda est.*

27. According to Cyprian those who live a virtuous life, but do not suffer martyrdom, receive a white crown (*De opere et eleemosynis* 26; *CSEL* 3.1.394.21–29, and *Ep.* 10.5; *CSEL* 3.2.495.1–5); Hummel, *The Concept of Martyrdom,* 135–36. There is probably also a reference here to the white robes of the newly baptized (Albert Blaise, *Le vocabulaire latin des principaux thèmes liturgiques* [Turnhout, 1966], 476). At the same time, the martyrs in heaven are dressed in white: *Pe.* 1.67, 4.145, 5.373–74 (cf. 13.86–87).

28. Horace, *C.* 3.2.21–22: *Virtus, recludens immeritis mori / caelum, negata temptat*

allusion to *Odes* 3.3 in *Pe.* 4, Prudentius has chosen to appropriate for the martyrs a passage describing the ascent to heaven of the Stoic hero. In so doing, he has also given a Christian reinterpretation to the military virtue praised by Horace in the Roman Ode.[29]

The bracketing effect of this Horatian reminiscence, *decorum* (25) and *dulce* (51), suggests a structural design competing with that presupposed up to now. While the phrase *forte tunc* (40) clearly marks the beginning of a *narratio,* yet lines 25–51 also cohere as a group, describing in general terms the nature of martyrdom, before the first mention of the two martyrs in line 52. The lines are also set off by ring composition; the section begins and ends with generalized accounts of death by martyrdom. In fact, lines 25–30, and the transitional stanza (22–24), which links the description of the martyr's death with the introductory section treating the contemporary cult, supply some of the detail concerning the significance of the passion that is missing from the narrative proper. A series of periphrases for death explore various aspects of the martyr's sacrifice. The shedding of blood (*sanguinis dispendio / sanguinis . . . damnum,* 23–24) is interpreted as a confession of God (*deum fateri,* 23), exploiting the specifically Christian sense of *confiteri* as "to suffer martyrdom."[30] It is also, in the military language pervasive in this poem, "to conquer the enemy" (*hostem vincere,* 27), and a baptism in blood (*lota mens in fonte rubro,* 30), by which the spirit receives release from the body (*sede cordis exilit,* 30), finds the way open to heaven (*porta iustis panditur,* 29), and receives the recompense of eternal light (*lux rependit longior,* 24). The variety of expressions for the martyr's death suggests something of the lexical riches available to Prudentius in describing the final moments of a passion. In this respect, too, *Pe.* 1 serves as an appropriate introduction to the whole collection, with its emphasis on the typical qualities of the martyr narrative. Even the specific detail that Emeterius and Chelidonius were former soldiers is not inappropriate, for in an extended sense every martyr is a *miles Christi.*[31] The three

iter via. Palmer, *Prudentius on the Martyrs,* 144–54, is fundamental; for Prudentius' reinterpretation of the Horatian concept of *virtus,* see Ilona Opelt, "Prudentius und Horaz," in W. Wimmel, ed., *Forschungen zur römischen Literatur: Festschrift zum 60. Geburtstag Karl Büchner* (Wiesbaden, 1970), 209–13.

29. See especially *Pe.* 1.32-33: *milites quos ad perenne cingulum Christus vocat, / sueta virtus bello et armis militat sacrariis.* Fortunatus, speaking of St. Maurice and the military martyrs of the Theban legion, has the line [*dogmate Pauli*] *nomine pro Christi dulcius esse mori* (*C.* 2.14.8).

30. Hoppenbrouwers, *Recherches sur la terminologie du martyre,* 209–10.

31. Jacques Fontaine, "La culte des martyrs militaires et son expression poétique au

canonical sections of the martyr narrative are represented in *Pe.* 1, albeit in some instances displaced or indirectly expressed. From the consideration of their role in this single poem I will move to examination of the three categories in the collection as a whole.

Verbal Examination

In the epigrams of Damasus verbal confrontation between persecutor and martyr plays a limited role. The constrained form allows only the briefest snatches of direct speech and in practice even that little is absent in Damasus' poems. Twice, instead, the formula *iussa tyranni* suggests a verbal content to the martyrdom. The persecutions took place when "there was oppression by the commands of the tyrant" (*premerent cum iussa tyranni, Epigr.* 35.1). The commands in question here are evidently the requirement that Christians perform an act of pagan sacrifice, for which some form of *iubeo* is regularly used by Prudentius.[32]

These commands can also be transferred from persecution in general to the circumstances of a particular martyrdom. So Eutychius is provided with the power to overcome "the cruel commands of the tyrant and the executioners' thousand ways of inflicting hurt" (*crudelia iussa tyranni / carnificumque vias pariter tunc mille nocendi, Epigr.* 21.1–2). The notion of requiring an act of apostasy is still present in the phrase *iussa tyranni,* but the qualification *crudelia* and the juxtaposition with the torturers' *vias mille nocendi*[33] evidently refer to the second category of speeches attributed to the prosecuting magistrate in Prudentius, those threatening and/or ordering tortures and, ultimately, execution. When

IVe siècle: L'idéal evangélique de la non-violence dans le christianisme théodosien," *Augustinianum* 20 (1980): 149, = *Études sur la poésie latine tardive d'Ausone à Prudence* (Paris, 1980), 339, suggests that military martyrs may have had a special appeal in the Theodosian period, when monasticism, which also could be interpreted as *militia Christi,* was gaining popularity in the West (cf. Ambrose, *Hymn* 10 Bulst, on Victor, Nabor, and Felix). For other military martyrs see Adolf Harnack, *Militia Christi: The Christian Religion and the Military in the First Three Centuries,* trans. David McInnes Gracie (Philadelphia, 1981), 89–99.

32. *Pe.* 1.41, 3.28, 5.68, 6.36, 6.41, 10.176, 13.37, 14.13. The phrase *iussa tyranni* also occurs in Damasus, *Epigr.* 8.3.

33. The phrase is modeled on Virgil, *Aen.* 7.338, *mille nocendi artes* (Ferrua *ad loc.*). For the Christian reception of this phrase, see Pierre Courcelle, "*Mille Nocendi Artes* (Virgile, *Aen.*, VII, 338)," in *Mélanges de philosophie, de littérature et d'histoire ancienne offerts à Pierre Boyancé,* Collection de l'École française de Rome 22 (Rome, 1974), 219–27.

this aspect of the verbal confrontation between prosecutor and martyr is uppermost, we hear not of "commands" but of "threats." So Agnes is said "to have spontaneously trodden underfoot the threats and rage of the cruel tyrant" (*sponte trucis calcasse minas rabiemque tyranni, Epigr.* 37.4).

The persecuting magistrate may use various tactics to extort an act of apostasy. The threat of torture, intended to intimidate the martyr, involves a speech of instruction (*iussa*) to the torturer. An alternative approach is more insinuating, seeking to persuade rather than compel. This distinction is fundamental to Augustine's Sermons on the martyrs, which are in part a set of meditative commentaries on passion texts. Speaking of the martyrdom of Vincent, Augustine identifies "a double-edged sword" that "the world draws against the soldiers of Christ. It cajoles [*blanditur*] in order to deceive. It intimidates [*terret*] in order to break."[34] The two forms of assault require different responses from the martyr: self-restraint (*continentia*) against *blanditiae,* and steadfastness (*patientia*) against *saevitia.*[35] For Augustine the distinction is important because it allows him to compare the experience of martyrdom and the everyday battle of the Christian against sin: "two factors entice or compel men to sin, pleasure or pain . . . Against pleasures, self-restraint [*continentia*] is required, against pain, steadfastness [*patientia*]." In this respect the martyrs provide a model to imitate for Christians of the period after the persecutions.[36]

No writer suggests that such *blandimenta* are easier for the martyr to overcome than physical torture. On the contrary, they can present a more serious test. In his commentary on the fourth book of Maccabees, an influential work in the Christian martyr tradition, Ambrose reports that Antiochus first used flattering persuasion with Eleazar "because he believed his tortures could be overcome."[37] Both physical and verbal

34. The full quote is: *Duplicem, dixi, aciem producit mundus contra milites Christi. Blanditur enim, ut decipiat; terret, ut frangat* (*Serm.* 276.2.2; *PL* 38.1256). For other references, see *Serm.* 274 (*PL* 38.1253), 283.1.1 (*PL* 38.1286), 284.4–5 (*PL* 38.1291–92), 304.1.1 (*PL* 38.1395), 311.1.1 (*PL* 38.1414), 328.7.6 (*PL* 38.1454), 335.1.1 (*PL* 38.1470).

35. *Illecebras dum ministrat, vincitur per continentiam: poenas et tormenta infligit, vincitur per patientiam* (*Serm.* 274; *PL* 38.1253).

36. *Duo sunt enim quae in peccata homines aut illiciunt aut impellunt; voluptas aut dolor. . . . Contra voluptates necessaria est continentia, contra dolores patientia* (*Serm.* 283.1.1; *PL* 38.1286).

37. Ambrose's commentary on the martyral sections of 4 Macc. concludes his *De Iacob et vita beata.* The passage in question is 2.10.43: *denique a blandimentis coepit, quia iudicabat tormenta sua posse superari* (*CSEL* 32.2; 59.5–6). For a discussion of Ambrose's

assaults can be described as trials of the martyr's resolution. But insofar as verbal blandishments employ deceitful cunning directly against the mind, they may represent a more dangerous threat to spiritual integrity than tortures that work on the body.

In Prudentius *blanditiae* play a subordinate role to *saevitiae,* but at least in the case of Agnes the interrogator alternates threats and soft words: *nunc ore blandi iudicis inlice / nunc saevientis carnificis minis,* 14.16–17. The content of the interrogation is supplied by *Pe.* 3, also addressed to a virgin martyr, Eulalia. There the presiding magistrate expresses his desire to recall Eulalia to the joys of marriage and indicates the instruments of torture standing ready before her to impel her to this choice (3.101–15). In the case of Lawrence, the Roman magistrate abandons physical threats and makes a reasonable request (*blande et quiete efflagito,* 2.63) for the wealth of the Church. Datian similarly masquerades as the voice of reason when he asks Vincent to hand over the Church's holy books. Lawrence's response is to agree, apparently, to go along with the request;[38] as a result the discomfiture of his opponent, when it comes, is all the more final. Vincent, however, is uncompromising in his rejection of Datian's request. He addresses his interrogator as *maligne* and *serpens,* while threatening him with a fiery end that far transcends what the judge has in mind for the sacred texts. Vincent's words echo the poet's introduction to Datian's speech. The praetor, we are told, "hisses from his treacherous mouth serpentine words" (*ore subdolo / anguina verba exsibilat,* 5.175–76). The association of the persecutor with the devil is, of course, pervasive in martyr texts. In the employment of *blanditiae* he is perhaps at his most diabolical. The phrase *anguina verba* recalls the temptation scene in the Garden of Eden, while the general deviousness of the presiding magistrate in such speeches has something in common with the temptations of Christ.[39]

Whether the persecutor is ordering or enticing, enjoining sacrifice to

treatment of his Jewish original see Gérard Nauroy, "Du combat de la piété à la confession du sang: Ambroise de Milan, lecteur critique du IVe livre des Maccabées," *RHPhR* 70 (1990/91): 49–68. I have been unable to see a companion study, "Les frères Maccabées dans l'exégèse d'Ambroise de Milan ou la conversion de la sagesse judéo-hellénique aux valeurs du martyre chrétien," *Cahiers de Biblia Patristica* 2 (1989): 215–45.

38. For such apparent capitulations to the persecutor, see 4 Macc. 12.8–9 and Delehaye, *Les passions des martyrs,* 190–91.

39. The comparison with the temptations of Christ is made explicitly by Augustine, *Serm.* 284.5 (*PL* 38.1291–92); in *Serm.* 309.3.5 (*PL* 38.1412) the judge at Cyprian's trial is said to speak with a *lingua subdola diaboli.* For the serpentine affiliations of the persecutor, see also *Pe.* 5.382 and 6.23.

the pagan gods or threatening torture, from the point of view of the larger pattern of the narrative, the martyr must show defiance. This may be expressed briefly, and in the later poems of the *Peristephanon,* leaving aside *Pe.* 10, the magistrate's interrogation is either vestigial or displaced on a secondary group.[40] When speeches are elaborated they tend to correspond to the categorization of Delehaye, as either direct response to the demands of the magistrate, presentations of Christian doctrine, especially confessions of faith, or prayers, though with a good deal of overlap among the categories.[41] Because from the perspective of the larger pattern of the martyr text expression of defiance is more important than the particular form that expression takes, martyrs' speeches are available to carry material of thematic importance for the text as a whole (e.g., Lawrence's prophecy of a Christian Rome, 2.413–84) or to lend a narrative something of the quality of a theological treatise. Thus, *Pe.* 10 takes on the nature of an antipagan polemic in the manner of the *Contra Symmachum,* while Lawrence's long speech in *Pe.* 2 on true wealth is an exercise in the Christian appropriation of Roman, largely Stoic, philosophical arguments (2.185–312).[42]

When speeches are multiplied, each exchange tends to take on the pattern of the martyrdom as a whole: conflict, followed by victory for the martyr and defeat for the magistrate. As a general rule, however, a progressive principle can be observed. Each expression of verbal defiance only intensifies the persecutor's fury. This is most fully differentiated in *Pe.* 5. Datian begins with "soft words of gentle persuasion" (*verba . . . mollia / suadendo blande effuderat,* 5.17–18). After Vincent's first response, he becomes more agitated (*iam commotior,* 5.41), and his

40. 9.33–42, but no direct address to the martyrs; 11.63–76, displaced on Hippolytus' followers, and 85–88; 13.90–94. Only *Pe.* 14 is an exception, though here the interrogation is given a special twist, appropriate to Agnes' sex.

41. Delehaye, *Les passions des martyrs,* 189–97: 1.58–69, response to (elided) demand to sacrifice; 2.113–32, response to interrogation, 185–312 and 413–84, exposure of doctrine, latter containing elements of prayer; 3.66–95, response to (implied) demand to sacrifice; 5.33–40, 56–92, 146–72 and 186–200, response to interrogation and confession of faith/exposure to doctrine; 6.44–47, confession of faith; 13.90–91, confession of faith; 14.31–37, response to interrogation/confession of faith, and 69–84, prayer. I omit speeches not delivered in the presence of the magistrate or addressed explicitly to the Christian community.

42. See Fridoff Kudlien, "Krankheitsmetaphorik im Laurentiushymnus des Prudentius," *Hermes* 90 (1962): 104–15, on Stoic medical metaphors. Barthes, "Introduction to the Structural Analysis of Narratives," 120 speaks of the capacity of narrative sequences, in our case the conflict sequence, with its various subsidiary constituents (called by Barthes "functional nuclei"), to "furnish intercalary spaces which can be packed almost infinitely."

agitation continues to grow (5.94–95), until after Vincent's final words he is "wounded, and grows pale, reddens and seethes, rolling his maddened eyes and gnashing his teeth and foaming at the mouth" (*saucius / pallet rubescit aestuat / insana torquens lumina / spumasque frendens egerit,* 5.201–4). The description suggests diabolical possession—there are verbal parallels with the description of possession in *Pe.* 1—while the Virgilian reminiscences suggest that Datian is by now more animal than human.[43] Datian's excited state continues after Vincent's death and helps to explain his vendetta against that saint's corpse (5.377–82, 429–32); he is now truly like a wild beast, preying on carrion. Indeed, so uncontrollable is his spirit (*inpotentem spiritum,* 5.430), that it even bursts the bonds of narrative propriety. When Prudentius exclaims in rhetorical question "Will no way be found to break your purpose?" (5.432), a not uncommon form of authorial intrusion in Christian Latin poetry, Datian astonishingly responds: "None, I shall never stop" (5.433).[44] Time of narrator and narrated are thoroughly confused. Yet such is the impassioned agitation of Datian that his response has a certain psychological, if not historical, plausibility. The continued verbal defiance of Vincent has aroused his fury. It is not surprising that he and Asclepiades, confronting the incorrigibly loquacious Romanus, direct their torturers' best efforts to silencing the organ of speech.[45]

Punishment and Torture

Prudentius speaks of *mille poenae* (1.70), Damasus of *viae mille nocendi* (*Epigr.* 21.2). In the epic passion the persecutor conventionally has a large number of methods available for inflicting pain. It is a principle of these texts that the glory of a martyr is proportionate to the cruelty of his suffering.[46] Multiplying punishments increases their cruelty and

43. *Torquens lumina* is used by Virgil (*G.* 3.433, *Aen.* 7.448–49) of a snake, *spumas aget* (*G.* 3.203) of a horse; cf. Christian Schwen, *Vergil bei Prudentius* (Leipzig, 1937), 76. For the parallels with *Pe.* 1, see verse 101 of that poem.

44. *Nullusne te franget modus? / "Nullus, nec umquam desinam"* (*Pe.* 5.432–33).

45. See this chapter, n.21, and *Pe.* 5.95–97. Elaine Scarry, *The Body in Pain: The Making and Unmaking of the World* (New York, 1985), 45–51 and 54, describing modern torture, emphasizes the significance of the torturer's monopolization of language and silencing or control of the victim's voice.

46. Cf. Ambrose, *De Iac.* 2.12.55, *talis haec pugna est, ut ille gloriosius vicerit, qui crudelius fuerit occisus* (*CSEL* 32.2; 67.20–21), of 4 Macc., Aug., *Serm.* 274 (*PL* 38.1252), 276.3 (*PL* 38.1256–57), and the passages collected by Rainer Henke, *Studien zum Romanushymnus des Prudentius,* Europäische Hochschulschriften, Reihe 15, Klassische Sprachen und Literaturen 27 (Frankfurt am Main, 1983), 102–14.

hence enhances the martyr's renown. The principle is enunciated in a typical Augustinian play on words: speaking of the resurrection of the flesh he says that "the martyrs' bodies, in which they suffered great torments [*tormenta*], will receivc great ornaments [*ornamenta*]."[47] The causal relationship, torments produce ornaments, though not directly stated, is implicit in the paronomasia. Variety of tortures is translated metaphorically and chromatically into the multicolored flowers or jewels of the martyr's crown, or the flowery meadows of the Paradise he or she now enjoys.[48] The trope itself figuratively embodies the close relationship between suffering and reward.

The multiple sufferings of the martyr are most briefly expressed as a series of nouns for punishments and tortures. Thus, Damasus enumerates some of the "thousand ways of giving hurt" in his epigram on Saint Lawrence:

verbera, carnifices, flammas, tormenta, catenas
  vincere Laurenti sola fides potuit.

(*Epigr.* 33.1–2)

[Scourgings, executioners, flames, tortures and chains, Lawrence was able to conquer all of them by faith alone.]

The presence of *carnifices* in this enumeration, personal agent rather than instrument, action or effect, may seem anomalous. Damasus implies that the torturer/executioner is as much an impersonal instrument of the persecuting magistrate as the rest of the paraphernalia of torture. This inference is borne out by Prudentius' treatment of the relationship between *iudex* and *carnifex,* as we shall see. But the half-line *verbera, carnifices* can also be treated diachronically, as a constituent of Latin poetic idiom. Lucretius, in accounting for human fears of punishment in the underworld, attributes these delusions to familiarity with the excesses of Roman judicial torture: *verbera, carnifices, robur, pix, lammina, taedae* (3.1017, "scourgings, executioners, the rack, pitch, the metal plate,

47. Aug., *Serm.* 328.6 *Corpora ipsa sua habebunt magna ornamenta, in quibus passi sunt magna tormenta* (*PL* 38.1454); cf. 280.5.5 (*PL* 38.1283).

48. Punishments as crown of flowers: John Chrysostom, *Oratio de S. Romano* 1.2 (*PG* 50.609), quoted by Delehaye, *Les passions des martyrs,* 149–50; punishments as flower-strewn meadow, Prudentius, *Pe.* 5.277–80 and 321–22.

torches").[49] Whether or not the imitation is a conscious one, the implication that the Roman technology of torture remained constant from Republican times to the late Empire is fully supported by the historical facts. Every one of the methods of torture enumerated by Lucretius finds a place in the *Peristephanon* with the exception of pitch, for which the boiling white lime into which the martyrs of the *Candida Massa* were thrown (13.76–87) is a kind of substitute.

The syntactical form of Damasus 33.1, asyndetic enumeration, is especially appropriate with its radical abbreviation to the brevity of the epigram. At the same time, by combining unity with multiplicity the figure is well suited to a martyr text. All the nouns in the enumeration are in a relationship of equivalence to each other; their literal juxtaposition in the line of verse corresponds to the semantic association of the words in question, despite minor variations in the nominal categories to which they belong (e.g., personal agent, physical instrument, action). To put it another way, all are parts of a larger generic whole, to which each specific noun may bear a synecdochical relationship.

Prudentius' lexical practice will help to exemplify this principle. When a single word is required to express the whole sequence of punishments, viewed collectively and stopping short of death, the singular *poena* is used. Encratis, for instance,[50] though cruelly tortured, survives her own "martyrdom" and is able to tell her tale. "You live and retrace the sequence of your punishment" (*poenae seriem retexis,* 4.117), Prudentius apostrophizes her. In so doing she usurps the role of the martyrologer, that is, in this collection, of Prudentius. The creating of a sequence (*series*) from the collective noun *poena* involves the opening out, or unravelling—the literal meaning of *retexo*—of that word's implications, i.e., the breaking up of *poena* (singular) into its constituent *poenae* (plural) or *supplicia.* So Vincent expresses his scorn of threatened punishments:

tormenta, carcer, ungulae
stridensque flammis lammina

49. The translation is Cyril Bailey's, *Titi Lucreti Cari De Rerum Natura Libri Sex,* 3 vols. (Oxford, 1947), 1: 355; the passage is quoted by T.P. Wiseman, *Catullus and His World: A Reappraisal,* (Cambridge, 1985), 5, whose brief account of Roman judicial tortures vividly portrays their cruelty and sometimes arbitrary, and illegal, application. For the imitation of Lucretius, see Ferrua, 167, *ad loc.*

50. Compare also *Pe.* 5.289–90, *decursa iam satis tibi / poenae minacis munia,* cited at the beginning of this chapter.

atque ipsa poenarum ultima,
mors, Christianis ludus est

(5.61–64)

[Tortures, imprisonment, claws and the plate hissing in the flames, even the ultimate punishment, death, are to Christians sport.]

Imprisonment and each individual torture are separately *poenae,* while the whole process can be referred to collectively as *poena.* Even the death itself can be seen as no more than the last in the sequence of *poenae* and from this perspective at least their metonymic equivalent. It is no accident that Vincent experiences all the punishments enumerated here. Lines 61–64 are an epitome of the martyr text as a whole (at least up to the death), and they supply the bare minimum of narrative sequence from which the text before us is unfolded.

In the concluding section of *Pe.* 5, Prudentius returns to the contemporary situation of the poet and sinning humanity whom he represents. He prays for Vincent's intercession at the throne of God. In doing so, he once more enumerates the instruments of Vincent's passion.

per te, per illum carcerem,
honoris augmentum tui,
per vincla, flammas, ungulas,
per carceralem stipitem,

per fragmen illud testeum
quo parta crevit gloria
. . . .
miserere nostrarum precum

(5.549–54 and 557)

[By yourself, by that prison, enhancer of your glory, by the chains, flames, and claws, by the prison stocks, and by those shards of pottery by which the fame you had already attained grew... have pity on our prayers.]

The enumeration of Vincent's punishments implies the whole sequence of the passion, called forth in the mind's eye of the worshipper by the mnemonic quality of the language, and in the case of Vincent, by the very presence of the bed he lay on after his tortures, and which the devotees tremblingly embrace (555–56). Word and physical object are equivalent here; both have the power to make present, in a small compass, the reality of the saint's suffering. In the case of relics Brown has called this principle the effect of inverted magnitude[51] and has emphasized the massive *potentia* derived from a tiny fragment that has the ability to transcend spatial distinctions of magnitude as well as the temporal division between time of the passion and time of the worshipper. From a literary perspective this is one more example of the synecdochical principle: the part standing for the whole. By multiplying the tortures inflicted on a saint, persecutors were in fact increasing that martyr's glory by the creation of new narrative fragments, each replete with the mystery of the whole passion, just as they ran the risk of creating new relics by multiplying objects that had come into contact with the martyr in his suffering. Relics might even be actual fragments of the instruments used to torture or execute a prisoner, the best known example being the nails and slivers of the Cross that were the proud possession of a number of western churches, which are included in an enumeration of the Instruments of the Passion in a poem of Sidonius Apollinaris.[52]

Of all the words used for specific punishments in the *Peristephanon* Prudentius selects *catenae,* "chains," to stand for the whole sequence of the martyr's sufferings prior to death. The martyrs are those "whom neither chains nor cruel death have frightened" (1.22). The association with death suggests that the two together (*catenae* and *mors*) stand for the whole course of the Passion. This is confirmed by the later passage in this same poem that amplifies the sequence *catenae,* followed by *mors,* 1.43–51.[53] The last of these three stanzas deals with the martyr's death, by fire or the sword; the first two with an amplification of the word *catenae.* That the second passage is to be read as a fuller version of the first is confirmed by verbal repetition: *nec . . . terruit,* 22, corresponds to *interrita,* 45. *Catenae* includes, then, rods and axes and two-forked claws (44), prison (46), and the torturer (47).

In *Pe.* 5, *catenae* is once again applied to the whole sequence of tortures. In the introductory section the poet recalls Datian's attempt to

51. Brown, *Cult of the Saints,* 78, 87, 96.

52. Sidonius, *C.* 16.48–49, *sustentans alapas, ludibria, verbera, vepres, / sortem, vincla, crucem, clavos, fel, missile, acetum*; cf. Fortunatus' hymn *Pange, lingua* (2.2 Leo) 19, *hic acetum, fel, arundo, sputa, clavi, lancea.*

53. Quoted earlier in this chapter.

force Vincent to sacrifice to the pagan gods: "he was trying with the sword and with chains [*ferro et catenis,* 5.16] to compel you to sacrifice." Here *ferro* is presumably metonymy for *mors,* and refers to Datian's initial threat (5.50–52) that Vincent must sacrifice or die. But there is little trace of *catenae* in the rest of the poem—the word does not recur. True, Vincent is thrown into prison (237–38), but only after a long sequence of tortures, interrupted by a respite to allow the torturers to catch their breaths (140). *Catenae* is again best taken as a collective noun, referring to the whole sequence of punishments Vincent suffered before his death, including both tortures and imprisonment.

The choice of *catenae* for this function has a number of explanations. One reason is that imprisonment, followed by death, is the irreducible minimum of a martyr's punishments: the martyrdom of Fructuosus and his two deacons, *Pe.* 6, is a good example of an elaboration of this simple pattern.[54] A second is that in order to experience *tormenta* a victim had first to be immobilized. Vincent, for example, is "bound with hands twisted behind his back" (*vinctum retortis bracchiis,* 5.109). While the word *catenae* never signifies such secondary restraint in the *Peristephanon,* the more general word *vincula* and its cognates convey both this sense and that of imprisonment. From this point of view, too, the use of *catenae* as equivalent of *poenae* has its own logic. Physical restraint is common to all stages in the martyrdom. The emotional force of the word dictates the choice of *catenae* rather than *vincula.* Chains are truly capable of inspiring fear; because *vincula* is more general in meaning it loses vividness, and it therefore is less well suited to convey the threats against the martyr.

Prudentius' emphasis on physical restraint and incarceration as constituents of the martyr text is by no means arbitrary. We have already seen in *Pe.* 1.70–72 that physical restraint can act as a foil to spiritual liberation. In contrast to the bonds put on the body, the martyr's voice, privileged organ of the spirit, can express itself freely in defiance (1.70) or prayer to God (13.53–54); even if his hands are immobilized, the martyr may raise his eyes to heaven (5.235–36). This radical disassociation of mind and body is characteristic of martyrdom. In Augustine's words, speaking of Vincent, "so extreme was the punishment of his

54. It is perhaps no accident that it is the only poem of the *Peristephanon* based on a text dating to the persecution period; Delehaye, *Les passions des martyrs,* 104–5, P. Tino Alberto Sabattini, "Storia e leggenda nel *Peristephanon* di Prudenzio I," *RSC* 20 (1972): 37–43.

limbs, so great was the composure of his words that it was as if one person was being tortured and another speaking."[55] The separation of mind and body prefigures the culminating liberation of death, when the mind is conclusively freed from the body (*Pe.* 5.359). The whole course of martyrdom is a dialectic between freedom and restraint, between the liberation of the spirit and enchainment of the body, between faith and suffering.[56]

Each stage in the process is, at a certain level of abstraction, equivalent. But this does not exclude some spatial and temporal progression. Metaphorically the stages in the passion can be described as steps on a ladder to heaven, recalling Perpetua's vision before her martyrdom of ascending a ladder that led up to God. For Fructuosus imprisonment is a step toward a martyr's crown (*gradus coronae,* 6.25; cf. 5.223–24). For Agnes the successful preservation of her chastity when exposed as a prostitute is her first step to heaven (*primum . . . gradum / caelestis aulae,* 14.61–62); execution follows as a second means of ascent (*alius . . . / ascensus,* 62–63). The temporal progression of the martyrdom is translated into a vertical spatial dimension, of increasing proximity to heaven. That special quality of the martyr's shrine as a place where heaven and earth meet is also written into the martyr narrative before the moment of death. The martyr's sufferings bring heaven and earth closer together; for the martyr punishment is a propaedeutic for death and a foretaste of the elevation that is to come. Free of the body yet still, however tenuously, implicated in it, still on earth yet close to heaven, the martyr is in that transitional state between life and death that anticipates the power he or she has even after death to bridge easily the division between heaven and earth, presence and absence.

In their temporal sequence of *tormenta* the poems of the *Peristephanon* do seem to presuppose a regular succession of tortures: binding, stretching, tearing with the double-forked *ungulae,* and exposure to fire,

55. *Tanta poena erat in membris, tanta securitas in verbis, tanquam alius torqueretur, alius loqueretur* (*Serm.* 275.1; *PL* 38.1254). Cf. *Passio Mariani et Iacobi* 6.1–2, *Creditis Christianos sentire carceris poenas et saeculares horrere tenebras, quos manet gaudium lucis aeternae? Spiritus cum fida spe venientis gratiae caelos mente conplexus, suis iam non interest poenis* (200.24–27 Musurillo).

56. Cf. *Pe.* 1.43, of persecution in general, *liberam succincta ferro pestis urgebat fidem,* especially the expression *liberam . . . fidem.* For the martyr's *libera mens,* see also *Passio Mariani et Iacobi* 12.4: *nullae tamen aciem liberae mentis clausere tenebrae* (210.16–17 Musurillo). Tertullian writes to *martyres designati,* who are confined in prison, *nihil crus sentit in nervo, cum animus in caelo est* (*Ad Mart.* 2.10; *CCL* 1; 5.6–7).

either on a bed of flame (*catasta, grabatum*), or by heated metal plates (*lamminae*). Binding is a necessary preliminary in order to secure the victim for torture; the sequence may be preceded by some kind of beating (*virgae, flagra, ictus*; *Pe.* 10.116–22 and 11.55–56).[57] Only Vincent suffers the canonical sequence: Lawrence is spared the claws, Eulalia is not specifically said to have been stretched on the rack, but it is likely that her defiant cry to the torturer "go ahead, burn, tear, break apart my limbs" (*adure, seca, / divide membra,* 3.91–92), that refers to the canonical sequence of three tortures in reverse order, implies that the torturer rises to the challenge in the last instance as well as in the first two. In Romanus' case the persecutor intends fire to be a method of death, not torture—intends because the flames are doused by a providential storm of rain (10.856–60). On the other hand, in *Pe.* 10 the motif of torture by *ungulae* is doubled. Torturers apply the claws first to the body (*pensilis latus viri,* 452—the word *pensilis* shows that Romanus was first stretched on the horse[58])—then to the face (548–60), the only such use of claws in the *Peristephanon* and an early index in the poem of Asclepiades' obsession with silencing Romanus.

Pe. 5, however, the martyrdom of Vincent, best illustrates how *tormenta* contribute to the temporal progression of the martyr narrative. Five stages can be distinguished in Vincent's *poenae*: 1) stretching on the rack, till his limbs dislocate (*conpago donec ossuum / divulsa membratim crepet,* 111–12)—the actual procedure is not described, but that it took place can be inferred from Datian's order;[59] 2) first use of the claws (113–22); 3) second use of the claws (173–74); 4) the ultimate torture (*extrema quaestio,* 206–8), a bed of fire and red-hot metal plates, the former equipped with sharp metal spikes, strewn with salt and smeared with molten fat (217–20, 225–32); 5) incarceration, and exposure to a new form of punishment,[60] a bed strewn with jagged fragments of pottery.

---

57. For the Roman technology of torture, see J. Vergote, "Folterwerkzeuge," *RlAC* 8 (1972): 120–40, especially 133–35, and for narrative ellipses in the description of torture in Prudentius, Rainer Henke, "Die Nutzung von Senecas (Ps.-Senecas) Tragödien in Romanus-Hymnus des Prudentius," *WüJb* 11 (1985): 142–44. The canonical sequence probably reflects normal Roman inquisitional practice.

58. Henke, "Die Nutzung," 143.

59. Ibid., 142.

60. The punishment and its description as a *nova poena* are found already in Damasus' epigram on Eutychus (21.4–5). Paulinus attributes the same punishment to Felix (*C.* 15.185–86).

Vincent's reaction to his *tormenta* provides a counterpart to Datian's response to the calm words of the martyr. While Datian increasingly loses control of his emotions, Vincent becomes ever more resolute and serene. After the first two tortures, treated together by the poet, Vincent is only made more joyful and sees Christ present before him (*ille tanto laetior . . . te, Christe, praesentem videns,* 125 and 128). The gap between heaven and earth is already closing, so much so that Vincent's joy can be described in meteorological terms: "he makes bright his clear brow, free of every cloud" (*omni vacantem nubilo / frontem serenam luminat,* 126–27). While *frons serena* is a clichéd manifestation of happiness, Prudentius has reanimated the metaphor in *serena* by insisting on its original meteorological sense, and in so doing he has represented the martyr as an antitype to Zeus or Jupiter as weather-god, whose brow is among the clouds. Vincent receives heavenly attributes because he is in some sense already in heaven. As in the use of Horace, *Odes* 3.3, in *Pe.* 4, pagan mythological speculation on heaven and the role of the gods finds a Christian reinterpretation in the ascent to heaven of the martyrs.

After the fourth torture the saint is once more only strengthened in his resolution. He is removed from the bed of fire still stronger (*fortior,* 237) and thrown into prison "lest free access to light inspire his lofty spirit" (*altum spiritum,* 240). Clearly, the description of Vincent's spirit as *altus* is no panegyric cliché. The elevation of his soul is insisted on throughout the poem. Subjection to physical abuse, even being thrown into the deepest prison (*imo ergastulo,* 241), only increases his resolution and his proximity to heaven (cf. *Pe.* 10.580). The vision Vincent receives in prison confirms this progression in fortitude and its association with heaven. Angels stand before him and one of them calls him to join their heavenly throng, addressing him as "bravest of the brave" (*fortissimorum fortior,* 294). Vincent's bravery has reached a high point, corresponding to the depths of uncontrollable passion into which Datian has been plunged. The effects of psychological *tormenta* can be read in Datian's facial expression (202–4), just as Vincent's serenity of countenance bears witness to his psychological composure.[61]

The persecutor's anger is a response to the saint's vocal expression of his *patientia.* Response to the victim's physical endurance is displaced

61. Augustine (*Serm.* 275.2; *PL* 38.1254–55 and 276.3; *PL* 38. 1257), in his sermons for Vincent's feast day, insists on the psychological *tormenta* suffered by Datian, and in him by Satan.

from the *iudex* to the *tortor,* who, along with the jailer, acts as an extension of the magistrate's power in its coercive aspect. The most obvious, even banal, manifestation of this is that the torturer frequently becomes exhausted by the unavailing exercise of his skills (5.122–23, 139–40); by contrast the martyr is always fresh and outstrips the torturers in his eagerness to move on to new tortures (5.210–12, 221).[62] There is nothing specifically Christian, still less Prudentian, in this. Both are topoi of the literature of torture. Regulus returned voluntarily to Carthage despite his knowledge of what the *barbarus tortor* had in store for him;[63] in Silius' *Punica* the heroic Spanish killer of Hasdrubal is subjected to the most hideous punishments, but "his mind remains untouched" (*mens intacta manet,* 1.179), and, like Vincent, "as if a spectator he rebukes the torturers who are wearied by their toil" (*spectanti similis, fessosque labore ministros / increpitat,* 1.180–81).

The description of the torturers found in the majority of manuscripts at 5.99–100 is typical of Prudentius: they are "fed on the flesh of criminals and skilled in hand" (*reorum carnibus / pastos manuque exercitos*). Whatever the original text, this reading, adopted by Cunningham but not by Bergman and Lavarenne, accurately reflects Prudentian usage.[64] The latter phrase in particular harks back to the first mention of the torturer in the collection: *barbaras forum per omne tortor* **exercet manus** (1.47). In *Pe.* 5 Prudentius regularly substitutes hand(s) or arms metonymically for *tortor(es)*:

nisusque anhelus solverat
fessos *lacertorum toros.*

(5.123–24)

[Breathless effort had exhausted the weary muscles of [their] arms.]

cohibete paulum *dexteras.*

(139)

62. Examples in the *Pe.*: (weariness of persecutors) 10.456, 809; (eagerness of martyr) 6.18, 10.69–75, 10.897, 14.19–20.

63. The expression *barbarus tortor,* from Horace's Regulus ode (3.5.49–50), is twice imitated by Prudentius (*Pe.* 1.47 and 4.121). In Silius Regulus' *patientia* (6.545) is hailed, and he is cited as an exemplary model of *fides* and *virtus* (547–49).

64. Cunningham's text is found in the majority of manuscripts, but not in the oldest group, which gives *illos reorum plutones / pastos resectis carnibus.* (There is a metrical problem in the quantity of the *o* of *plutones.*) For my purposes it is enough that the expression is Prudentian in the broader sense of "in the manner of Prudentius."

[Check for a while your hands]

[ulcera] *manus* resulcans diruet.

(144)

[The hand will furrow and tear open the scars once more.]

The reduction of an individual to his physical *membra* provides an appropriate contrast to the martyr, whose spiritual integrity survives the dismemberment of his body. At the same time, as depersonalized hands the torturers become one more instrument in the magistrate's arsenal of coercion. When Vincent invites Datian to dip his hands into the wounds (*manus et ipse intersere,* 151), he is doing no more than asking the magistrate to act out in person the role that his "hands," i.e., the *carnifices,* have already been performing for him. As Vincent tells him, "you yourself are the greater torturer" (*carnifex,* 148). It comes as no surprise that Datian is described as "a skilled practitioner of torture" (*crucis peritus artifex,* 1.254) when he has the novel idea of scattering Vincent's prison bed with jagged fragments of pottery.

We now see why Damasus includes *carnifices* among instruments of torture in his epigram on Lawrence. The reverse of this assimilation of person to thing is the attribution of emotion to the *tormenta* themselves. Vincent so intimidates his "cruel and savage tortures" (*saeva et aspera / tormenta,* 295–96) that they "tremble before their conqueror" (*victorem tremunt,* 296).[65] In the ritualized combat of martyrdom, divisions between human and nonhuman are subverted; persecutor and his agents become depersonalized instruments, the martyr in his transcendence of his body approaches the sphere of the divine.

The persecutor and his agents are also depersonalized by their assimilation to wild animals. The topos is common to pagan, Jewish, and Christian martyr texts,[66] and receives support from the lexicon of torture. *Ungulae* is used not only of the torture instrument; it may also mean the claws of birds or wild animals. The comparison between torturers and wild beasts is explicit in the Theodosian Code.[67] This may explain why of the three canonical forms of torture it is the claws that receive the fullest description in the *Peristephanon.*

65. See also 6.101–2 and 106.

66. Silius 6.531; 4 Macc. 9.28, 12.13; Delehaye, *Les passions des martyrs,* 162 and 178.

67. *CTh* 9.12.1.

In both transmitted texts at 5.99–100 the torturers are said to be fed on flesh. Once again the language is thoroughly Prudentian. The *carnifex* who takes Fructuosus and his companions off to prison is "fed on blood" (*pastus sanguine,* 6.17) and in *Pe.* 5, when Vincent is released from prison, he is to recover so that he may provide "fresh nourishment" (*pastum novum,* 331), whether for the torturers or Datian is left unclear. By this stage the distinction can scarcely be maintained. The same language can be used at any level in the hierarchy of persecutors. In *Pe.* 3 it is the emperor Maximian who is said to feed on innocent blood (3.87).[68] And once more Vincent urges Datian to act out the implications of his persecution not only by plunging his hands into his victim's body but also by drinking the rivers of hot blood (*rivosque ferventes bibe,* 152).

Such a diet of flesh and blood immediately puts the *tortor/iudex* beyond the pale of human civilization. Vincent, then, quite appropriately calls his torturers Datian's hounds (146–47); in *Pe.* 10 they are carrion-eating dogs and vultures (10.806–10). In Prudentius' version, Lawrence's famous last words also allude to his persecutor's habitual diet. Ambrose quotes his words as *assum est, . . . versa et manduca* ("it is roasted, turn me over and eat," *Off.* 1.41.207); in the Ambrosian Hymn[69] they are *versate me . . . , / vorate, si coctum est* ("turn me over, eat, if it is cooked," 13.31-32), and in Augustine *iam . . . coctum est . . . versate me, et manducate* ("it is cooked now; turn me over, and eat," *Serm.* 303.1; *PL* 38.1394). Prudentius rationalizes this speech by splitting it into two. Lawrence first asks to be turned over (401–4); the prefect complies (405). Then he announces he is cooked and ready to eat.

68. The passage exemplifies the application of the language of torture at a high level of generality to persecution as a whole. While the language of feeding is metaphorical, the shift is primarily synecdochic, involving the assimilation of the church as a whole to its individual members: *Dux bonus, arbiter egregius, / sanguine pascitur innocuo / corporibusque piis inhians / viscera sobria dilacerat / gaudet et excruciare fidem* (3.86–90). Compare Damasus' favorite phrase for the time of the persecutions, *tempore quo gladius secuit pia viscera matris* with *Epigr.* 46.7, *cum lacerat pia membra,* which appears to refer to a specific act of torture (Ferrua 189 ad loc.).

69. Manlio Simonetti, "Studi sull' innologia popolare cristiana dei primi secoli," *MAL,* ser. 8a, 4, 6 (1952): 397–98, concludes that this hymn is not by Ambrose and detects an imitation of Prudentius (vs. 3–4: *Pe.* 2.25–28). Gérard Nauroy, "Le martyre de Laurent dans l'hymnodie et la prédication des IVe et Ve siècles et l'authenticité ambrosienne de l'hymne 'Apostolorum supparem'," *REAug* 35 (1989): 44–82, argues for the authenticity of the hymn and discusses Lawrence in the literary tradition of the fourth and fifth centuries (53–60 on Prudentius).

Coctum est, devora
et experimentum cape
sit crudum an assum suavius.

(2.406–8)

[It is cooked, eat, and put to the test whether raw or roast is sweeter.]

The last two lines are Prudentius' addition. Only *assum* has Ambrosian authority. They are included to evade the difficulty in the traditional story that, on this occasion at least, a persecutor is found eating cooked flesh. Line 408 implies that raw flesh is his normal diet. The conduct of the *iudex/carnifex* elsewhere in the *Peristephanon* bears out the implication.

We are now able to add something more to our discussion of Datian's treatment of the martyr's corpse. In exposing the body to carrion-eating animals (387–88) or to the fish of the sea (444), Datian becomes bestial himself (*efferata,* 380). But this bestiality is nothing new. It is rather the most overt manifestation of that dehumanization of the persecutor evident throughout the poem. In anticipating Vincent's corpse being torn by wild animals (*carpendum dare,* 388) or his flesh ripping and bursting on rocks (445–48), Datian is attempting to reenact, this time against a dead body, the assaults he made on the saint's physical integrity while he was alive. That Datian fails, that he is defeated once more by the saint's "bones and empty limbs" (*ossibus / vacuisque . . . membris,* 5.427–28), is a measure of the last great mystery of martyrdom: that even after death, which is the final separation of spirit and body, the martyr's mortal remains—indeed any place or object stained with the blood of his suffering (cf. 4.89–96)—retain the power to thwart the forces of the devil and the secular world. This power is derived from the sufferings of the martyr, while spirit and flesh were still, however tenuously, together. From the point of view of the cult of the saints, the "psychodrame" of the martyr's suffering,[70] not the fact of death, is the guarantee of posthumous *potentia.* That is why this section of the martyr text is most elaborated in the epic passions. Although she survived the most horrible tortures, Encratis has the title of a martyr and receives the crown because her punishment was complete (*plena . . . / poena,*

70. Brown, *Cult of the Saints,* 82–83 describes Prudentius' poems as "psychodrames."

4.135-36). Viewed from this perspective death may be no more than the last in a series of *poenae,* the final act in that disassociation of body and spirit that characterizes the whole sequence of the passion.

Death

Elidit illic fune collum martyris
lictor nefandus. Sic peracta est passio.
Anima absoluta vinculis caelum petit.

(10.1108–10)

[The wicked executioner then crushed the martyr's neck with a rope. The passion was over. His soul freed from its bonds made its way to heaven.]

With these words Prudentius recounts the death of Romanus. Despite the length of the poem, the moment of death is subject to radical abbreviation. Three elements are present: method of death, announcement of completion of life/passion, and separation of soul from body and spiritual ascent. All three elements are routinely present in the poems of the *Peristephanon,* though it is the last, with its representation of death as a continuation and fulfillment of the whole course of the passion that receives most play.

Prudentius recognizes three standard forms of martyrdom: *ferrum, flammae,* and *ferae,* the sword, fire, and wild beasts (3.116–18, 7.11–13). A majority of his martyrs die either by the sword (Emeterius and Chelidonius, Cyprian, Agnes) or by fire (Lawrence, Eulalia, Fructuosus and his deacons). *Pe.* 7, devoted to the martyr Quirinus, who was drowned in a river (*fluvius,* 7.23; cf. 14),[71] acts as a kind of footnote and qualification to the more common methods of martyrdom. The comparison of the flood in which the martyr was drowned and the floods of blood associated with the typical passion (7.16–20) further helps to set up the assimilation of martyrdom and baptism in *Pe.* 8. More uncommon modes of death tend to cluster in the later poems (the martyrdoms of Cassian,

71. Cf. *ILCV* 976.6–8, *sub pedibusque iacet passio cuique sua: / ferrum, flamma, ferae, fluvius, saevumque venenum. / Tot tamen has mortes una corona manet* (fifth century, from Rome) and Cyprian, *Hab. Virg.* 6 (*CSEL* 3.1; 192.10): *ignes aut cruces aut ferrum aut bestias patitur ut coronetur.* The fourth method of execution, the cross, is found in the *Peristephanon* only in the special case of Peter (*Pe.* 12.9–18).

Hippolytus, and the *Candida Massa* in *Pe.* 9, 11, and 13). Vincent is unusual in that his death comes when he is no longer subject to punishment; Datian intends to give him time to recover before he is submitted to new tortures (5.329–32). In this, as in everything else, Vincent thwarts his persecutor's intentions. Finally, the third of Prudentius' standard forms of martyrdom, *ferae,* is not literally represented in the *Peristephanon.* It has undergone a metaphorical displacement. No literal wild beasts tear the martyr's bodies; rather it is the *iudex* and his henchmen who torture their victim's flesh with bestial cruelty.

From one point of view, death, when it comes, represents a break with what has gone before, the end (*finis*) of sufferings and trials (5.527–28, 6.117, 14.90),[72] the final chapter of the passion. But the concept of death as the soul's release from the body and its ascent to heaven receives greatest emphasis in the *Peristephanon,* i.e., just those elements that assimilate death to the whole course of the martyr's suffering. Not that the language of release and ascent, when speaking of death, is unique to the martyrs. On the contrary, it is a commonplace of Christian sepulchral inscriptions.[73] Damasus makes extensive use of the motif of heavenly ascent, but without discriminating between martyrs and nonmartyred Christians. He applies very similar language to his sister Irene and to the martyr Protus.[74] Death for the martyr has the same consequences as for the virtuous Christian—ascent of the soul to heaven. (Sepulchral inscriptions assume that the inhabitant of a tomb is virtuous.[75]) From this perspective the life and death of the martyr serve as a model for the post-persecution Christian, a model of spiritual combat against the forces of the devil and of its celestial reward. Ambrose and Augustine emphasize this aspect of martyrdom in their homiletic.[76] What

72. For the word *finis* of death, see also 2.485–87, 4.128, 10.813, 12.25.

73. Gabriel Sanders, *Licht en Duisternis in de christelijke Grafschriften: Bijdrage tot de Studie der latijnse metrische Epigrafie van de vroegchristelijke Tijd,* Verhandelingen van de k. vlaamse Academie voor Wetenschappen, Letteren en schone Kunsten von België, Klasse der Letteren, Jaarg. 27, nr. 56 (Brussels, 1965), 2: 447-621; Charles Pietri, "La mort en Occident dans l'épigraphie latine: De l'épigraphie païenne à l'épitaphe chrétienne, 3e-6e siècles," *La Maison-Dieu* 144 (1980): 34–35 and 44–48.

74. *Epigr.* 11.11 (on Irene): *quem sibi cum raperet melior tunc regia caeli* and 47.3: *te Protum retinet melior sibi regia caeli.* Cf. 1.11–13, 7.3, 16.3, 20.4–5, 25.2 and 5, 31.3, 32.5, 33.1.4, 35.4, 39.1–2, 4, and 8–9, 43.5, 51.8, 71.9, 72.1.5–6 and 9. Jacques Fontaine, "Images virgiliennes de l'ascension céleste dans la poésie latine chretienne," *JbAC,* Ergänzungsband 9 (Münster, 1982), 56–58, analyzes the influence of Virgilian language on Damasus.

75. The observation is Pietri's, "La mort en Occident," 47.

76. Ambrose: Ernst Dassmann, "Ambrosius und die Märtyrer," *JbAC* 18 (1975): 63–

distinguishes the experience of the martyr from that of the ordinary Christian is that he or she has already, while alive on earth, given proof of that disassociation of body and spirit, of that ascent to heaven that is promised to all Christians after death. Once again it is the endurance of suffering rather than the actual moment of death that sets the martyr apart. Whatever the uncertainties and fears of the individual Christian about the afterlife, in the case of the martyrs there could be no doubts. The accounts of their passions, related each year at the saints' annual festivals, and the continuing presence of the saints at their shrines, manifested by the miracles and other blessings performed there, guaranteed that the martyrs experienced the spiritual transcendence familiar from the sepulchral formulary.

Every poem of the *Peristephanon* contains a formula of heavenly ascent; for Prudentius death is preeminently the culmination of the martyr's spiritual elevation. The main area of lexical invention is in the language for heaven. Prudentius especially favors language that suggests parallels with terrestrial architecture and furnishings. The martyrs, wearing their crowns, ascend to "lofty courts" (*ardua . . . / atria,* 8.9–10)[77] or to the "seat of Christ" (*Christi . . . sedile,* 6.9), the "tribunal on high" (*celsum tribunal,* 5.224),[78] or the "throne of the Father" (*solium patris,* 3.17, 7.55; cf. 10.639, of Christ).[79] This opening out of the single word *caelum* contributes new dimensions to the description of the martyr's death, implying further equivalences with the trial of the martyr and opening new semantic possibilities that transcend the historical moment of death.

Prudentius uses the word *atria* most often of church architecture. The implied parallel between terrestrial basilica and the halls of heaven is reinforced by the expression *sedile Christi.* The noun *sedile* is used in one other passage in the *Peristephanon,* of Cyprian's election as bishop.

His igitur meritis dignissimus usque episcopale
provehitur solium doctor, capit et sedile summum.

(13.33–34)

66; Aug., *Serm.* 297.8.11 (*PL* 38.1364–65): [*martyres*] *sic celebremus, ut amemus; sic amemus, ut imitemur; ut imitati ad eorum praemia pervenire mereamur.* The sentiment is repeated often throughout Augustine's martyr sermons.

77. Cf. *Epigr.* 72.1.6, not by Damasus, though included in Ferrua's edition.

78. Cf. Prudentius, *C.* 9.104, *arduum tribunal alti victor ascendit patris.*

79. The phrase *solium patris* is also found in *C.* 3.189, *A.* 585, and *D.* 98.

[And so, most worthy because of these virtues, he was advanced to the episcopal throne as teacher and occupied the highest seat.]

Sedile here has an almost abstract sense, "highest honor." The figure of *interpretatio* (theme and variation) guarantees that *sedile summum* means the same as *episcopale solium,* i.e., the office of bishop. But the word inevitably evokes the presence in the church of the episcopal throne, elevated above the seats of his fellow priests.[80] Cyprian is elevated metaphorically to high dignity; he is elevated literally on the bishop's *cathedra.* And that elevation enacts in the African church and before the congregation of Carthage his subsequent elevation through martyrdom to the throne of Christ. The verb used—*provehitur*—is one used often of heavenly ascent.[81] The bishop is the representative of Christ on earth, seated on his high throne; but also his ascent to office makes present in the here and now that other ascent to celestial beatitude that is promised at death to the virtuous Christian and assured to the martyr by martyrdom.

The word *tribunal* enlarges the connotative range of Prudentius' language for heaven still further. In *Pe.* 11.225–26 the *sublime tribunal* of a church is the raised area of the apse, "from where the priest preaches of God" (*antistes praedicat unde Deum*). The sense is presumably the same in *Pe.* 2.500: Rome abandons its pagan shrines and hurries "to the *tribunal* of Christ." The antithesis with *sacellis* in the previous line establishes that *tribunal* refers to a part of the church; it stands by synecdoche for the Christian basilica as a whole.[82] But the slippage of language allows a second level of meaning: *Christi tribunal* as heaven. Church and heaven, the religious experience of the Christian community and celestial afterlife, are inseparably intertwined.

The normal classical meaning of *tribunal,* however, is the platform from which a Roman magistrate gave judgment, and it is from this sense that other meanings of the word derive. In the *Peristephanon* the word is used four times (3.64, 6.32, 10.916, 11.77) of the dais from which the examining magistrate presides. It is "lofty" (*celsum,* 11.77), the *tribunal*

80. Cf. Albert Blaise, *Dictionnaire latin-français des auteurs chrétiens,* 2d ed. (Turnhout, 1967), 139, s.v. *cathedra.*

81. In the *Pe.*, 6.26, 8.2; for the simple verb *veho* and other compounds, see 1.90, 5.7, 10.639, 13.86.

82. *Tribunal* is not a "pulpit" *strictiore sensu.* Pulpits are first introduced into Roman churches in the seventh century from the East (Richard Krautheimer, *Rome: Profile of A City, 312–1308* [Princeton, 1980], 91).

not of Christ but of "the cruel foe" (*trucis . . . hostis,* 6.32), terrestrial representative of the universal enemy of humanity, Satan. In appearing before the magistrate's tribunal the martyr is already enacting at the very beginning of his passion a scene that will be repeated at his death when he ascends to heaven to appear before the tribunal of Christ. The relationship is one of similarity and contrast; by his endurance at the tribunal of the enemy of Christianity he wins a glorious heavenly reward.

The word *solium* is used by Prudentius in the same contexts as *sedile* and *tribunal*: of the episcopal throne (13.34, passage quoted above) and of the magistrate's platform. In the martyrdom of Hippolytus the persecutor sits above the others (*celsior*) on an elevated throne (*extructo . . . in solio,* 11.50). But *tribunal,* with its standard sense of judgment seat, also anticipates the Last Judgment (cf. Prudentius, *C.* 6.98), and the special role of the martyr at that time as intercessor for ordinary Christians. This eschatological dimension is also present in *solium.* The throne is a common iconographical motif in Christian art. It communicates majesty and is frequently found in an eschatological context symbolizing the glory of Christ's Second Coming.[83] Although the iconographic image is not univocal, its association with the Parousia and Last Judgment makes the phrase *ad solium patris* an especially suggestive formula for a martyr's ascent to heaven. Prudentius' language of heavenly ascent gives verbal expression to that collapse of temporal distinctions characteristic of the martyr cult. In his use of the words *sedile, tribunal,* and *solium,* the past, the moment of the martyr's first appearance before the judge's tribunal and of his or her ascent to heaven after death, the present, the experience of worship in the Christian basilica, and the future, the Last Days, coalesce in a single lexical formula that can be interpreted at all these semantic levels.

Because of the importance of spiritual elevation in Prudentius' martyr narrative, readers will be sensitive to any expression that implies height or ascent. Prudentius himself recognizes the principle when he describes Vincent mounting his bed of fire (*conscendit rogum,* 5.221) "as if, already sensing the martyr's crown, he was climbing the lofty tribunal" (*ceu iam coronae conscius / celsum tribunal scanderet,* 5.223–24). The verbs

83. Josef Engemann, "Zu den Apsis-Tituli des Paulinus von Nola," *JbAC* 17 (1974): 42–46, protests against the exclusive interpretation of the image of the throne as referring to the eschatological future. His argument is that other interpretations may coexist with the eschatological, i.e., the image is polysemous (see the examples he cites). See also Geir Hellemo, *Adventus Domini: Eschatological Thought in 4th-Century Apses and Catecheses,* Vigiliae Christianae, suppl. 5 (Leiden, 1989), 102–8.

scando and *conscendo* are regularly used by Prudentius of the heavenly ascent of the spirit after death.[84] In this case he explicitly compares the saint mounting the pyre and his spirit mounting to heaven. In fact, the martyr narrative multiplies such "heavenly ascents." Even the most apparently trivial gestures may be interpreted as instances of spiritual elevation, the equivalents of the final release of the soul at death. Hands, eyes, and especially voice, in the form of prayers, are raised to heaven.[85] When Lawrence dies his spirit bursts out of his body, following the path his voice had already taken (*erupit volens / vocem secutus spiritus,* 2.487–88)—he has just finished a speech prophesying Rome's conversion, that contains a triple address and prayer to Christ (2.413, 433, 453). One special case of the heavenly ascent is the vision that accompanies a martyr's death, and that serves as confirmation of the release of his spirit. The vision may symbolize the soul of the martyr, the spiritual qualities he or she embodies (1.82–90, 3.161–65), or, as in the case of Fructuosus and his deacons, the saints themselves may be seen joining the heavenly choir (6.122–23). The language of ascent is undistinctive, but by attributing the vision to an eyewitness rather than recounting the elevation in his own person, the poet wins extra authenticity for his narrative and acquires a new perspective on the saint's spiritual elevation. (In *Pe.* 3 the observer is the executioner; there are two witnesses in *Pe.* 6, a servant and the daughter of the presiding magistrate.)

In Damasus' epigrams formulas of heavenly ascent are frequently combined with an antithetical expression of victory over the powers of the world (*contempto / superato principe mundi*).[86] While the language of victory is frequent in the *Peristephanon* too, Prudentius more often elaborates on the body : soul antithesis, which, as we have seen, informs the whole of the Prudentian martyr narrative. The simple inclusion of the adjective *liber* in a formula of heavenly ascent is enough to invoke the idea of liberation from the constraints of the flesh, without any further specification (e.g., 5.304, *liber in caelum veni*).[87] But the account of Romanus' death is more typical: "his soul freed from its bonds [*anima absoluta vinculis*] made its way to heaven" (10.1110). The verb *solvo* or its compounds feature regularly in such passages; the bonds may be

84. *Scando*: 6.98, 7.88, 8.9; *conscendo*: 8.7.

85. 5.235–36, 6.106–8, 13.53–54; for the language of heavenly ascent used of prayer, see Paulinus of Nola, *C.* 16.35–37 and 26.182–85.

86. *Epigr.* 7.2, 31.2, 39.7, 43.4.

87. Also *Pe.* 2.270, 5.359, 14.92; cf. Prudentius, *Praef.* 44–45 and Damasus, *Epigr.* 11.12.

specified as those of the flesh (2.486–87). In this its simplest form, the language of release from the body can be abundantly paralleled in sepulchral inscriptions.[88] Prudentius elaborates the implications of conventional language far beyond the ambitions of the epigraphic formulary.

From the Christian perspective all human beings are released at death from the *vincula carnis*. For the martyrs this language takes on added significance. During their passion they have experienced literal *vincula,* the chains of prison, the bonds that restrained them during examination. Take the case of Vincent. His death follows shortly after his miraculous release from prison, when stocks fell from his legs and the jail was flooded with light; Vincent experiences an angelic vision summoning him to heaven. Although he survives this release to die in the care of the Christian community—Datian wishes him revived to suffer more tortures—the actual moment of death comes about as an afterthought. He has already experienced the exaltation of heaven. Lying on the bed his fellow Christians have prepared for him, he has now "achieved rest" (*quietem contigit,* 5.354). There is no more common formula for death in Christian inscriptions than an expression involving *quies,* its compounds, or cognates.[89] As observed in the previous chapter, Vincent is in a liminal state between heaven and earth: he is already the object of cult from the Christian community, while enjoying the peace of heaven.

When death comes it is described simply: "his victorious spirit left his limbs and ascended to heaven" (*victor relictis artubus / caelum capessit spiritus,* 5.367–68). But the lengthy sentence that contains this clause also includes a parenthetical meditation on the theological significance of the martyr's death (353–60). It is death

quae corporali ergastulo
mentem resolvit liberam
et reddit auctori deo.

(5.358–60)

[that releases the mind and frees it from the prison-house of the body and restores it to its creator, God.]

---

88. *Solvo* and its compounds: *Pe.* 2.270, 5.303 and 359, 9.86, 12.26 (a paraphrase of 2 Tim. 4:6); sepulchral inscriptions: Sanders, *Licht en Duisternis,* 1: 309–18.

89. Sanders, *Licht en Duisternis,* 1: 320–46, Pietri, "La mort en Occident," 41–42. In the *Peristephanon,* 4.127.

In the context in which Vincent has just been released from literal prison, the equivalence between *vincula carnis* and *vincula carceris* could scarcely be more emphatic.

Vincent's death repeats and fulfils the events of his incarceration. There an angel had summoned him to heaven in a speech that concludes with a combination of the language of bodily release and spiritual ascent.

> Pone hoc caducum vasculum,
> conpage textum terrea,
> quod dissipatum solvitur,
> et liber in caelum veni.
>
> (5.301–4)

> [Lay aside this mortal vessel compacted of earthly fabric, which is dispersed and breaks apart, and come freely to heaven.]

Flesh is mortal (cf. 2 Cor. 4:7 = *Pe.* 5.163), but the spirit lives. The phrase *quod dissipatum solvitur* is a general truth. But it has a special relevance for the martyr. He or she, unlike the ordinary Christian, experiences the dissolution of the flesh while still in the body. The frame (*compago*) of Vincent's bones cracks as it is torn apart limb by limb (5.111–12). Eulalia bids her torturer "burn, tear, separate limbs compacted of mud" (*coacta luto,* 3.91–92).[90] Each torture is a death in miniature; the dissolution of the frame of the body (*membra morti obnoxia / dilancinata interficis,* 5.155–56), while the spirit remains "free, at peace, untouched, not subject to bitter pain" (*liber, quietus, integer, / exsors dolorum tristium,* 5.159–60). The martyr experiences death in life as he will experience life in death. The persecutor's frustration mounts because he fails to recognize the saint's spiritual integrity or to evaluate correctly the relationship of body and soul in the human makeup. Viewed diachronically, torture is actually a benefit to the martyr since it accelerates that final separation of body and spirit at death for which the whole course of the *passio* is practice.[91]

90. Similar language is used by Lawrence of the effect of disease on the body (2.209 and 219; cf. 1.26 and 10.887–90).

91. Tertullian, *Mart.* 2.9, describes the spiritual freedom the martyr experiences while subject to incarceration: *Etsi corpus includitur, etsi caro detinetur, omnia spiritui patent. Vagare spiritu, spatiare spiritu, et non stadia opaca aut porticus longas proponens tibi, sed* illam viam, quae ad deum ducit. *Quotiens eam spiritu deambulaveris, totiens in carcere non eris* (*CCL* 1; 5.2–6).

Prudentius' martyr texts are characterized by intensity rather than individuality. Narrative components are few and, at a certain level of generality, repetitive. Death can be seen as just one more punishment, albeit the last. Verbal and physical examination are complementary; the martyr is exalted by physical suffering, the persecutor enraged (i.e., debased) by his victim's vocal defiance, while the characteristic sequence of combat followed by victory for the saint and defeat for the magistrate or his representative holds good for the smaller narrative units, as it does for the passion as a whole. Intensity depends on the variety of semantic levels and narrative situations at which the same pattern is repeated. The critic of English literature Stanley Fish has noticed a similar pattern of narrative repetition in another work of Christian devotion, John Bunyan's *The Pilgrim's Progress.* There the basic figure of pilgrimage, which relies on the idea of spatial and temporal extension, is called into question by the near-identical pattern of each successive episode. Fish describes the process of interpreting such a text as follows:[92]

> The truth about the world is not to be found within its own confines or configurations, but from the vantage point of a perspective that transforms it. It is Christian's duty to meet his trials in terms of that perspective, and it is the reader's duty to perform his acts of interpretation in the same way.

Readers of the *Peristephanon* are in the same situation. They must interpret the martyr texts from a perspective that transcends the spatiotemporal confines of worldly narrative.

Two recurrent themes dominate the Prudentian martyr narrative: the bringing into proximity of heaven and earth, and the dialectic between body and soul. Both have a bearing not just on the historical meaning of martyrdom, but also on the late fourth-century martyr cult with its belief in the martyr's privileged access to heaven and capacity to transcend divisions between heaven and earth, life and death. In his choice of language for the ascent of the martyr's soul to heaven, Prudentius expresses the special qualities of the martyr cult: place of martyrdom, basilica, and heaven, past, present, and eschatological future are all collapsed into a single turn of phrase. Metaphor, descriptive passage,

92. Stanley E. Fish, *Self-Consuming Artifacts: The Experience of Seventeenth-Century Literature* (Berkeley, 1972), 237. The discussion of this aspect of *The Pilgrim's Progress* extends from 224 to 238.

and biblical example, as we shall see in the next chapter, far from serving as extraneous ornamentation, return to the basic themes of the standard Prudentian martyr narrative and further intensify the poems' meditations on the themes of martyrdom and martyr cult.

CHAPTER 3

The Road to Heaven

In the previous chapter we saw the word *catenae* used by Prudentius to encapsulate the martyr's sufferings short of death; physical restraint is essential to the martyr text. But imprisonment, a special form of restraint, has particular significance in the *Peristephanon.*

Three of Prudentius' martyrs are thrown into jail: Vincent, Fructuosus (with his deacons), and Cyprian. There are passing references elsewhere to imprisonment,[1] but only in these cases does the subject receive any elaboration. In the case of Fructuosus, the third-century prose *Passio* that provided Prudentius with much of his material survives.[2] There Fructuosus and his deacons "were taken to prison" (*recepti sunt in carcerem,* 1.4), where they baptized one Rogatianus. Prudentius' version intensifies the emotional force of the narrative: "an executioner dragged them off to the chains of imprisonment" (*ad carceream viros catenam / . . . carnifex trahebat,* 16–17). At the same time, it incorporates an address by Fructuosus to his deacons, not found in the prose text, that contains a eulogy of imprisonment as a step to heaven.

Carcer christicolis gradus coronae est,
carcer provehit ad superna caeli,
carcer conciliat deum beatis.

(6.25–27)

[Prison for Christians is a step to the crown, prison carries them to heaven's heights, prison wins God's favor for the blessed.]

---

1. *Pe.* 1.46 (cf. 71–72), 10.794, 11.53.

2. Cf. P. Tino Alberto Sabattini, "Storia e leggenda nei *Peristephanon* di Prudenzio I," *RSC* 20 (1972): 37–43.

Anaphora of *carcer,* with tricolon, gives special emphasis to Fructuosus' eulogy of prison. As a stage in the martyr's suffering, incarceration involves spiritual elevation. But its metaphorical implications transcend the physical and spiritual experiences of the individual martyr and lend an exemplary quality, valid for the whole Christian community, to his achievement of salvation.

In *Pe.* 6 Prudentius goes on to describe the baptism performed by Fructuosus while in prison. The account is generalized from the prose Passion. There is no mention of the candidate's name; instead, periphrases for baptism amplify its redemptive, cleansing power (*mysticum lavacrum,* 29; *purgamen aquae,* 30). Nor is the setting neutrally presented. Prison is now a "cave of the accused" (*specus reorum,* 28). *Rei* is a natural word to use of literal prisoners, but it is also used by Christian authors, including Prudentius, of human sinfulness.[3] In the context of the sacrament of baptism, this second meaning is certainly present; prison is a "cave of sinners," to whom Fructuosus brings purgation. It is a cave because it is dark,[4] and, I suspect, subterranean. Though a literal cave could be used for the confinement of prisoners, Prudentius probably means here a cell with cavelike qualities. The darkness of prisons was sufficiently notorious for the emperor Constantine to enact that the incarcerated "must not suffer the darkness of an inner prison, but must be kept in good health by the enjoyment of light."[5] When confronted with the endurance of the martyrs, the darkness of prison, like the instruments of torture, reacts to the spectacle before it: it is astonished by the mystical purgation of baptism (*purgamen aquae stupent tenebrae,* 3.30). In both cases the forces of evil are discomfited.

The allegorical dimensions of imprisonment are already beginning to emerge. Two spiritual interpretations of incarceration were theologically acceptable at the beginning of the fifth century. The first associates the earthly world with a prison; it is expounded in Augustine's commentary on *Ps.* 141:8 *educ de carcere animam meam.*[6]

3. See Albert Blaise, *Le vocabulaire latin des principaux thèmes liturgiques* (Turnhout, 1966), 559–60, for the liturgical use of *reus/reatus*; in Prudentius, *Pe.* 2.582, 13.60.

4. Lavarenne 221, *ad loc.,* "ainsi nommée [*sc. specus*] . . . à cause de son obscurité," comparing *Pe.* 5.237. *Specus* is also used of a prison in *Pe.* 13.53. The prison of the martyrs Marianus and Jacobus is also described as a cave (*antrum caligans, Passio Mariani et Iacobi* 6.3; 200.28 Musurillo).

5. *CTh* 9.3.1 *Nec vero sedis intimae tenebras pati debebit inclusus, sed usurpata luce vegetari.* The translation is Clyde Pharr's, in *The Theodosian Code and the Sirmondian Constitutions* (Princeton, 1952), 228. For the darkness of prison, see also *ThLL* 3.438.41–45.

6. *PL* 37.1843. See the passages collected in *ThLL* 3.438.21–27 and Jacqueline Amat,

Quibusdam ergo visum est quod spelunca et carcer mundus iste sit; et hoc orat ecclesia, ut de carcere educatur, id est, de hoc mundo, de sub sole, ubi omnia vanitas . . . . Anima nostra per fidem et spem in Christo est, sicut paulo ante dixi: "Vita vestra abscondita est cum Christo in Deo." Corpus autem nostrum in isto carcere, in isto mundo. Si diceret: "Educ de carcere corpus meum," securi acciperemus carcerem mundum. Fortasse tamen propter aliqua quae nos tenent desideria terrena, contra quae luctamur et dimicamus, quia "Video aliam legem in membris meis, repugnantem legi mentis meae" [Rom. 7.25], recte dicimus: "Educ animam meam de hoc mundo," id est, de laboribus et pressuris huius saeculi. Non enim caro quam tu fecisti, sed corruptela carnis, et pressurae, et tentationes carcer mihi sunt.

[Some people have thought that the cave and prison are this world, and for this reason the Church prays that it be led from prison, that is, from this world, from under the sun, where all is vanity . . . . Our soul is, as I have said before, in Christ by virtue of faith and hope: "Your life is stored with Christ in God." Our body, however, is in this prison, in this world. If the psalmist said "Lead my body out of prison" we would readily understand prison as the world. Yet perhaps because of some earthly desires which grip us, and against which we struggle and contend, for "I see one law in my body, in conflict with the law of my mind," we rightly say "Lead my soul out of this world," that is, from the trials and tribulations of the world. For it is not the flesh which you created, but corruption of the flesh, tribulations and temptations which are my prison.]

"The trials and tribulations of the world": prison is associated with the terrestrial, the worldly, the desires of the flesh, i.e., the sinful world of fallen humanity. Prison in the martyr texts is a microcosm of the world, populated by sinners (*rei*), the realm of darkness, and the demonic, in the person of *carnifices* (cf. 5.137, where the torturers are described as *alumni carceris*). Fructuosus' performance of baptism in prison takes on special significance as the cleansing of the Christian from the consequences of

Songes et Visions: L'au-delà dans la littérature latine tardive (Paris, 1985), 260–63: for example, *Passio Mariani et Iacobi* 6.1, *carceris poenas et saeculares . . . tenebras* (200.24–25 Musurillo). Tertullian, *Ad Mart.* 2.1–3, elaborates on the parallel between *carcer* and *mundus.* See especially *Ad Mart.* 2.3, *plures postremo mundus reos continet, scilicet universum hominum genus* (*CCL* 1; 4.8–9).

Original Sin, consequences that may be represented metaphorically as incarceration. At the same time, in liberating Christians from imprisonment in the sinful world through baptism, Fructuosus reenacts in miniature Christ's own victory over Satan at the Crucifixion that made redemption possible.

One aspect of the Crucifixion story resonates particularly strongly in the martyr texts' treatment of prison: Christ's descent to the underworld (*descensus ad inferos*).[7] And indeed, the second theologically acceptable interpretation of *carcer* was precisely Hell (*inferi / infernum*). The association of ideas is already found in Old Latin manuscripts of 2 Pet. 2:4, *carceribus caliginis inferi* (cf. 1 Pet. 3:18–20), leading to the observation in a sermon included in a homiliary of Caesarius of Arles that "frequently the Holy Scriptures have the habit of calling Hell [*infernum*] a prison."[8] Prudentius himself describes Christ's descent to Hell in *C.* 9.70–81 and, while the realm of the dead is not represented in so many words as a prison, the language used shows a number of parallels with the description of Fructuosus' jail cell. God "illuminates the cave of death with golden light" (*luce fulva mortis antra inluminat, C.* 9.76). The underworld, like the martyr's prison, is a dark cave (cf. *Pe.*5. 238, 13.51).[9] When Christ's light shines in the murky depths, "the darkness is astounded," *stupentibus tenebris* (77), a phrase that parallels exactly the response of Fructuosus' dark prison to the mystery of baptism (*Pe.* 6.30).[10] Christ's descent to Hell is an aspect of his redemption of the human race from the consequences of Original Sin. Baptism makes that salvation available to the individual Christian through a liturgical act that reenacts the victory of light

7. For the history of this item of faith in the early church, see H. Quilliet, "Descente de Jésus aux enfers," *DThC* 4 (1924): 565–619, and Josef Kroll, *Gott und Hölle: Der Mythos vom Descensuskampfe,* Studien der Bibliothek Warburg 20 (Leipzig, 1932), 1–125.

8. *Frequenter divina scriptura infernum carcerem appellare consuevit* (Mai 136.5). For the theological problems raised by 1 Pet. 3:18–20 and Augustine's interpretation, see Quilliet, "Descente," 590–93.

9. The Virgilian underworld is also described as an *antrum* (*Aen.* 6.262, 400, 418, 423). Ambrose, *Hex.* 1.8.32 makes an etymological association between cave and darkness: *unde antrum clausum undique huiusmodi locum vocarunt, nisi quod atro inhorrescat situ atque offusione tenebrarum?* (*CSEL* 32.1; 34.4–6).

10. Prudentius' language is almost certainly influenced by the liturgy (cf. Kroll, *Gott und Hölle,* 17–18 and 126–28), in which the *descensus* is described in terms of illumination of dark by light, and liberation from chains and death is said to be "astonished"; cf. *Sacr. Gel.* (564 Muratori): *Mors quae olim fuerat aeterna nocte damnata* **inserto veri fulgoris lumine** *captivam se trahi Dominicis triumphis* **obstupuit.** These features are already found in Hippolytus' *Apostolic Tradition* (cf. Kroll, 17–18).

over darkness associated with Christ's descent. The martyr, too, enjoys the consequences of that original victory.

At the same time, the martyr, by being plunged into dark subterranean depths from which his spiritual integrity allows him to emerge victorious, repeats Christ's own descent. Christ's soul descended to the underworld while his body was in the tomb.[11] The martyrs' ability to transcend physical suffering and restraint through spiritual resources assures them of their release and ascent to heaven.

The drama of the martyrs' imprisonment finds its fullest development in the *Peristephanon* in the case of Vincent. There Datian, after failing to break Vincent's resolve by torture, throws his tormentor into prison:

Sublatus inde fortior
lugubre in antrum truditur,
ne liber usus luminis
animaret altum spiritum.

Est intus imo ergastulo
locus tenebris nigrior,
quem saxa mersi fornicis
angusta clausum strangulant.

Aeterna nox illic latet
expers diurni sideris;
hic carcer horrendus suos
habere fertur inferos.

In hoc baratrum conicit
truculentus hostis martyrem
lignoque plantas inserit
divaricatis cruribus.

(5.237–52)

[Still firmer in his resolve, the martyr was taken away and thrown into a gloomy cave so that no free enjoyment of light should inspire

11. Augustine, *De fide ad Petrum* 11, *in sepulcro secundum solam carnem idem Deus iacuit, et in infernum secundum solam animam descendit* (*PL* 40.757); cf. *Tract. in Ioh.* 47.10 (*PL* 35.1738).

his lofty spirit. There in the depths of the jail was a place blacker than darkness itself, which the confining stones of an underground vault held enclosed in a throttling grip. There was the hidden realm of eternal night, untouched by the sun's daytime star; this terrible prison, it is said, had an underworld of its own. Into this pit the fierce enemy hurled the martyr and put his feet in wooden stocks that held his legs apart.]

Physical reality is here dematerialized into a spiritual "landscape." By transference of language (metonymy) the poet leaves the location of Vincent's incarceration uncertain. It is prison, *carcer / ergastulum*—the two words are used interchangeably in late antiquity—but also a cave (*antrum*) and a pit (*baratrum*), both words used of the underworld in classical and Christian authors.[12] Untypically, Prudentius makes the identification with Hell explicit: "the prison is said to have an underworld of its own" (247–48), rather than leaving it to be inferred. *Inferi* is regularly used of the place in Christian Latin,[13] the immediate sense in the present passages. But originally it meant personnel, the dwellers in the nether world, and that sense is present here too. We do not need to look far for the demonic forces that populate this underworld: Datian himself, the "fierce enemy" (250), is the Satan of this realm, the torturers and executioners, described elsewhere in the poem as "children of the prison" (*alumni carceris,* 137), his agents. While Lucretius, in *De rerum natura* (3.978–1023), denies the reality of an underworld of punishments, arguing that humans falsely imagine such on the basis of emotional perturbations in life, for the Christian poet the punishments of Hell and the temptations and tribulations of the world, of which martyrdom is a special case, are both real and inseparable. *Inferi* and *mundus* are interconnected realms; both are prisons in which the soul is confined when it succumbs to sin, but neither have power over the spirit of a resolute Christian, who is proof to temptation and suffering.

Substantial features of Vincent's cell merge into an affective, impressionistic picture of the infernal and demonic. Two features are stressed, darkness and depth, the latter in the words *imo* (241) and *mersi* (243), which culminate in the description of prison as a pit (*baratrum,* 249).

12. For *antrum* see *ThLL* 2.192.17–22 and above n.9; in Prudentius, *C.* 9.76 and *Pe.* 2.288 (*antrum Tartari*). For *baratrum, ThLL* 2.1723.77–1724.28, Prudentius, *C.* 11.40, *A.* 785, and Blaise, *Le vocabulaire latin,* 56.

13. *ThLL* 7.1.1390.27–52, Blaise, *Le vocabulaire latin,* 456–58.

The realm of the devil/persecutor is a world of secrecy and concealment (cf. *intus* 241; *latet,* 245). But in the dialectic of inner and outer that runs through the martyr text, it is the inner spiritual strength of the martyr in resisting assaults on his external frame that is able to break open the secret recesses of the infernal and turn the tables on the devil and his agents. Prison/hell is a world of darkness (239) and eternal night (245–46); it is of a surpassing blackness (242), appropriate to an *antrum,* a word associated etymologically by Ambrose with the adjective *ater* ("black").[14] When release comes this darkness is flooded by "the brilliance of light" (*splendore lucis,* 270). The careful system of enclosure and concealment cannot hold against the flood of light; doors give way before the brilliance within as the light finds a way through tiny cracks (*clausas fores / interna rumpunt lumina / tenuisque per rimas nitor / lucis latentis proditur,* 305–8). Unlike the spiritual integrity of the martyr, the fabric of the prison gives way.

Prudentius' description of the breaking of the prison doors illustrates well how apparently realistic detail serves an allegorical purpose. The point that the light is visible through cracks in the door appears to be naturalistic. But in the context of the association of the diabolical with concealment and secrecy, the detail bears a heavy load of significance. A tiny crack of light is in the world of the martyrs, where part stands for whole, the equivalent of breaking down the doors (*fores / . . . rumpunt lumina,* 305-6). The devil's secret redoubt is betrayed. The juxtaposition of the words *latentis proditur* (308), though they are not in an immediate syntactical relationship, encapsulates the defeat that the infernal/internal powers have suffered.

Returning to the pre-illuminated state of the prison, we find that the description proper begins with the familiar introductory ecphrastic formula *est . . . / locus* (241–42). However, instead of giving a realistic description of Vincent's prison, Prudentius selects visual elements that communicate the spiritual significance of the situation. The detail that Vincent's cell is vaulted (*saxa . . . fornicis,* 243–44) might seem an exception. But the rest of the words of the relative clause in which this detail is contained belie this impression. The adjectives all insist on characteristic qualities of the diabolical: depth (*mersi,* 243) and enclosure (*angusta clausum,* 244). The sense of claustrophobia thus created culminates in the verb *strangulat*—the prison walls themselves become

14. See this chapter, n.9.

executioners, a characteristic Prudentian confusion of animate and inanimate. In the present case, the verbal play of **ang***usta* : *str***angu***lant* lends further credibility to the threat.

Prudentius' description of Vincent's cell has much in common with perhaps the most famous prison ecphrasis in Latin literature, Sallust's description of the Tullianum (*Cat.* 55.3–4), the underground death cell in the Carcer Mamertinus where the Catilinarian conspirator Lentulus and his comrades were executed by strangulation. The Tullianum, too, in Sallust's account, is below ground (*humi depressus*), confined (*eum muniunt undique parietes*), vaulted (*insuper camera lapideis fornicibus iuncta*), and dark. Although the verbal parallels are not absolutely compelling, I am inclined to believe that Prudentius remembered the Sallustian passage when writing his own account of an underground cell, whose walls and ceiling "strangle" the space within, as the Catilinarian conspirators were literally strangled.[15] The analogy with the two-story prison at Rome gives some support to my translation of *tenebris* in 242 as an ablative of comparison rather than specification. I suspect Prudentius has in mind such a double-tiered prison in which darkness is proportionate to depth. At the same time, the account in Acts of the imprisonment of Paul and Silas probably played a role (Acts 16:22–34). There the apostles are confined to an inner prison (*interiorem carcerem,* Acts 16:24), where, like Vincent's, their feet are bound "with wood" (*pedes eorum strinxit ligno*). In *Pe.* 5 Prudentius habitually assimilates extension downwards and inwards (i.e., infernal : internal; cf. the juxtaposition *intus imo,* 241); accordingly, he translates the distinction in Acts into a vertical dimension.

The second specific detail in the account of Vincent's imprisonment, that his legs were put in stocks, looks as though it too was inspired by the same passage in Acts. Whether or not the detail is Prudentian or taken from a prose source,[16] it has an important function in the economy

15. The Sallust passage also begins *est locus*: *Est locus in carcere, quod Tullianum appellatur, . . . circiter duodecim pedes humi depressus; eum muniunt undique parietes atque insuper camera lapideis fornicibus iuncta; sed incultu tenebris odore foeda atque terribilis eius facies est*; see too Daremberg-Saglio 1.917–18 s.v. *carcer* and Ernest Nash, *Pictorial Dictionary of Ancient Rome* (New York, 1961–62), 1: 206–8. Apart from the reference to the darkness of the prisons (*tenebris*), which is a commonplace, the closest similarities in language are in the descriptions of the arched roofs (*lapideis fornicibus*: *saxa fornicis*) and of the enclosing effect of walls and ceiling (*eum muniunt undique parietes*: *quem [locum] saxa . . . clausum strangulant*). In the last case there is no verbal coincidence, but there is a close similarity in syntax and structure of thought.

16. Opinions differ on the relationship between surviving versions of the prose *Passio Vincentii* and Prudentius; for summaries of the situation, see P. Tino Alberto Sabattini,

of the narrative. Vincent does not escape from prison; he does not even, like Paul and Silas, have the prison gates come miraculously open for him. The expected liberation is transferred synecdochically to a smaller scale: "the double teeth of the stocks break apart, as their chambers burst open" (271–72).[17] The Latin for the last phrase is *ruptis cavernis.* While not unparalleled in the general sense of aperture,[18] the word *caverna,* used of the leg-holes of the stocks, evokes all the associations of the cavernous in the context as a whole: prison, underworld, and death. Once more, realistic detail is retained because it lends itself to spiritual interpretation.

The saint's conversion of his jailer represents a final parallel with the imprisonment of Paul and Silas. As Vincent's stocks spring apart, his jail cell is flooded by light.

> nam carceralis caecitas
> splendore lucis fulgurat,
> duplexque morsus stipitis
> ruptis cavernis dissilit.
>
> (269–72)

> [For the darkness of prison blazes with a brilliant light, and the double teeth of the stocks break apart, as their chambers burst open.]

Caecitas is here translated "darkness." It is the natural meaning in the context: absence of physical light. But as the account proceeds, a second meaning emerges—absence of spiritual light, i.e., spiritual blindness. The phrase *carceralis caecitas* is reinterpreted as metonymy, abstract for animate. It is the spiritually blind jailer, described later as "custodian of the black threshold" (*obsessor atri liminis,* 310) and "master of the jail" (*manceps carceris,* 345), whose *carceralis caecitas* receives illumination. He undergoes conversion—*repente Christum credidit* (348)—an

---

"Storia e leggenda nei *Peristephanon* di Prudenzio II," *RSC* 20 (1972): 193, n. 18, Amat, *Songes et visions,* 224 and 283, and most thoroughly Victor Saxer, "La passion de S. Vincent diacre dans la première moitié du Ve siècle: Essai de reconstitution," *REAug* 35 (1989): 275–97. Sabattini is right to stress the great freedom with which Prudentius handles his sources.

17. *duplexque morsus stipitis / ruptis cavernis dissilit.*

18. *ThLL* 3.646.19–39. *Caverna* may be used also as a near-synonym for *rima*; see Tertullian, *Nat.* 1.7.15, *domesticorum curiositas furata est* **per rimulas et cavernas** (*CCL* 1;19.10–11).

experience that is immediately reinterpreted in terms of the illumination of the prison: "he had seen the enclosed cave of thick darkness shine with the brilliance of a foreign light" (350–52).[19]

The jailer's conversion depends on his reaction to the first evidence of what is happening inside the prison, the chinks of light (305–8), and the voice of the martyr, which echoes off the confined walls of his cell, as he sings hymns (313–16). Like the darkness in *Pe.* 6, the gatekeeper is astonished (*stuperet territus,* 309). He peeks fearfully in "as far as his eyesight [*acies*], brought close to the door, can enter through the narrow joints of the hinges" (318–20).[20] The awkwardness in the translation of *acies* is intentional and reflects a difficulty in the Latin. Does the word signify a part of the body, the eyes, which can literally be "brought close to the door" (*admota . . . postibus*), or does it have an abstract sense, "eyesight," for only vision not eyes can be said to enter (*intrare*) the cell? The difficulty replicates on a small scale the theme that informs the whole text: the dialectic between corporeal and intellectual/spiritual, body and mind/soul. The *ianitor* outside the cell is the mirror image of the martyr within; for both darkness is illuminated. Chinks of physical light penetrate the doors of the martyr's prison (305–8); the constricted line of sight/insight of the jailer brings mental illumination to his own carcereal darkness. Like the double bite of the stocks, the narrow joints of the door cannot hold. The jailer, charged with maintaining the distinction between inner and outer inviolable—he must keep what is in in and what is out out—is himself implicated in transgressing those boundaries, in opening out what is closed. Spatial distinctions of inclusion and exclusion give way under the powerful solvent of the martyr's realignment of the opposition between body and soul.

The story of the jailer's conversion is a subtext that Prudentius has interwoven with the main narrative concerning Vincent in a manner unparalleled in the recensions of the prose passion.[21] In this way the reader experiences in his or her own person the tension between inner and outer that directs the scene. Events are viewed from within, from the perspective of the martyr (cf. *agnoscit,* 273 and *cernit,* 277), and from without (cf. especially 321–24, a doublet of 277–80). The juxta-

19. *densae specum caliginis / splendore lucis advenae / micuisse clausum viderat.*

20. *admota quantum postibus / acies per artas cardinum / intrare iuncturas potest.*

21. Technically this is achieved by transposing Datian's orders to remove Vincent from prison and to allow him some respite so that they precede rather than follow the jailer's conversion.

position implies at a certain level of generality an equivalence between the conversion of an individual Christian and the victory of the martyr; both are experiences of spiritual transcendence and illumination.

In the case of Vincent, the opposition between life and death is dissolved. Descent into the "gloomy cave" (*lugubre in antrum,* 238) of the prison is a form of death, an association reinforced by the description of tombs as *antra* in biblical and classical literature (cf. Gen. 23:20; Lucan 8.694 and 10.19). In the transformation of the jagged potsherds on which he must lie into paradisiacal flowers (277–80, 321–22) Vincent experiences a foretaste of heavenly bliss while still alive. He is, as described in the previous chapter, suspended between life and death, his body in the depths of prison but his soul already on high (cf. *altum spiritum,* 240). For the persecutor life is associated with physical freedom—"free enjoyment of the light" (*liber usus luminis,* 239). He wishes to deprive Vincent of this freedom by incarcerating him and in so doing deprive him of his spirit/life (*ne liber usus luminis / animaret altum spiritum,* 239–40), i.e., kill him, a regular sense of *exanimare.* But for the martyr spiritual well-being, like life, does not depend on physical freedom. His spirit is proof against the body's confinement. For him death itself is a liberation, the final realization of the spiritual freedom he has demonstrated throughout the passion. If life involves the "free enjoyment of light," then the martyr's death is, as Prudentius implies (*si mors habenda eiusmodi est,* 357), no death at all but life.

The final use of prison language occurs in the account of Vincent's death; death is said to release the free spirit from "the prison of the body" (*corporali ergastulo,* 358). The association of the body with a prison is recorded first in Plato; it is found in classical and early Christian authors.[22] In Prudentius' day the orthodoxy of the doctrine, espoused by Origen, had been called into question. In the passage quoted above from Augustine's Psalm commentary,[23] the African father is careful to make clear that the body is not evil in itself—that would involve attributing the creation of evil to God—but only becomes so when corrupted by the carnal sins of the world: *non enim caro quam tu fecisti, sed corruptela carnis et pressurae et tentationes carcer mihi sunt.*

Prudentius' use of *ergastulum* here of the body is no doubt influenced

22. The material is collected by Pierre Courcelle, "Tradition platonicienne et traditions chrétiennes du corps-prison (*Phédon* 62b; *Cratyle* 400c)," *REL* 43 (1965): 406–43.

23. Augustine goes on to consider in more detail the theological problems involved in describing without qualification the body as a prison.

by the conservatism of epigraphic formulary, which continued to speak of the prison of the body in sepulchral contexts.[24] At the same time, the actual physical fabric of the body, its articulated structure (cf. *conpage textum,* 302), will have promoted the idea of it as a kind of bondage. Nonetheless, Prudentius is sensitive to a too-radical opposition between body and soul, an opposition that is contradicted by the expectation of Resurrection in the flesh.[25] The implications of the phrase "prison of the body" are clearer in a second instance of a martyr's incarceration, the case of Cyprian.

> Antra latent Tyriae Carthaginis abditis reposta,
> conscia tartareae caliginis, abdicata soli.
> Clausus in his specubus sanctus Cyprianus et catena
> nexus utramque manum nomen patris invocat supremi.
> . . . .
> "Si luteum facili charismate pectus expiasti,
> vise libens tenebris *ergastula caeca* dissipatis,
> eripe *corporeo de carcere vinculisque mundi*
> hanc animam. . . ."
>
> (*Pe.* 13.51–54 and 61–64)

> [Hidden in remote regions of Tyrian Carthage were secret caves, privy to infernal gloom and denied all sunlight. Shut up in these caverns, though both his hands were bound with chains, holy Cyprian called upon the name of the highest Father . . . . "If you have purified by your ready grace my earthly heart, deign to visit this dark jail and dispel its blackness, rescue this soul from its bodily prison and the bonds of the world . . . ."]

For Prudentius the prison of the body and the bonds of the world (*vincula mundi*) are synonymous. In Cyprian's case it was the "madness of indulgence" (*luxuriae rabiem,* 25), in particular magic practices and adultery (21–24), that represented worldly temptation. It is these carnal temptations that permit description of the body as a prison.

Prudentius says of Cyprian's abandonment of his former sinful life,

24. *ILCV* 3427.3, *ICUR,* n.s. 2.4220.5.

25. *C.* 3.196–200: *credo equidem, neque vana fides, / corpora vivere more animae; / nam modo corporeum memini / de Phlegethonte gradu facili / ad superos remeasse Deum.* For the effect of corrupt flesh on the spirit, see *H. pr.* 55–56.

"Christ checked the madness of his indulgence . . . and dispelled the darkness from his heart" (*discutit et tenebras de pectore,* 26). The parallelism of language suggests an equivalence between changing the style of life, dispelling the darkness of the prison cell, and rescuing the soul from the *vincula carnis* or *mundi.* Christ's saving activity is described again in Cyprian's prayer, verse 61; the word *pectus* is repeated from the earlier context (26, *pectore*), this time qualified by *luteum* as a reminder of the carnal quality of the saint's sin. Now the saint calls for the dispelling of darkness, language that was applied in the earlier passage to the martyr's mending of his ways, for his prison cell (*discutit tenebras,* 26—*tenebris dissipatis,* 62). Both activities can be described in similar language. In addition, the logic of Cyprian's prayer, the parallel imperatives of 62 and 63, points to an equivalence between illuminating the cell and rescuing the soul from the *vincula mundi.* Put in other terms, incarceration is a model of the soul's exposure to temptation in this life. Vincent's and Cyprian's liberations from the prison of the body at death are only special cases of the spiritual freedom all Christians can achieve in their everyday life by resisting tribulation and temptation. From this point of view the saint's incarceration and final liberation through death are an inspiring example of the conquest of sin, an experience that can be imitated in the life of the ordinary Christian. Prison, as we have seen, is just one more punishment, replicating the pattern of the passion as a whole. At the same time, insofar as the martyr in his jail cell repeats the pattern of Christ's descent to Hell, it adds a further dimension to the martyr narrative. Imprisonment transcends divisions of place and time: prison is the underworld, the everyday world of sin and temptation, the literal place of incarceration of the martyr and the tomb; the martyr's experience unites the original saving resurrection of Christ with the individual Christian's victory over sin in his or her own life and the promise of posthumous salvation in the life to come. Viewed from this perspective, prison is "the path to heaven" (cf. *Pe.* 6.26).

In the language of incarceration, distinctions of time and place are focused on a particular place and event: the martyr in his jail cell. In particular, incarceration can stand for the entire experience of the Christian in this world. In the case of a second metaphor for resistance to worldly temptation, contained in Prudentius' poem for the virgin martyr of Mérida, Eulalia (*Pe.* 3), some temporal and spatial sequence is retained. Eulalia's devoted parents attempt to protect their daughter from persecution by hiding her on their country estates. Their efforts are in vain. Eulalia breaks out and travels through the night to the city to confront the tribunal. Eulalia's nighttime journey is described as follows.

> Illa perosa quietis opem
> degeneri tolerare mora
> nocte fores sine teste movet
> saeptaque claustra fugax aperit,
> inde per invia carpit iter.
>
> Ingreditur pedibus laceris
> per loca senta situ et vepribus
> angelico comitata choro
> et, licet horrida nox sileat,
> lucis habet tamen illa ducem.
>
> (3.41–50)

> [Repelled by the thought of enduring the benefits of retirement in ignoble sloth, unobserved, at nighttime, she pushed open the doors and slipped the enclosing bolts, then took to her heels, making her way over trackless wastes. She walked, with torn feet, through rough and desolate areas overgrown with brambles, a choir of angels at her side, and though the silence of the night was fearful, she had light to show her the way.]

The passage has attracted the attention of a number of scholars as an example of the use of Virgilian phrases to convey spiritual landscape in Prudentius.[26] Aeneas, too, encountered "rough and desolate areas," *loca senta situ,* in his descent to the underworld (*Aen.* 6.462). The parallel suggests that one interpretation of Eulalia's journey is a descent *ad inferos.*[27] The presence of light in darkness and of a company of angels

26. Reinhart Herzog, *Die allegorische Dichtkunst des Prudentius,* Zetemata 42 (Munich, 1966), 26–28; G. Richard, "L'apport de Virgile à la création épique de Prudence dans le Peristephanon liber," *Caesarodunum* 3 (1969): 191; Jean-Louis Charlet, "L'apport de la poésie latine chrétienne à la mutation de l'épopée antique: Prudence précurseur de l'épopée médiévale," *BAGB* (1980): 213.

27. The phrase *per invia carpit iter* (3.45) further supports this interpretation; cf. Virgil, *Aen.* 6.154–55 *sic demum lucos Stygis et* **regna invia** *vivis / aspicies* and 629 *sed iam age,* **carpe viam** *et susceptum perfice munus.* Neither phrase in itself would be sufficient to evoke the Virgilian context—they are so much a part of the common poetic idiom—but in proximity to the distinctive *per loca senta situ,* and in the light of the obvious relevance of Aeneas' *catabasis* to Eulalia's situation, the Virgilian reminiscence would probably be perceptible.

recalls Vincent's prison cell. But it is a second interpretation, the association of Eulalia's nighttime travels with the sinful world, which I intend to explore. We must remember the specific situation of Virgil's *loca senta situ*: Aeneas is addressing, or attempting to address, Dido in the part of the underworld set aside for those who had experienced unhappy love. The phrase is probably meant by Aeneas to be a characteristic of Hades *tout court,* equivalent to *has . . . per umbras* (461) and *noctemque profundam* (462). But the fact that it occurs in a speech to Dido, among the shades of unhappy lovers, is more likely to be memorable than its precise connotation in the *Aeneid.* The relevance to Eulalia is immediately obvious. Prudentius imagines her, as a virgin of marriageable age (cf. 16–18), exposed to sexual temptation. The praetor, in cross-examination, attempts to persuade her to marry (101–15). There could be no better illustration from the Christian perspective of the snares of love, and the uncertain distinction between sexual temptation and marriage, than Dido. For the Christian reader, I suggest, the *loca senta situ* of Virgil's underworld represent both the temptations and tribulations of earthly love and the consequences of indulgence in such love in the hereafter.

Petruccione has made a similar point in discussing another Virgilian parallel in *Pe.* 3.[28] After the praetor's attempt to persuadc Eulalia to marry, he makes arrangements for the girl to participate in an act of sacrifice. Images are set up, salted meal is brought in censers to her. Her response is twofold: she spits in the tyrant's face, thus indicating that she recognizes his diabolical aspect, and she kicks over the images and censers: *simulacra dehinc / dissipat inpositamque molam / turibulis pede prosubigit* (128–30). It has long been recognized that the locution *pede prosubigit* is Virgilian (*G.* 3.256). But Petruccione is the first, to my knowledge, to point out the contextual relevance of the *Georgics* passage. There Virgil is describing the effect of sexual desire on the animal kingdom. Eulalia reverses the connotation of the Virgilian phrase. She is trampling underfoot the images of the pagan gods, but also, in an association established in the praetor's speech between idolatry and marriage, treading down sexual temptation. There is a suggestion here that the habitual ferocity of Eulalia's resistance to her persecutors[29] is,

28. John Francis Petruccione, "Prudentius' Use of Martyrological Topoi in Peristephanon" (Ph.D. diss., University of Michigan, 1985), 156–57, and "The Portrait of St. Eulalia in Prudentius' *Peristephanon* 3," *AB* 108 (1990): 97–98.

29. She is described as *aspera* (14), *severa* (23), *ferox* (32), *animosa* (37), *fera* (39),

from the Christian perspective, a benign deflection of the powerful sexual drive described by Virgil.

Eulalia's trek through the rough, bramble-overgrown landscape of her nighttime flight is the equivalent of her rejection of idolatry/sexual desire before the praetor. In the former case, too, the martyr treads temptation underfoot; this is the implication of *pedibus laceris* (46). The details of her unobserved escape from her parents' house are strongly reminiscent of Thisbe's flight in Ovid, *Met.* 4.84–86 and 93–95, to meet her lover Pyramus; compare especially *nocte silenti / fallere custodes foribusque excedere temptent, Met.* 4.84–85 with *nocte fores sine teste movet, Pe.* 3.43. Here again the context in the pagan author, in this case Ovid, is relevant and again the same point is made: the contrast in attitudes to sexual love between heroines of pagan mythology and the Christian virgin Eulalia, who slips out of her house not to meet a lover but to trample sexual temptation underfoot.

Thorns, weeds, brambles and, in general, agricultural disuse and uncultivation have a well established allegorical meaning in Christian writings. The application of such language to the husbandry of the soul goes back to Jesus' parable of the sower (Matt. 13:3-23), a biblical text that Prudentius expounds in *C. Symm.* 2.1020–63. There the poet speaks of "uprooting rough brambles from the heart" (*extirpamus enim sentos de pectore vepres,* 1040) and of the "thorny brier of wicked deeds choking the fruit and harvest of the soul with frequent sin" (*ne frugem segetemque animae spinosa malorum / inpediat sentix scelerum peccamine crebro,* 1042–43).[30] Brambles and thorns are a metaphor for sin in general; in the language of the biblical text "the care of the world and the indulgence of riches" (*sollicitudo saeculi huius et voluptas divitiarum,* Matt. 13:22). Sexual temptations are subsumed under worldly cares. Paulinus of Nola in his tenth *Natalicium* for Felix (*C.* 28), traditionally dated to 404, enumerates the "thorns" (*spinae*) or "rubble" (*rudera*) of the soul, which must be extirpated/cleared away by the Christian. The latter image of spiritual edification is inspired by Paulinus' own literal building activities at Felix' shrine at Cimitile. He first lists the sins of "idle indulgence, indecent love, corrupt passion" (*luxus iners, inpurus amor, maculosa*

superba (64), and *torva* (103). See also Martha Malamud, "Making a Virtue of Perversity: The Poetry of Prudentius," *Ramus* 19 (1990): 72–78, and Petruccione, "Portrait of St. Eulalia," 85–104.

30. For the "thorns of the soul" in Prudentius, see Herzog, *Die allegorische Dichtkunst,* 23–24, and in the liturgy, Blaise, *Le vocabulaire latin,* 549. Petruccione, "Portrait of St. Eulalia," 91–93, elaborates on my interpretation of this passage.

libido, C. 28.285). The three are set off syntactically as a coherent group. Together they can be summed up as *luxuria*; the same *luxuriae rabies* that Cyprian was called upon to eliminate from his own life (*Pe.* 13.25). Paulinus' enumeration concludes with the desire for wealth, corresponding to *voluptas divitiarum* in the Gospel text. Sexual *luxuria* is implicitly understood as an aspect of the biblical "worldly temptation" (*sollicitudo saeculi huius*).[31] For the fourth-century Christian the martyrs had most triumphantly overcome such assaults of the *saeculum,* in their case upon the physical flesh. Prudentius' contemporaries felt the assaults of the "sins of the flesh"; for a Christian virgin of marriageable age, the thorns of sexual temptation were sharpest. A virgin martyr gloriously exemplified the victory that could be achieved over temptations of the body.[32]

Like Aeneas, Eulalia is on a journey (*iter,* 45; *viam,* 56). The Trojan hero comes to a fork in the road. On the left is Tartarus, where he sees the place of punishment of the damned, but he continues on the right-hand road to the abode of the blessed (*Aen.* 6.540–43, 637–39). The Virgilian passage receives a systematic Christian interpretation from Lactantius (*Inst.* 6.3–4).[33] The fork in the road represents a choice between two ways of life. In this way, Aeneas' situation is assimilated to the philosophical myth, going back to Prodicus, of the choice of Herakles, and to Christ's parable of the two ways (Matt. 7:13–14).[34] Lactantius, though, believes that Virgil is wrong to situate the choice among the dead; it is a choice made by the living (*Inst.* 6.3.9). The two paths between

---

31. The full enumeration runs:

luxus iners, inpurus amor, maculosa libido
rudera sunt animae; sic corporis anxia cura,
livor edax et avara fames, gravis ira, levis spes,
prodiga et ambitio proprii, sitiens alieni,
spinae sunt animo, quia semper inanibus angunt
ancipites animas stimulis, quas iugiter urit
defectus miseri metus et miser ardor habendi.

(*C.* 28.285–91)

There is no need to see any distinction between the vices labeled *rudera* and those labeled *spinae.* The two metaphors are used interchangeably (cf. 296–97). For Paulinus' relatively untroubled views on sexual continence, see Peter Brown, *The Body and Society: Men, Women, and Sexual Renunciation in Early Christianity* (New York, 1988), 409.

32. Prudentius reflects the attitude characterized by Brown, *The Body and Society,* 397: "Italian writers [of the late fourth century] found it difficult to imagine female martyrs other than as young virgins, intent, above all, on preserving their virginity."

33. On this passage, see Pierre Courcelle, "Les pères de l'église devant les enfers virgiliens," *Archives d'histoire doctrinale et littéraire du moyen âge* 22 (1955): 21–24, Amat, *Songes et visions,* 363–65.

34. Lactantius cites the Pythagorean symbol of the *bivium,* the letter Y (*Inst.* 6.3.6).

which humans must choose still lead to the abodes of the blessed or the damned, that is, in Christian terminology, to heaven or hell (*Inst.* 6.3.1 and 10). The traveller must choose between a path that is steep, rough, and thorny (*clivosa . . . vel spinis horrentibus aspera vel saxis extantibus impedita, Inst.* 6.4.6), but leads to heaven, or one that initially appears much more level and attractive (*amoena multoque tritior,* 6.3.3), but leads to hell. It is a choice between virtue and vice, salvation and sin, or, as Lactantius terms it, between *frugalitas* and *luxuria* (6.3.6).[35]

Prudentius was aware of this passage in Lactantius. His account of the two ways in the *Hamartigenia* (789–801) shows its influence.[36] There he describes the right-hand road as "narrowed by a forest of thorny briers" (*cum dextrum spinea silva / sentibus artaret, H.* 792–93). The language looks like a variation on the *loca senta vepribus* of Eulalia's journey. Here is one more aspect of the presence of Virgil in this Prudentian passage, and further confirmation of the allegorical dimensions of Eulalia's journey. Though the young martyr does not literally have to choose between two roads, in quitting her parents' house she does choose a style of life, one that, in the language of Lactantius, describing the right-hand way, leads "by combat with the enemy" (*cum hoste certamen,* 6.4.15) to the "crown of virtue" (*corona virtutis,* 6.4.11).[37] The analogy between martyrdom and the struggle with sin in the post-persecution world is clear. Both involve treading underfoot the thorns of worldly temptation (cf. Lactantius 6.4.6 *cum summo labore ac* **pedum tritu** . . . *sit cuique gradiendum*).

In the parable of the two ways the right-hand road leads to heaven. So Eulalia's soul/a dove is seen to leave earth and "make for the stars" (*astra sequi,* 163, a Virgilian locution [*Aen.* 12.893]). The poet does not here attempt to transform heaven into a spiritual landscape, counterpart to the wasteland Eulalia traversed to reach her reward. But there is such a *locus amoenus* in the poem. It is transferred to the here and now, the basilica in which the annual festival of Eulalia was celebrated in the depths of winter (December 10).

Tecta corusca super rutilant
de laquearibus aureolis
saxaque caesa solum variant,

35. *omnis ergo haec de duabus viis disputatio ad frugalitatem ac luxuriam spectat.*

36. Cf. Courcelle, "Les pères de l'église," 24.

37. Lactantius 6.4.16–19 elaborates on this language of *terrena militia.*

floribus ut rosulenta putes
prata rubescere multimodis.

(196–200)

[The brilliant roof glitters overhead with golden coffering and multicolored marble slabs decorate the floor, so that you imagine rose-red meadows, abundant with flowers.]

Brilliance of light and flowered meadows recall Virgil's Elysian fields with their fertile swathes (*locos laetos et amoena virecta, Aen.* 6.638).[38] The decoration of the church evokes Eulalia's reward in Paradise, imagined, as often, as a brilliant springtime landscape.[39] In entering the basilica at the time of Eulalia's festival, the individual worshipper experiences in the here and now that heavenly bliss that the martyr won by her own spiritual journey—the bliss that is promised to all who fight the same fight against worldly temptation. The Christian basilica is the "gateway to Paradise" (*exitus in paradisum*), as it is described by Paulinus of Nola (*Ep.* 32.12) in verses he composed for an entrance to the pre-Paulinian basilica at the shrine of Felix.[40] Although there is nothing similar to the golden coffering of Eulalia's shrine in Virgil's underworld, the *Aeneid* does offer a close verbal parallel in the gilded ceilings (*laquearibus aureis, Aen.* 1.726) of Dido's palace. Gilded ceilings were not an unusual architectural feature (cf. Pliny, *N.H.* 33.18.57). But given the context of the Virgilian passage, a scene of luxury and love, and the earlier evocation of Dido in *Pe.* 3, it is difficult to avoid the impression that the Virgilian reference is intentional. Dido is the supreme example of someone who fails to resist the temptations of *luxuria* and suffers in the life to come; Eulalia enjoys posthumous *luxuria* as a reward for her *frugalitas* in this world.[41]

---

38. For the light of Virgil's Elysian fields, see *Aen.* 6.640–41, *largior hic campos aether et lumine vestit / purpureo.*

39. Cf. Prudentius, *C.* 3.101–5, 5.113–24, and 8.41–48, with the comments of Jacques Fontaine, "Trois variations de Prudence sur le thème du Paradis," in W. Wimmel, ed., *Forschungen zur römischen Literatur: Festschrift zum 60. Geburtstag von Karl Büchner* (Wiesbaden, 1970), 96–115, = *Études sur la poésie latine tardive d'Ausone à Prudence* (Paris, 1980), 488–507.

40. The full inscription runs: *caelestes intrate vias per amoena virecta, / Christicolae; et laetis decet huc ingressus ab hortis, / unde sacrum meritis datur exitus in paradisum. Amoena virecta* is from Virgil's description of the Elysian fields (*Aen.* 6.638). For other Christian uses of this phrase, see Courcelle, "Les pères de l'église," 33–34. Paulinus exploits the fact that the entrance in question is from an orchard-garden (*de hortulo vel pomario*).

41. Prudentius tends to see Paradise and the life of sinful indulgence as equal but

Prudentius has not concluded his description of the paradisiacal qualities of Eulalia's shrine. He moves from the floral appearance of the basilica to the flowers the worshippers bring to the celebration of the saint's festival.

> Carpite purpureas violas
> sanguineosque crocos metite!
> Non caret his genialis hiems,
> laxat et arva tepens glacies,
> floribus ut cumulet calathos.
>
> (201–5)

> [Gather purple violets and pick crocuses the color of blood. Festive winter has no shortage of these, as the ice warms and unbinds the fields so that it piles baskets with flowers.]

The passage presents problems of interpretation. Readers have usually thought of literal gifts of flowers, offered to the saint at her annual festival.[42] But although such blooms may have been available in December in Mérida, by combining Virgilian language for winter (*genialis hiems, G.* 1.302), when the only outdoor activities are hunting and collecting acorns and berries, with that for spring (*laxat et arva,* cf. *G.* 2.330), Prudentius draws attention to the extraordinary nature of the springtime in winter that he is attributing to Eulalia's shrine. As Richard has pointed out,[43] the epithet *sanguineos* (202) is not merely a color term, equivalent to *purpureos.* Blood-colored blooms are an appropriate offering to a martyr. The epithets describing the violets and crocuses already suggest a spiritual meaning for the flowers. So what, then, is it that the worshippers bring? Since martyrdom is associated throughout the poem with the conquest of sin and temptation in the everyday experience of the individual Christian, the flowers here probably have the

---

opposite states; he uses the Virgilian *amoena virecta* of both (*C.* 3.101, *H.* 795). On the possible evocation of Dido's palace, see Anne-Marie Palmer, *Prudentius on the Martyrs* (Oxford, 1989), 173–74.

42. See especially Klaus Thraede, *Studien zu Sprache und Stil des Prudentius,* Hypomnemata 13 (Göttingen, 1965), 34, who denies any spiritualization of the offerings, and Isidoro Rodriguez-Herrera, *Poeta Christianus: Prudentius' Auffassung vom Wesen und von der Aufgabe des christlichen Dichters* (Speyer, 1936), 70–71.

43. Richard, "L'apport de Virgile," 188–89; see also Palmer, *Prudentius on the Martyrs,* 174–75.

allegorical meaning of virtues. It is the spiritual virtues of the individual soul that are brought as offerings to Eulalia's shrine, in particular, since the offerants are identified in the next stanza as adolescent girls and boys (*virgo puerque,* 207), sexual continence. Elsewhere Prudentius refers to chastity as a flower (*A.* 574, *H.* 956–57, *C. Symm.* 2.253).[44] By their offerings the worshippers bring the "landscape" to bloom. Spring and winter are united in the devotion of the celebrants of Eulalia's anniversary, just as at Nola on Felix' feast day (January 14) "winter breathes the color of spring" (*C.* 14. 111; cf. 23.1–3).

One last element is at work here in Prudentius' *genialis hiems.* Not only is the locution a Virgilian reminiscence; it also combines two phrases that have occurred earlier in the poem, *glacialis hiems* (176) and *genialis honor* (105). The latter phrase occurs in the praetor's speech when he attempts to persuade Eulalia to marry. *Genialis* has its original sense of "nuptial." The reference is suggestive; celebration of the saint's festival day involves not only a *natalicium,* but, in the case of a virgin, an epithalamium. The virgin is the bride of Christ, *sponsa Christi.*[45]

Viewed in this light, the details of Prudentius' account, especially the motif of springtime in winter, take on further significance. It was a principle of the epithalamium, enunciated by Sidonius Apollinaris in his epithalamium for Ruricius and Hiberia, that whatever the real time of year, in the bridal chamber it was always spring.

> Proxima quin etiam festorum afflata calore
> iam minus alget hiemps, speciemque tenentia vernam
> hoc dant vota loco quod non dant tempora mundo.
> (*C.* 11.126–28)

---

44. The association of *flos* with *virginitas/pudicitia* goes back to classical authors (*ThLL* 6.935.56–72). Virtues in general are more usually described as jewels, adorning the temple of the soul, but flowers and jewels are often interchangeable in late antique literature; both are brilliant and multicolored. The reference to *flos pudicitiae, C. Symm.* 2.253, however, comes in a description of a *templum mentis*; see also Jerome, *Ep.* 64.22.1, *diversis coloribus et gemmis floribusque virtutum* and *ThLL* 6.936.19–44. See also Petruccione, "The Portrait of St. Eulalia," 99–100.

45. *Pe.* 14.79, J. Schmid, "Brautschaft, heilige," *RlAC* 2 (1954): 559–62, and Blaise, *Le vocabulaire latin,* 515. Petruccione develops my suggestion of the epithalamial content of *Pe.* 3, detecting references to the Song of Songs and persuasively suggesting that the *sanguineos crocos* of line 202 are intended to evoke the color of the Roman bridal veil. The ceremony of *velatio,* the veiling of the consecrated virgin, echoes the Roman marriage ceremony (Brown, *Body and Society,* 356); white is prominent in the *velatio* (white robes, white marble railing), as it is at Eulalia's martyrdom, when a snowfall covers her body.

[Though winter is near, yet still its cold is reduced by the warm breath of the festival, and the marriage, bearing a springtime appearance, brings to this spot what the seasons refuse the world at large.]

The language could be adopted, word for word, for the festival of a saint; *vota* may be used both of marriage vows, and hence marriage, and of the prayers of worshippers at a martyr's tomb (e.g., *Pe.* 1.9). The symbolic association of marriage and springtime finds expression in the epithalamium of Prudentius' contemporary, Claudian, for the emperor Honorius, when he situates Venus' temple in a grove of perpetual spring (*Nupt.* 54–55 and 60–61). Flowers, too, real or symbolic, regularly deck the bridal chamber (e.g., Claudian, *C. Min.* 25.116–20), as they do Eulalia's shrine. One further parallel between saint's day and marriage ceremony, though not emphasized in *Pe.* 3, is the ability of each to unite social classes in a single celebration, to restore a form of community (cf. Statius, *Silv.* 1.2.233–35 and *Pe.* 11.199–202).[46] When we remember that *flores/munera* are brought to Eulalia's shrine by a choir (*choro,* 208) of unmarried girls and boys, the analogy with the secular wedding ceremony is unmistakable. *Luxuria* is a key word in Claudian's epithalamium for Honorius and Maria; it embodies the ideology of the epithalamium and all that Venus stands for—luxury, luxuriance of vegetation, and sexual indulgence (cf. *Nupt.* 54, of Venus' grove: *luxuriae Venerique vacat*). This is exactly the ethos that Eulalia has vanquished in her life/nighttime journey. The festival of the saint is a marriage ceremony in reverse, celebrating the victory of *frugalitas* not *luxuria,* and translating the material display of the latter into the spiritual qualities of the soul and heavenly salvation.[47]

No pre-Prudentian prose Passion of Eulalia survives. Petruccione makes the attractive suggestion that the poet has created her *acta* for himself out of the traditions available to him about the Roman virgin

46. Cf. Menander Rhetor 2.6 (404.16–17).

47. Paulinus of Nola also protested against the emphasis on *luxuria* in secular marriage ceremony in a poem written for the wedding of children of clergy, Julian and Titia,

absit ab his thalamis vani lascivia vulgi,
Iuno Cupido Venus, nomina luxuriae.

(*C.* 25.9–10).

See Michael Roberts, "The Use of Myth in Latin Epithalamia from Statius to Venantius Fortunatus," *TAPA* (1989): 337–38.

Agnes.[48] It certainly seems probable that there is a large element of invention in the *Peristephanon,* consistent with what Prudentius considers the basic themes and message of martyrdom. I would prefer to speak of *Pe.* 3 and 14 as complementary. They are meant to be read as a pair. This relationship would hold good even in the unlikely event of a prose source for Prudentius' Eulalia poem being discovered.

We have already proposed that the blandishing enticements of Agnes' judge (*ore blandi iudicis inlice, Pe.* 14.16) are exemplified in *Pe.* 3, where the praetor attempts to persuade Eulalia to marry. While *Pe.* 3 implies that the desire for martyrdom is a quasi-erotic impulse, this becomes explicit in the erotic language of *Pe.* 14 (71–78), where the executioner is greeted as a lover (74).[49] Agnes' victory over lust, when she is exposed in a brothel, repeats the theme of virginity and sexual temptation that underlies Eulalia's nighttime journey. But closest to the Spanish martyr's journey is the ascent of Agnes' spirit to heaven after her execution, and the vision of the secular world that accompanies it. Both are journeys accompanied by an angelic host (*Pe.* 3.48, 14.92–93). Agnes' vision begins with a cosmic panorama reminiscent of the ascent of Pompey's spirit in Lucan's *Pharsalia* (9.11–14), but it soon takes on a specifically Christian moral tone as the martyr's soul sees the transient vanity of the world (*quod vana saecli mobilitas rapit, Pe.* 14.99).[50] There follows an enumeration of idle human passions: ambition for kingdom, empire, and political power, greed for wealth and material possessions, anger, fear, longing and jealousy, and, what summarizes them all, idolatry (100–111). The list is reminiscent of Paulinus' list of *spinae animi,* which also includes jealousy, greed, ambition, idle hope, and the passion to acquire and fear of losing material possessions (*C.* 28.286–91).[51] We are reminded once more, at the end of the Eulalia-Agnes diptych, that the sexual is only a special case of the whole realm of worldly temptation. A victory in this particular sphere is a victory over all sinful passions. Like Eulalia,

48. Petruccione, *Prudentius' Use of Martyrological Topoi,* 100–115, and "The Portrait of St. Eulalia," 83–85; see also P. Tino Alberto Sabattini, "Storia e leggenda nei *Peristephanon* di Prudenzio III," *RSC* 21 (1973): 42–47.

49. Martha Malamud, *A Poetics of Transformation: Prudentius and Classical Mythology* (Ithaca, N.Y., 1989), 149–77, makes the erotic elements of *Pe.*14 central to her interpretation of that poem.

50. For the influence of Lucan, see G. Sixt, "Des Prudentius' Abhängigkeit von Seneca und Lucan," *Philologus* 51 (1892): 505. The passage also owes something to the *Somnium Scipionis,* and to the Stoic tradition of posthumous revelations; in addition to Lucan, Seneca, *Ep.* 102.28, *Cons. Marc.* 25–26, *Cons. Polyb.* 9.3.

51. See this chapter, n.31.

Agnes treads underfoot the demons (*Pe.* 3.130 *pede prosubigit, Pe.* 14.112 *pede proterit*). In so doing she fulfils as antitype the figure of Eve, treading with her heel on the serpent's head (*haec calcat . . . / stans et draconis calce premens caput,* 111–12; cf. Gen. 3:15 *ipsa tuum calcabit caput et tu observabis calcaneum eius*). Eve, by succumbing to temptation, introduced sin into the world; Agnes, by resisting temptation, reasserted human supremacy over the fallen world (cf. 114–18).

Eulalia's nighttime journey also corresponds to an Old Testament type, which it reenacts in the era of the persecutions. Aeneas in descending to the underworld had the Sibyl as his guide; Eulalia, in passing at night over rough, overgrown terrain, has light to lead her (*lucis habet tamen illa ducem, Pe.* 3.50), light that the poet compares with the column of fire that accompanied the Israelites in their escape from Egypt (Exod. 13:21–22).

> Sic habuit generosa patrum
> turba columniferum radium,
> scindere qui tenebrosa potens
> nocte viam face perspicua
> praestitit intereunte chao.
>
> (51–55)

> [In the same way the noble followers of the patriarchs had a ray of light, in the shape of a column with the power to tear apart the darkness, that showed the way at night with brilliant torch, as the blackness perished.]

The illumination of darkness by light recalls the language of Vincent's imprisonment. Once again the infernal powers suffer defeat, *intereunte chao* (55). While *chao* operates at one level as metonymy for darkness, the word is regularly used by Latin poets of the underworld. The polysemy of the passage derives from the poet's choice of language. Eulalia's journey and the Exodus from Egypt are also victories over Hell, victories that receive their authoritative prefiguration/fulfillment in Christ's own Crucifixion and Resurrection. A further item of vocabulary suggests Prudentius has just this event in mind. The word *scindere* (53) is used metaphorically with the object *tenebrosa.* It is used literally in the Gospel story of the tearing of the veil of the temple (Matt. 27:51 *ecce velum templi scissum est* = Mark 15:38), an act that symbolizes the superseding of the Old Dispensation by the New, and accompanies Christ's descent to and vanquishing of Hell. Divisions of time are once more temporarily dispelled; the Exodus from Egypt, Christ's *catabasis,* and Eulalia's journey merge into a single atemporal pattern, so much so that in the next stanza the virgin martyr can be said to flee from "the Egyptian realm" (*regna Canopica,* 59). There is no question of a literal setting in Egypt. Eulalia's martyrdom is set in Mérida.[52] She, nevertheless, can be described both as fleeing from Egypt and on her way to heaven (*super astra pararet iter,* 60). Such language demands a readjustment of reading. As a literal, historical account of Eulalia's circumstances it makes no sense. The reader must understand the text at a higher level of generality, where Egypt, the underworld and the country near Mérida are synonymous. At that level, multiple meanings become one. Prudentius' achievement as a composer of martyr poems is to create an idiom, in large part by resources of lexicon, that gives expression to this plenitude of meaning present in the worship at a martyr's shrine.

At the same time, Christian exegetes regularly interpreted the Exodus from Egypt as the struggle with and eventual victory over sin. Egypt is the world, Pharaoh the devil, Israel the *populus Christianus,* and the column of light, Christ who illuminates the way from past sins to the brightness of salvation through baptism.[53] The interpretation coheres with that of the spiritual landscape through which Eulalia passes. It is an interpretation that unites biblical past and the time of the martyrs with the experience of the individual worshipper in the here and now. Each Christian soul pursues a similar itinerary through the darkness/wasteland of worldly sinfulness. The martyr both shows how that path should be traversed and has the power to aid in the journey (cf. 3.214–15). Christ as the column of light illuminates the way, as God, in Lactantius' interpretation of the two ways (*Inst.* 6.3.16), is leader on the right-hand road to heaven.[54]

Prudentius' assimilation of Eulalia's journey to the Exodus from

---

52. Herzog, *Die allegorische Dichtkunst,* 26–28, has some interesting remarks on the movement from metaphor to religious allegory, as exemplified by this passage.

53. Zeno of Verona, *Tract.* 2.54, *Aegyptus mundus est iste. Pharao, cum populo suo diabolus et spiritus omnis iniquitatis. Israel, populus christianus . . . . Columna viam demonstrans Christus est Dominus* (*PL* 11.510A). See also Tertullian, *Bapt.* 9.1, (*CCL* 1.283.33–284.8), Ambrose, *Sacr.* 1.6.22 (*CSEL* 73; 24.14–21), and in general Jean Daniélou, *Sacramentum Futuri: Études sur les origines de la typologie biblique* (Paris, 1950), 131–200.

54. *Nos autem homines omnis sexus et generis et aetatis in hoc caeleste iter inducimus, quia deus, qui eius viae dux est, immortalitatem nulli homini nato negat.*

Egypt raises the more general question of the use of biblical *exempla* in the *Peristephanon.* Leaving aside biblical citations and allusions, and considering only passages that evoke a particular event or episode, three broad, though not entirely discrete, categories can be identified:[55] biblical martyrs, miraculous reversals of nature, and the assimilation of martyrs to patriarchs and leaders of the Jewish people, especially Moses. For the first group, biblical martyrs, Cyprian provides a list of available models in his *Letter to Fortunatus* (11). He includes Abel, Jacob, Joseph, David, Elijah, Zachariah, the three Hebrews in the furnace, Daniel, Tobias, the seven Maccabee brothers, and Eleazar. Of these Abel, Elijah, the three Hebrews, and the Maccabees occur in the *Peristephanon,* as well as Isaiah, and from the New Testament, John the Baptist, the Innocents and Stephen, who, though not included in Cyprian's list, are frequently found among biblical martyrs.[56] References cluster in two poems, *Pe.* 5 (Abel, John the Baptist—also incarcerated like Vincent—Isaiah, and the Maccabees) and *Pe.* 10 (the Innocents, Isaac, the Maccabees, and Abel).[57] The two poems are the most complete martyr texts in the collection and it is not surprising that they should include such biblical parallels. Elijah, the biblical exemplar of the persecuted prophet,[58] also figures in *Pe.* 5 (405–6), but in the story of his feeding by a raven, an illustration of the marvellous obedience of nature rather than of martyrdom. In addition, the brilliance of Stephen's face is compared to Lawrence's as he prepares for martyrdom (*Pe.* 2.369–72), and Fructuosus and his two deacons, like the three Hebrews in the furnace, are untouched by the flames until they pray for their souls' release (6.109–17). The martyrs of the Church renew and participate in the sufferings and death of the biblical figures. Old Testament figure, apostle, and martyr, all preenact/reenact the supreme Passion of Christ and his victory

55. For Prudentius' use of the historical books of the Old and New Testaments as sources of *exempla,* see Jean-Louis Charlet, "Prudence et la Bible," *RecAug* 18 (1983): 91–92. In addition to Charlet's invaluable study, Natale Grasso, "Prudenzio e la Bibbia," *Orpheus* 19 (1972): 79–170, studies Prudentius' use of the Bible.

56. Simone Deléani-Nigoul, "Les *exempla* bibliques du martyre," in Jacques Fontaine and Charles Pietri, edd., *Le monde latin antique et la Bible,* Bible de tous les temps (Paris, 1985) 2: 246.

57. *Pe.* 5.371–72, 375–76, 523–36; 10.737–40, 748–50, 751–80, 828–30. The story of the martyrdom of Isaiah is apocryphal but common in Christian exegesis (Charlet, "Prudence et la Bible," 83) and derived from Jewish tradition (Deléani-Nigoul, "Les *exempla,*" 246–48.

58. Deléani-Nigoul, "Les *exempla,*" 255–56.

over sin and death, an event that is actualized afresh in the liturgical celebration of a martyr's festival.[59]

The second group of biblical *exempla* concerns the marvelous obedience of nature and is confined to *Pe.* 5 and 7. Vincent's body is protected from carrion-eating creatures by a bird, thus recalling Elijah's protection by ravens (5.405–8); carried out to sea and thrown overboard in a sack weighted with rocks, the body floats back to shore, demonstrating the same divine control of the element of water as was shown by Christ's walking on the Sea of Galilee and by the crossing of the Red Sea (5.473–84). That a body can continue to be the beneficiary of God's miraculous powers even after death has an obvious relevance to the cult of the saints as practiced in Prudentius' own day, when miracles of healing frequently took place at the shrines of the martyrs (e.g., at Nola, as recorded by Paulinus). By comparing these miracles of divine protection with biblical episodes, Prudentius emphasizes the continuity and common origin of such reversals of nature. In the words of Ambrose, referring to miracles performed by the relics of martyrs, "the miracles of former times are reenacted."[60]

The situation is rather similar in *Pe.* 7, but here it is a live saint who is thrown into a river in a sack weighted with rocks—he floats. In praying for release from life, Quirinus cites two biblical examples of Christ's power over water, once again from the New and Old Testaments respectively: Christ holding out his hand to Peter to keep his feet above the waves (Matt. 14:29–31), and the reversal of the course of the Jordan (Josh. 3:13–17; Ps. 113:3–5).[61] Here the relevance to the contemporary cult of the martyrs is less marked, since it is the live person of Quirinus that is buoyed up, not his dead body, though the ability of the saint's body to transcend its physical properties and float on the water is an illustration of the superiority of spiritual over corporeal that is also demonstrated by Peter, and fundamental to the martyr's *potentia.* The New Testament miracles in *Pe.* 5 and 7 emphasize the treading underfoot of a stormy sea (*terga calcans aequoris* and *vasti viator gurgitis,* 5.477 and 480; *calcare fremitum maris,* 7.59). Both, especially in the verb

59. See especially Simone Deléani-Nigoul, "L'utilisation des modèles bibliques du martyre par les écrivains du IIIe siècle," in Jacques Fontaine and Charles Pietri, edd., *Le monde latin antique,* Bible de tous les temps (Paris, 1985) 2: 334-38.

60. *Ep.* 77(22).9, *reparata vetusti temporis miracula* (*CSEL* 82.3; 132.86).

61. Prudentius' reference to the turning back of the Jordan derives from Psalms; cf. *C.* 12.178, *H.* 482, *D.* 57–58, and Charlet, "Prudence et la Bible," 46–48.

calcare, employ language appropriate to the victory over sin and the world. The two Old Testament examples are commonly interpreted in Christian exegesis of baptism,[62] itself a victory over sin, and, as in *Pe.* 6 (28–30), an illumination of darkness by light. The association is especially clear in *Pe.* 7, where Prudentius equates martyrdom in a flood of blood with martyrdom in a flood of water (16–20). The next poem, written probably as an inscription for a baptistery at Calahorra, then depends entirely on the equivalence between martyrdom in blood and baptism in water.[63] Viewed in this light, Quirinus joins the Old Testament types for the saving role of baptism. It is tempting to wonder whether *Pe.* 8, shorter than and different in nature from the other poems, was not included in the collection just to clinch this association of ideas.

The final group of biblical examples overlaps with those already treated, but merits separate treatment because of the contribution it makes to the themes of the *Peristephanon.* In *Pe.* 1 (40) the persecuted Christians are described as "second descendants of Israel" (*secundos Istrahelis posteros*). If the Christian community is a second Israel, the martyrs who hold ecclesiastical office are likened to the Jewish patriarchs and prophets, and particularly to Moses, who led his people from bondage in Egypt to the Promised Land. This theme is most marked in *Pe.* 2. In the brilliance of his face, as he prepares for martyrdom, Lawrence is not only likened to the New Testament martyr Stephen but also to Moses as he descends from Mt. Sinai after receiving the law, only to find his people worshiping a gold calf (2.361–68).[64] The worship of gold[65] is an appropriate subject for a poem in which Lawrence's persecutor, in his desire for wealth, has attempted to appropriate the riches of the church. The language of 365–68 equates the city prefect and the pagan values he represents with the idolaters of Exodus. Lawrence is cast in the role of Moses bringing enlightenment to his people. Prudentius goes on to distinguish further between those Christians, cleansed by baptism, who can see the brilliance of Lawrence's face, and the blindness of his persecutors (*inpiorum caecitas,* 377) that prevents them from doing so. He draws the parallel with the ninth plague of Egypt (Exod. 10:21–23), when darkness enveloped the Egyptians, called *barbari* (382) by Pru-

62. Herzog, *Die allegorische Dichtkunst,* 90.

63. Cf. Willy Schetter, "Prudentius, *Peristephanon* 8," *Hermes* 110 (1982): 110–11.

64. Prudentius here conflates details from Exod. 32 and 34:29–35; cf. *A.* 321–37.

65. Cf. *D.* 40, of the worship of the golden calf: *forma sed his vituli solus deus et* **deus aurum**.

dentius, while the Israelites enjoyed the light of day (383–84). In this case the pagans are associated not with the idolatrous Hebrews, but with the Egyptians; Christians now play the role of *Hebraei,* enjoying illumination. By calling the Egyptians *barbari* Prudentius assimilates the Jewish : Egyptian and Christian : pagan antitheses to a third opposition, that between Romans and non-Romans (cf. *C. Symm.* 2.816, *sed tantum distant Romana et barbara*).[66] Although in the historical circumstances of the martyrdom Christian to pagan is not as Roman to non-Roman, the poem as a whole anticipates and celebrates the time, in Prudentius' own day, when that would be the case, when the western Roman Empire is united in a single Christian community under the patronage of the saints, as adumbrated in *Pe.* 4. By the roles attributed to the Hebrews and their leaders in this passage and to the Egyptians/idolatrous Israelites, Prudentius converts Old Testament history into a political allegory of the conversion of Rome to Christianity under the leadership of the martyrs.

The final reference to Moses occurs in Prudentius' poem on Bishop Fructuosus of Tarragona (*Pe.* 6.86–90). Before entering the fire that is his punishment Fructuosus takes off his shoes—so much is in Prudentius' prose source (3.4–5). But the prose text does not contain the comparison with Moses, who removed his shoes before approaching the burning bush (Exod. 3:5). The identity of the two actions no doubt prompted the comparison in the *Peristephanon.* But there are further points of similarity; like the burning bush (Exod. 3:2–3), Fructuosus and his deacons will not be consumed by the fire they are about to enter. They will, once their feet are bare, be able to "tread on the sacred fire" (*calcare sacram cremationem—calcare* with reference to Fructuosus' punishment, *sacram* to the burning bush). The burning bush, in which God appeared to Moses, also draws attention to the special proximity Moses and Fructuosus enjoy to the divine (*adstare deo,* 89). In a poem that, like its prose source, devotes special attention to Fructuosus' role as bishop, there is perhaps the further point that in the new world of Roman

66. The association of pagans with barbarians is habitual in Prudentius; see Marianne Kah, *"Die Welt der Römer mit der Seele suchend . . ." : Die Religiosität des Prudentius im Spannungsfeld zwischen 'pietas christiana' und 'pietas romana',* Hereditas 3 (Bonn, 1990), 178–9, citing *A.* 194, *H.* 456, *C. Symm.* 1.44, and *Pe.* 1.47, in addition to the present passage. For a discussion of *C. Symm.* 2.816–21 and the complications of the analogy between Romans and non-Romans and believers and nonbelievers, see Hans Arnim Gärtner, "Rome et les barbares dans la poésie latine au temps d'Augustin: Rutilius Namatianus et Prudence," *Ktema* 8 (1984): 118–20.

Christianity the role of Moses as leader of the Israelites devolves on the bishops of the Church. In the same way the deacon Vincent inherits the sacral functions of Old Testament priests and is described as "from the sacred tribe of Levi" (*levita de tribu sacra,* 5.30).

This chapter has been devoted to a range of strategies for amplifying the narrative scope of martyr texts. Vincent/Fructuosus in prison, Eulalia escaping from her parents' custody, and the Israelites escaping from Egypt all experience a journey whose common goal is heaven. Whether spatially and chronologically extended, as Eulalia's trek, or confined in time and place in the manner of incarceration, the journey narratives repeat the synecdochical pattern we have already observed by containing in themselves the whole course of the martyrdom. At the same time, the narratives replicate the supreme act of suffering and redemption, Christ's Passion and victorious Descent, and map out the path for the souls of all Christians in their struggles with sin and temptation. In the case of Eulalia, this journey narrative is further enriched by material appropriate to her as a Christian virgin. Reminiscences of classical poetry evoke a contrast with unhappy mythological lovers, while the description of her festival explores the opposition between indulgence and chastity in the language of late antique ceremonial. Biblical *exempla* establish a universal atemporal type to which the martyrs conform. In particular, Lawrence, as teacher, and Fructuosus, as bishop, fulfill roles prefigured by Moses. This theme of martyr as bishop and teacher, which plays a significant role in a number of the poems, will be the subject of the next chapter.

CHAPTER 4

The Martyr as Bishop and Teacher

The poems of the *Peristephanon* contain all sorts of verbal and thematic cross-references that defy any attempt to specify the interrelationships between them according to a single organizing principle. This aesthetic is characteristic of late antiquity, which delights in the rich patterning created by a multiplicity of effects of similarity and opposition.[1] Readers are at liberty to group together poems according to a variety of organizing criteria. Yet one principle that does receive some prominence is association by ecclesiastical status of the martyr. *Pe.* 3 and 14 are both about Christian virgins, and 2 and 5 have deacons as their subjects. A third, less pronounced, grouping is of poems about martyr-bishops. *Pe.* 6, 7, and 13 clearly belong to this category—they all concern bishops. *Pe.* 11 and 12, though concerned with martyrs who can only be described as bishops with some qualification, share some of the same themes as the unambiguously episcopal poems, as does *Pe.* 9, a poem about a teacher.

The first bishop to play a role in the *Peristephanon,* as conventionally ordered, is Sixtus, bishop of Rome during the persecutions of 258. It is he who, from the cross where he is suffering martyrdom,[2] predicts the passion of Lawrence, his own deacon.

"Desiste discessu meo
fletum dolenter fundere!
Praecedo, frater; tu quoque

1. See Michael Roberts, *The Jeweled Style: Poetry and Poetics in Late Antiquity* (Ithaca, N.Y., 1989).

2. Prudentius is the first to describe Sixtus as crucified rather than beheaded. The confusion is plausibly explained as a misunderstanding of Damasus, *Epigr.* 25.3 and 7. Damasus' own epigram on Sixtus (17.4 and 6) seems to presuppose beheading, though it is not unambiguous (cf. Ferrua's edition and commentary, 125 and 154).

post hoc sequeris triduum."

(*Pe.* 2.25–28)

["Do not shed sorrowful tears for my departure. I am going ahead, my brother; you too will follow on the third day from now."]

The words here attributed to Sixtus are an amplification of Ambrose's version of the same speech in *De officiis* 1.41.206: "*mox venies, flere desiste, post triduum me sequeris*" ("you will soon come, stop weeping; in three days you will follow me").[3] Such speeches addressed by a martyr to the clergy or Christian community, either in direct or indirect speech, are only given to bishops in the *Peristephanon,* a reflection of the bishop's function as teacher and pastor.[4] Sixtus in *Pe.* 2 is typical. He goes ahead of his deacon Lawrence, instructing by example and words. As bishop he is the first to meet his death—a point also emphasized by Damasus (*Epigr.* 17.6); his last words foretell Lawrence's glory (cf. *Pe.* 2. 29–30, *Extrema vox episcopi, / praenuntiatrix gloriae*). Ambrose insists on the pupil-teacher relationship implicit in this exchange between deacon and bishop. Lawrence shows that he is a good student by imitating his instructor's example, even in the latter's absence.

Infirmi discipuli magistrum praecedant, fortes sequantur ut vincant sine magistro qui iam non indigent magisterio.

(*Off.* 1.41. 206)

[Let weak pupils go before their teacher, but let the brave follow to be victorious without a teacher since they no longer need instruction.]

In times of persecution the bishop must lead by example, show the way, if necessary, to martyrdom, and act as teacher of his community. So Bishop Fructuosus of Tarragona is described as *dux et praevius et magister* (6.10) to the two deacons who suffer martyrdom with him. As instructor (*praeceptor,* 20) he strengthens his companions' resolve lest they be gripped by fear (*ne quis socios timor feriret,* 19) and ignites their ardent faith in Christ (*incenditque fidem calore Christi,* 21). All these

3. See also the hymn to Lawrence attributed to Ambrose (13 Bulst), verses 7–8: *maerere, fili, desine, / sequere me post triduum.* For the authorship of this hymn, see above chap. 2, n.69.

4. *Pe.* 6.22–27, 54–60, 77–84, 94–99; 7.41–45, 11.29–34, 13.38–48.

details of the bishop's role are absent from Prudentius' prose source. They indicate the poet's sensitivity to the responsibilities of episcopal status.

Something similar is evident in the account of Bishop Quirinus' martyrdom in *Pe.* 7. Prudentius is here primarily concerned with the allegorical significance of martyrdom by water. But set roughly in the middle of the poem is a vignette dramatizing the relationship between bishop and community.[5]

Spectant eminus e solo
doctorem pavidi greges;
nam Christi populus frequens
riparum sinuamina
stipato agmine saepserat.

Sed Quirinus ut eminens
os circumtulit, heu, suos
exemplo trepidos videt;
nil ipse proprii memor
inter stagna periculi,

confirmat pia pectora,
verbis mitificis rogans
ne quem talia terreant
neu constans titubet fides
aut poenam putet emori.

(7.31–45)

[From far off on dry land the flocks fearfully watch their teacher; for the people of Christ *en masse* packed the curving river banks in a dense column. But when Quirinus, his head above water, glanced around, alas, he saw his followers alarmed by his situation. With no thought for his own danger among the waters he strengthened their

5. The prose version of the passion, which may well date to the fourth century (cf. P. Tino Alberto Sabattini, "Storia e leggenda nei *Peristephanon* di Prudenzio 1," *RSC* 20 [1972]: 43), passes over this scene with the minimum of detail: *cum spectantibus locutus est, ne suo terrerentur exemplo, Passio Sancti Quirini episcopi et martyris* 5 (= P. Tino Alberto Sabattini, "Storia e leggenda nei *Peristephanon* di Prudenzio 111," *RSC* 21 [1973]: 63). Prudentius refers to Quirinus' episcopal status also in verses 22 (*sanctae plebis episcopus*) and 51 (*martyr episcopus*).

righteous hearts with calming words, asking that no one be terrified by such happenings, nor that resolute faith waiver or think death a punishment.]

The situation here and Quirinus' words recall Fructuosus' speeches in *Pe.* 6. Both bishops are concerned to strengthen their addressees' resolve (*confirmat,* 7.41; *firmat* 6.20), to prevent or assuage fear (7.32, 38, 43; 6.19), and to bolster faith (7.44; 6.21). Quirinus' argument that death is no punishment (7.45) repeats Fructuosus' last words to his Christian audience, "believe me, what you see is not a punishment" (*non est, credite, poena quam videtis,* 6.94). The emphasis on eminence and distance in the description of Quirinus' position as he addresses his people (cf. 7.21–22) is probably meant to reproduce the situation of the bishop in church, separated from and raised above the congregation on his elevated *cathedra* in the apse. Quirinus' concern with the spiritual well-being of his flock at the moment of his martyrdom is a special instance of the everyday pastoral responsibilities of the bishop.

A bishop-martyr continues his protection of his city even after death. At the same time, the special access to heaven he then enjoys makes him an effective intercessor for Christians everywhere. Asked by his devoted attendants (*pii sodales,* 6.73) in Tarragona whether he will remember them after death, Fructuosus' answer is "I shall petition Christ for all peoples" (*cunctis pro populis rogabo Christum,* 6.84). The prose passion is even more emphatic. The bishop's response there to his interrogator, a certain Felix, is "I must keep in mind the Catholic Church from east to west" (3.6).[6] Martyrdom generalizes the bishops' power and makes it available to the entire Christian community. But while in principle the martyr's power is available to all, it is the people of the immediately surrounding Pyrenees region who enjoy special protection through Fructuosus and his deacons (*exultare tribus libet patronis, / quorum praesidio fovemur omnes / terrarum populi Pyrenearum,* 145–47) and the prestige that redounds to the city of Tarragona from its martyrs exalts it above all other *Spanish* communities (*nostrae caput excitatur urbis, / cunctis urbibus eminens Hiberis,* 143–44; cf. 1–3). The power of the martyr is stronger in the immediate vicinity of his place of martyrdom. It is as though waves of influence radiate out from that location, but get progressively weaker the further removed from the point of transmission one is.

6. *In mente me habere necesse est ecclesiam catholicam ab oriente usque in occidentem.*

In this respect bishops are no different from other martyrs. What sets bishops apart is that most martyrs derive their power to intercede for the Christian community from the circumstances of their death. Bishops, on the other hand, by reason of their office have a duty to pray for their congregations in this world. So Bishop Valerian of Calahorra, to whom *Pe.* 11 is addressed, prays to Christ on behalf of his people (*Pe.* 11.239–40: *sic te pro populo, cuius tibi credita vita est, / orantem Christus audiat omnipotens.*) At the moment of martyrdom bishops continue to enact their role as pastor and teacher by addressing their clergy and Christian community. Fructuosus, Quirinus, and Hippolytus (*Pe.* 11.29–38) all remember this important function at the time of their passions. The office of bishop finds model and legitimation in those of its number who during the time of the persecutions continued to lead, instruct, and preach to the very end.

The best example of the episcopal martyr in the *Peristephanon,* however, is Cyprian. He is in many ways a model bishop. Prudentius sums up his qualities in a passage that takes as its point of departure the contrast in Cyprian's personal appearance before and after conversion.

Exuitur tenui vultus cute, transit in severam.
Deflua caesaries conpescitur ad breves capillos.
Ipse modesta loqui, spem quaerere, regulam tenere,
vivere iustitiam Christi, penetrare dogma nostrum.
His igitur meritis dignissimus usque episcopale
provehitur solium doctor, capit et sedile summum.

(*Pe.* 13.29–34)

[His face lost its soft complexion and took on an austere appearance. His flowing hair was cropped to a short cut. He was restrained in speech, his aim the hope of salvation, his life in accordance with the rule and the justice of Christ, with deep insight into our doctrine. And so, most worthy because of these virtues, he was advanced to the episcopal throne as teacher and occupied the highest seat.]

The passage is a *speculum episcopi* in miniature. Many of the qualities attributed to Cyprian can be paralleled in fourth- and fifth-century writings on the role of the clergy. Ambrose, in the *De officiis,* advocates moderation of language (1.3.12–13) and modesty of appearance (1.19.83). The *Statuta Ecclesiae Antiquae,* a Gallic compilation of the second half of the fifth century, but based on earlier material, requires that clergy have short hair; this was already the practice of Augustine at the beginning of the century.[7] The combination of eloquence of speech, intellectual understanding of the Scriptures and of Christian doctrine, and an exemplary life, as attributed to Cyprian in *Pe.* 13.31–32, conforms to the ideal Christian preacher described by Augustine in the fourth book of his *De doctrina Christiana.* Cyprian is here a model bishop, "most worthy because of his virtues" of the episcopal throne.

Like Fructuosus and Quirinus, Cyprian urges his charges to show resolute faith in the face of persecution (13.38–40). There follows a passage of indirect speech (41–48), an exhortation to martyrdom, that with its predominance of emphatically end-stopped lines constitutes a lapidary summation of the rewards that await the resolute Christian. Like Fructuosus and Sixtus, Cyprian will show the way to martyrdom; he will be "the originator of glorious death and lead the way to bloodshed" (*se fore principium pulchrae necis et ducem cruoris,* 46); "he who wishes to be united in spirit with Christ should follow Cyprian as his companion" (*Qui sociare animam Christo velit, ut comes sequatur,* 48). As complement to this passage Cyprian also remembers his flock in his prayer requesting speedy release for his soul, and he prays that their faith not waiver (67–69). As a bishop he is responsible for the souls entrusted to him.

Cyprian's prayer is answered. Set within the account of Cyprian's passion is a section that recounts the death of the *Massa Candida* (70–87), a group of martyrs normally said to have been executed at Utica by being thrown into a pit of quicklime.[8] In the *Peristephanon* they are

7. *Statuta Ecclesiae Antiqua* 44. For the circumstances of compilation of the *Statuta Ecclesiae Antiqua,* see Jean Gaudemet, *L'église dans l'empire romain (IVe-Ve siècles),* Histoire du droit et des institutions de l'église en occident 3 (Paris, 1958), 42–43, and for the practices of Ambrose and Augustine, F. Van der Meer, *Augustine the Bishop: The Life and Work of a Father of the Church,* trans. Brian Battershaw and G.R. Lamb (London, 1961), 235–36. Paulinus (*Ep.* 22.2) also believes hair should be kept short (*nec inproba adtonsi capitis fronte criniti sed casta informitate capillum ad cutem caesi*). Martha Malamud, *A Poetics of Transformation: Prudentius and Classical Mythology* (Ithaca, N.Y., 1989), 122–27, makes a good deal of this passage in *Pe.* 13. I am not sure that it can bear the weight of meaning she puts on it.

8. For the legend of the *Massa Candida,* see Pio Franchi de' Cavalieri, "I martiri della massa candida," in *Nuove note agiografiche,* Studi e testi 9 (Rome, 1902), 37–51. Malamud, *Poetics of Transformation,* 127–48 presents an interpretation of the *Massa Candida* in *Pe.* 13 that is diametrically opposed to mine. She understands Prudentius to be critical of the mass suicide of Cyprian's followers, and she would associate them with the excesses of contemporary Donatists. Both Cyprian and Carthage are suspect in her reading. Readers

transferred to Carthage and become the followers of Cyprian. Prudentius' version of the legend is surprising and contradicts African tradition. It raises the question why the poet—or his source—would wish to combine what were originally two separate martyr narratives.

One obvious benefit is to the characterization of Cyprian as bishop. Sixtus and Fructuosus had led the way to martyrdom for their subordinate clergy; Quirinus had preached to the laity that there was nothing to fear in martyrdom, though there is no statement in that poem that his people then followed him to their deaths. Now in the case of Cyprian the two models are combined: a bishop shows the way to martyrdom to the laity, the *populus Carthaginis* (71). Cyprian's teaching and prayer have their effect. Indeed the fate of the Christian community under their bishop's leadership forms a prominent subplot in the central sections of *Pe.* 13. The text shows the ideal bishop in operation and demonstrates his concern for the spiritual well-being of his flock, a concern that finds a triumphant outcome in the self-devotion of the *Candida Massa.*

This happy outcome is achieved by two closely related processes, teaching and prayer. Cyprian, as inspired teacher, is a privileged mouthpiece of the Holy Spirit: "the spirit of God . . . descending from heaven watered you [Cyprian] with springs of eloquence" (9–10).[9] Later God's spirit, actuated by the bishop's prayer, flowed into the people of Carthage and impelled them to resist to death (70–73).[10] At the same time, there is a causal relationship between the two interventions of the Holy Spirit. It is Cyprian's heaven-inspired teaching that prepares his flock for martyrdom by arousing ardent love for Christ (*his ubi corda virum Christo calefacta praeparavit,* 49). His ability to evoke by his words the warmth of Christian devotion in his audience ensures a similar reception for the direct stimulus of the Holy Spirit, when it is called forth by their bishop's prayer. Once again their hearts are warmed (*pectora . . . calerent,* 72: *corda . . . calefacta,* 49).

Cyprian is unique in the *Peristephanon* in his ability to act as mouthpiece of the Holy Spirit even before his martyrdom, in the conduct of his normal episcopal duties; this capacity reflects his special status as

will be able to judge for themselves between the two interpretations. To take a particular point, I cannot see how the phrase *candor vehit ad superna mentes* (86) can be made to square with an ironic reading of the passage.

9. *Spiritus ille dei . . . / fontibui eloquii te caelitus actus inrigavit* (*Pe.* 13.9–10).

10. *Vocibus his dominum permoverat, influebat inde / spiritus in populum Carthaginis auctor acrioris / ingenii, stimulis ut pectora subditis calerent / ad decus egregium discrimine sanguinis petendum* (*Pe.* 13.70–73).

teacher. The case of Fructuosus illustrates that bishops at the time of martyrdom might have this power to speak to their Christian audience as organs of the Holy Spirit. His final words are introduced as follows:

> Stabat calce mera; resultat ecce
> caelo spiritus et serit loquellam,
> quae cunctos tremefecit audientes.
>
> (*Pe.* 6.91–93)

> [He stood there in bare feet, when suddenly the Holy Spirit echoed from heaven and inspired a speech that struck fear in all the audience.]

There is a typical difficulty here for the translator of Prudentius. Who are we to imagine speaking in this passage, the Holy Spirit or Fructuosus as inspired by the Holy Spirit? The phrase *resultat . . . / caelo spiritus* and the fearful reaction of the audience suggest the former. On the other hand, *serit loquellam,* though it can be read as a periphasis for *loquitur,*[11] is more naturally taken to mean "inspires speech" in the martyr, as I have translated it. *Serit loquellam* would then be a less emphatic equivalent of *fontibus eloquii . . . inrigavit* of *Pe.* 13.10. The consequent confusion of speakers is not one that should be explained away by a unitary interpretation. The coexistence of both senses is essential to Prudentius' understanding of the passion. When a martyr speaks to his people at the moment of death it is the Holy Spirit speaking. The two are, in an important sense, inseparable. This is one consequence of the spiritual elevation that the martyr experiences as death approaches. Indeed the reader may initially be inclined to take *spiritus* in *Pe.* 6.92 of Fructuosus' spirit: "his spirit leapt up to heaven," understanding *caelo* as dative of end of motion.[12] The apparent antitheses between *stabat* and *resultat, calce mera* (i.e., a part of the body) and *spiritus* would support this. On reading further, this interpretation will, I think, seem less likely, especially because the descent of the Spirit is frequently associated with baptism—both of Christ and the individual Christian—to which martyrdom is often compared.[13] But the rejected sense still plays a role in

11. Lavarenne, Thomson, and Anne-Marie Palmer, *Prudentius on the Martyrs* (Oxford, 1989), 219, take *serit loquellam* in this way.

12. For examples of such a dative in Prudentius, see Maurice Lavarenne, *Étude sur la langue du poète Prudence* (Paris, 1933), 140–41.

13. So *Pe.* 8.11 (on the parallels between baptism and martyrdom) *spiritus aeterno solitus descendere lapsu* and *D.* 119–20 (Christ's baptism) **Spiritus aethere missus** / *testatur tinctum qui tinctis crimina donet.*

the interpretation of the passage, reinforcing the impression of the indeterminate realm in which the martyr moves as he approaches death. Finally, it is significant that the prose passion has no such ambiguity. Fructuosus himself speaks, inspired by the Holy Spirit (*monente pariter ac loquente Spiritu sancto, Fructuosus ait* . . . 4.1). The phrase *monente pariter ac loquente spiritu* would serve as an appropriate gloss to Prudentius' *serit loquellam.* Although the Holy Spirit is still said to speak, the unambiguous phrase *Fructuosus ait* makes abundantly clear that this speech is delivered from the mouth of the martyr. Prudentius, instead, deliberately injects uncertainty about the speaker, reawakening in his readers through the language of the text an awareness of the special quality of a martyr's last words as he goes to his death. Since in the case of *Pe.* 6 we do possess the prose passion used by Prudentius, this particular text is a specially convincing illustration of how the poet intentionally introduces such polysemy into his text and by so doing creates a poetics of martyrdom.

Cyprian, like the other bishops of the *Peristephanon,* is example and leader to his flock. He shows pastoral concern by his last prayer for the *populus Carthaginis,* as he prepares for his own martyrdom. But he is a slightly anomalous *dux et praevius.* Sixtus suffers martyrdom before his deacon Lawrence; Quirinus in front of his own people. Fructuosus is martyred together with his two deacons, and he shows particular eagerness to go to his death. Cyprian, on the other hand, though first to face judgment (50), dies *after* his own congregation, the *Massa Candida.* The reversal of the normal order is all the more in need of explanation, since there is no necessary connection between the two legends here united by Prudentius. When narrative elements are arranged in a sequence that deviates from the normal pattern, the question of meaning is inevitably raised. What, then, is the significance of this anomalous sequence, death of people–death of bishop? The question is all the more acute since in his reported speech to his people Cyprian claims to be "originator of glorious death" and to "lead the way to bloodshed" (46).

The answer must be that the bishop leads primarily not by example and action but by words. By interpolating the account of the *Massa Candida* within the passion of Cyprian, Prudentius emphasizes the power of the martyr's teaching. His preaching alone is sufficient to lead the way to martyrdom for his flock. Words speak louder, or at least as loud as, actions in the case of an inspired teacher like Cyprian. This analysis of the significance of the *Massa Candida* episode finds ample support in *Pe.* 13 as a whole. Words from the root *doc-* ("teach") are frequently applied to Cyprian.[14] The martyr's particular receptivity to the Holy Spirit, a receptivity attributed to other martyrs only at death, ensures special power for his teaching. He is elevated to the episcopal throne as *doctor* (*usque episcopale / provehitur solium* **doctor,** 33–34). Of the three titles attributed to Bishop Fructuosus in *Pe.* 6, *dux et praevius et magister* (6.10), the last predominates in the case of Cyprian and subsumes the others. The requirement that the bishop be a teacher goes back to deutero-Pauline precepts (1 Tim. 3:2, Titus 1:9). Ambrose speaks of the clergy's *officium docendi* (*Off.* 1.1.2), and Augustine writes a treatise on the *doctrina* appropriate to the Christian preacher. Cyprian's own exemplary learning makes him an especially appropriate episcopal model for the post-persecution age, when bishops no longer had the opportunity for dramatic acts of Christian resolution and when struggles with diabolical powers were more often conducted in private and their results were less obvious to the public eye.

This emphasis on the martyr's learning and skill as a teacher perhaps accounts for a second deviation from the authentic accounts of Cyprian's life and martyrdom contained in the Life of Pontius and the *Acta Consularia,* the attribution to the Carthaginian bishop of skill in magic arts and the seduction of women.

> Unus erat iuvenum doctissimus artibus sinistris:
> fraude pudicitiam perfringere, nil sacrum putare,
> saepe etiam magicum cantamen inire per sepulcra
> quo geniale tori ius solveret aestuante nupta.
>
> (21–24)

[He was the single most learned man of his young contemporaries in the black arts, skilled in the seduction of the chaste by deceit, regarding nothing as holy, often even performing a magical incantation in a cemetery to break the law of the marriage bed and cause a wife to seethe with passion.]

Cyprian himself in the *Ad Donatum* (3–4) gives the impression of a misspent youth; and Augustine speaks of the change in the saint's manner

14. *Pe.* 13.17, 21 (*doctissimus*), 34, 38, 74, 96, 97, 101, 105; cf. *discet* (8), *dogma* (32).

of life after dissolute early years.[15] But the details Prudentius gives, devotion to *artes sinistrae,* and in particular to their use for erotic purposes, fit better, as has often been pointed out, a second Cyprian, Cyprian of Antioch. That Cyprian, according to the legend, was a distinguished practitioner of magic arts who attempted to use his skills to seduce a Christian virgin. Foiled, he converted, and later became a bishop and martyr. Gregory of Nazianzus had already confused the two legends, leading Delehaye to posit a common source for Gregory and Prudentius that was responsible for the assimilation.[16]

By comparison with Gregory, however, Prudentius gives few circumstantial details derived from the legends surrounding Cyprian of Antioch. He is content with a general reference to the martyr's mastery of magic arts and to the erotic purposes to which those skills were put. Whatever the source of this material in Prudentius, it accords well with the larger thematic of *Pe.* 13 and provides links, too, with the surrounding poems (notably 9, 11, and 14). The stories surrounding Cyprian of Carthage's Eastern namesake conveniently fill out the vague references to youthful misdemeanors in the *Ad Donatum.* Prudentius will have chosen to include such material about the life of the saint prior to martyrdom, an unusual procedure in the *Peristephanon,* because it suited his conception of the particular qualities of Cyprian as martyr.

First, and most evidently, Cyprian's preconversion activities relate to the poem's larger theme of the use and misuse of learning. The bishop of Carthage, supreme teacher and expounder of *apostolica scripta* (16), the *volumina Pauli* (18), and the *mystica vel profunda Christi* (20),

15. Augustine, *Serm.* 311.7.7 *Mutatus est Cyprianus, cuius hodie memoriam frequentamus. Ipse scribit, ipse testatur, cuius vitae fuerit aliquando, quam nefariae, quam impiae, quam improbandae ac detestandae* (*PL* 38.1416). Malamud, *Poetics of Transformation,* 115–16, makes the attractive suggestion that Cyprian's association with the erotic depends on the etymological association of his name with *Cypris,* one of the titles of Venus. Unlike Malamud, though, I would say that Cyprian, through his Christian conversion, transcends, or at least transvalues, the erotic connotations of his name. If, as Malamud claims, Cyprian's episcopal rhetoric still has a quasi-erotic force, it is, at least in the poet's mind, redeemed by its Christian purpose. Although I could imagine a deconstructive reading that laid bare the rhetorical strategies of Prudentius' own text, I am reluctant to attribute such a critical attitude to Christian rhetoric to the poet himself.

16. Hippolyte Delehaye, "Cyprien d'Antioche et Cyprien de Carthage," *AB* 39 (1921): 331–32. Delehaye dismisses the possibility that Prudentius could have known Gregory's panegyric. The text of the latter is found in *PG* 35.1169–94. John Francis Petruccione, "Prudentius' Portrait of St. Cyprian: An Idealized Biography," *REAug* 36 (1990): 230, thinks the intermediary may have been Rufinus, directly or more likely indirectly, who translated a number of Gregory's speeches.

already showed a precocious talent when young, but one devoted to *magica cantamina* (23) and *artes sinistrae* (21). Cyprian is a case of a successful teacher whose enormous intellectual talents were ultimately turned to benefit not fornicators and adulterers, but the Christian community of which he was bishop, and ultimately the whole Christian world. In this he contrasts with the subjects of *Pe.* 9 and 11, Cassian and Hippolytus. Both are in some sense failed teachers. Cassian's learning is technical and ethically neutral. It can do nothing to benefit his pupils, unlike the preaching of Cyprian. The saint pays the price of this lack of moral content in his instruction when he falls victim to the unreformed paganism of his charges. Hippolytus, by contrast, is a schismatic, whose teaching is in conflict with the Catholic faith (*Pe.* 11.19–24).[17] Only at the moment of his death does he reject the sect of Novatus with all the authority of a martyr and urge orthodoxy: "What I taught, I now regret" (*quae docui, docuisse piget,* 11.33). Hippolytus' teaching during his life has gone for nothing; only at the moment of his death does he redeem himself by his final words and by his example.

The case of Cyprian as bishop and teacher thus gains further force by its juxtaposition with the more problematic *doctores* Cassian and Hippolytus. Why, then, the particular emphasis on the erotic in *Pe.* 13.21–24? Various answers can be given. Young men (*iuvenes,* 21) might be presumed to be especially susceptible to sexual indiscretion. Such youthful sexual misadventures play a recurrent role in Christian confessional literature, not only in the *Confessions of Cyprian of Antioch* but also in the *Confessions* of Augustine and later the *Eucharistichos* of Paulinus of Pella.[18] At the same time, the theme of male sexuality, which is touched on briefly in *Pe.* 13, plays a larger role in the following poem, dedicated to Agnes. There it is the martyr's own *pudicitia* that is subjected to temptation and "tried by many arts" (*temptata multis . . . artibus, Pe.* 14.15.) Agnes' persecutor plays the role of the preconversion Cyprian. The youth who looks at her with lustful eyes when she is exposed as a prostitute is blinded (14.46–51). In the case of *Pe.* 14 we see an assault on chastity from the perspective of the female victim. We see too that the dedicated Christian virgin (cf. *Pe.* 14.23–24 and 31–35) is capable of resisting diabolical temptation, whether it takes the form of the su-

17. This tradition is already found in Damasus, *Epigr.* 35.2.

18. Delehaye, "Cyprien," 316–21; Augustine, *Conf.* 6.15–25; Paulinus of Pella, *Eucharistichos* 169–75. Prudentius himself speaks of his *lasciva protervitas / et luxus petulans* (*Pr.* 10–11).

perior power of a pagan *iudex* or the *magica cantamina* of an adept in *artes sinistrae.* (In the legend of Cyprian of Antioch, the object of the future martyr's magic is also a Christian virgin, Justa or Justina. She successfully resists Cyprian's diabolical assaults.) *Pe.* 13 and 14 complement each other; the latter treats more fully, and from the standpoint of the female object of lust, the issues of male sexuality and of the ability of the Christian virgin to resist seduction that are implicitly posed, but not resolved, in *Pe.* 13.

Hitherto in my treatment of Cyprian as bishop and teacher I have concentrated on the narrative sections of *Pe.* 13. But the introductory and concluding sections to the poem (1–14 and 96–106, with 15–20 as transitional), though they are concerned, as those sections normally are, with the posthumous cult of the saint, put a still more intense emphasis on Cyprian as teacher than do the central portions of the poem. The two aspects of the Carthaginian bishop's fame, as martyr and exegete, are played off against each other in the nonnarrative sections of *Pe.* 13.

The poem begins:

Punica terra tulit quo splendeat omne quidquid usquam est,
inde domo Cyprianum, sed decus orbis et magistrum.
Est proprius patriae martyr, sed amore et ore noster.
Incubat in Libya sanguis, sed ubique lingua pollet,
sola superstes agit de corpore, sola obire nescit.
Dum genus esse hominum Christus sinet et vigere mundum,
dum liber ullus erit, dum scrinia sacra litterarum,
te leget omnis amans Christum, tua, Cypriane, discet.

(*Pe.* 13.1–8)

[The land of Carthage brought forth a man from whom everything everywhere was to receive illumination; Carthage was Cyprian's home, but he was the glory and teacher of the whole world. Though his native country possesses him as its martyr, in love and speech he is ours. His blood lies in Africa, but his tongue's power extends everywhere; it alone of his body survives, it alone is incapable of death. As long as Christ allows the human race to survive and the world to flourish, as long as there are still books and libraries of sacred texts, everyone who loves Christ will read you, and will learn your teachings, Cyprian.]

The prophecy of immortality for Cyprian's writings in the last three and a half lines of this passage takes a form that recalls the claims of pagan poets for the survival of their own works. Horace in the last ode of the third book sets the scarcely imaginable future as limit to his expected fame. His praise will remain fresh "as long as [*dum*] a priest climbs the Capitoline in the company of a silent maiden" (*Odes* 3.30.8–9). Prudentius similarly qualifies his claims for Cyprian's writings with a series of temporal clauses, introduced by *dum* (6–7).[19] He equates the continued influence of the martyr's works with the survival of the world of human beings and of Christian texts and readership, conditions that are intended to be coextensive.[20]

Geographically Cyprian's influence is equally wide. Ovid claimed a readership for the *Metamorphoses* that extended to the limits of the Roman empire (*Met.* 15.877–78); Cyprian is "glory and teacher of the world" (*decus orbis et magistrum,* 2). But while Prudentius describes the chronological extent of the bishop's fame in the language of literary immortality, albeit Christianized, he defines its geographical extension in terminology that owes more to the tradition of martyr literature.

Like the majority of the poems of the *Peristephanon, Pe.* 13 begins with a reference to the specific place of burial of the martyr. Each of the first four lines of the poem begins with a reference to the African fatherland of Cyprian, and contrasts it with his universal power, expressed in a separate, antithetically formulated clause. Although the bishop's blood was shed in Africa, his teaching makes him in a special sense the property of the whole Christian world; he is "in love and speech ours" (*amore et ore noster,* 3).[21] By using the first person plural

19. Such clauses are traditional, so Hans Peter Syndikus, *Die Lyrik des Horaz: Eine Interpretation der Oden,* Impulse der Forschung 7 (Darmstadt, 1973), 2: 277 on Horace 3.30.8–9 "Der abschliessende, mit 'solange' einsetzende Temporalsatz ist in Beteuerungen dichterischer Unsterblichkeit Tradition," citing Theognis 252, Anacreon fr. 1.5 Diehl, Ovid, *Am.* 1.15.9–12; cf. Virgil, *Aen.* 1.607–9.

20. The consensus of modern editors is to punctuate with a period after verse 6, thus separating the two verses containing *dum* clauses. I prefer to follow Arevalo and punctuate strongly after verse 5, thus associating 6 with what follows rather than what precedes. The anaphora would then gain in force, and the succession of temporal clauses would serve to interpret each other rather than, as is the case with the standard punctuation, being in tension.

21. Compare Gregory of Nazianzus, *Or.* 24.12: οὐ γὰρ τῆς Καρχηδονίων προκαθέζεται μόνον ἐκκλησίας οὐδε τῆς ἐξ ἐκείνου καὶ δι᾽ ἐκεῖνον περιβοήτου μέχρι νῦν ᾽Αφρικῆς, ἀλλὰ καὶ πάσης τῆς ἑσπερίου σχεδὸν δὲ καὶ τῆς ἑῴας αὐτῆς, νοτίου τε καὶ βορείου λήξεως, ἐφ᾽ ὅσα ἐκεῖνος ἦλθε τῷ θαύματι. Οὕτω Κυπριανὸς ἡμέτερος γίνεται (*PG* 35.1184B). This passage is cited by Delehaye, "Cyprien," 332 as evidence for

Prudentius is speaking for the whole Western Church, as defined at the end of the poem (102–6).

All martyrs can unite distinct communities through their veneration, and in so doing dissolve distinctions of place. That veneration is focused on a specific *locus,* however, the place where the martyr's blood was shed. Cyprian's blood still stains the earth of Africa (*incubat in Libya sanguis*); his cult is geographically localized. But he differs from other martyrs because, as teacher and writer, he is also the *immediate* property of all the world. Prudentius describes this special status in terms appropriate to the martyr cult. Alone of the parts of his body Cyprian's tongue survives and has power after death (4–5). As Malamud observes, it is a kind of relic that continues to be a source of *potentia* even after the saint's life is over;[22] but it is not a literal relic,[23] for *lingua* is also metonymy for speech, or in Cyprian's case for the written record that preserves his speech after death. Cyprian is a kind of "super-martyr" or "super-bishop" who, because of his writings, becomes after his death the common property of the worldwide Christian community, and whose pastoral care to instruct Christian souls extends beyond his immediate Carthaginian see to embrace all who read his works. Prudentius here elevates the status of Christian writing by attributing to it a power equivalent to that of martyrs after their death. If the symbol of the martyr's *potentia* is ever-flowing blood, the symbol of the Christian author's vigor is the ever-talking tongue. Cyprian's experience of the transcendence of the physical by the spiritual is the reverse of Romanus' in *Pe.* 10, and is played out on a wider stage. The latter's tongue is

---

a source common to Gregory and Prudentius. Pontius also attributes worldwide influence to Cyprian's teaching, *Vita Cypriani* 1 (*CSEL* 3.3.xc.5–7).

22. Malamud, *Poetics of Transformation,* 117–20. The comparison that I make below with Romanus' amputated tongue is also made by Malamud (118–19). I differ from Malamud, however, in making the conflation of language derived from the martyr cult with the traditional pagan claims for the survival of works of literature central to my reading of the poem. In *Pe.* 13 the classical (the language of poetic immortality), Christian tradition (the role of bishop as teacher), and contemporary cult (veneration of relics) intersect in the figure and writings of Cyprian. I would not describe Cyprian's tongue as "grotesque" (so Malamud, 118–20). Prudentius' language is inspired by a combination of the normal system of beliefs informing the cult of relics with his own characteristic metonymic fluency. There are certainly no grounds for imagining Prudentius is here hinting at criticism of Cyprian's rhetoric.

23. Literal relics do not play a particularly prominent role in the *Peristephanon,* despite the synecdochical fragmentation to which the martyr's body and the martyr text are subjected, and there is no reference to the translation of relics as a means of propagating a saint's cult.

amputated from his body, but he can still speak his defiance; Cyprian's tongue is the only part of his body to survive, still speaking to the world through his writings after his death.

The point is made with special force at the end of *Pe.* 13. Prudentius describes the burial that "sad Africa" (*maesta Africa,* 96) gives to Cyprian's body. He then turns to address *Africa* directly.

> Desine flere bonum tantum; tenet ille regna caeli
> nec minus involitat terris nec ab hoc recedit orbe.
> Disserit, eloquitur, tractat, docet, instruit, profetat.
> Nec Libyae populos tantum regit, exit usque in ortum
> solis et usque obitum. Gallos fovet, inbuit Britannos,
> praesidet Hesperiae, Christum serit ultimis Hiberis.
> Denique doctor humi est, idem quoque martyr in supernis;
> instruit hic homines, illinc pia dona dat patronus.
>
> (99–106)

> [Weep no more for so great a blessing; he inhabits the realm of heaven, yet nonetheless skims over the earth and has not left this world. He discourses, addresses, discusses, teaches, instructs, prophesies. He not only directs the people of Africa, but has gone out to the rising and setting of the sun. He cherishes the Gauls, instructs the Britons, watches over Italy, and propagates the worship of Christ in distant Spain. In sum he is teacher on earth, and also martyr on high. Here he instructs men, from there as patron he distributes holy gifts.]

In his ability to bridge the gap between heaven and earth, life and death, Cyprian is like any other martyr. But once more he differs from the other martyrs of the *Peristephanon* in that his posthumous influence is generalized over the whole world, rather than focused on a privileged *locus.* The striking asyndetic series in line 101 makes the point with great emphasis that the universality of Cyprian's power and its survival after death depend on his writings and teachings. As a martyr Cyprian performs the typical role assigned to such figures in the *Peristephanon* as patron, intermediary between heaven and earth and distributor of gifts. There is nothing unusual in the language with which these activities are described in the second half of lines 105–6. But the clauses antithetical to these, in the first half of each line, express the distinctive qualities of Cyprian, his role as teacher and his continuing ability to perform that role on earth in the here and now through his writings. Pagan writers traditionally claimed immortality for their works by asserting their ability to transcend limits of time and place. Prudentius makes the same claim for Cyprian's writings, but by assimilating and comparing the traditional language of poetic immortality with the idiom of the cult of the martyrs he Christianizes the pagan topos. In so doing, he elevates the dignity of Christian literature by investing it with the *potentia* of the martyrs, a *potentia* that is immediately available to the entire Christian community through Cyprian's writings.

This entire Christian community is specified in the geographic catalog of 102–4. Although Prudentius claims Cyprian's influence extends from East to West (*exit usque in ortum / solis et usque obitum,* 102–3),[24] the countries specified are all western. In part, this no doubt reflects a realistic recognition that a Latin author is unlikely to be read in the Greek-speaking East. But it also is true to Prudentius' own bias. His account in *Pe.* 4 of the Christian world united by the cult of the martyrs is also confined to the West, as are the poems themselves. (*Pe.* 10, on Romanus, who was martyred at Antioch, might seem an exception, but his place of martyrdom is never referred to and the poem is wholly western in conception, as the similarities with the *Contra Symmachum* and the martyr's own name suggest.)[25] The verbs used in this catalog—*regit, fovet, inbuit, praesidet, Christum serit*—remind the reader not only of the similarities between teacher and martyr, but also of the connections between teacher and bishop, for teaching, of course, is a prime episcopal function. The verb *fovet,* as we have seen in chapter 1, is regularly used of the relationship between a community and its martyr. In the *Peristephanon* it is specific to the cult of the martyrs. On the other hand, *regit* is not used elsewhere of this relationship, and it is a more natural word to choose of the supervisory duties of a bishop. It seems to imply a continued episcopal supervision of Africa by Cyprian through his writings even after his death. The two ideas are combined in the verb

24. The phrase *in ortum / solis et usque obitum* is a variation of the biblical *a solis ortu usque ad occasum* (Ps. 49:1, 112:3, Mal. 1:11). The verb *exeo* is frequently used of the distribution of literature/teaching in classical and Christian Latin (*ThLL* 5.1366.15–30); see especially Tert., *Adv. Iud.* 5.4 *in omnem terram exire habebat praedicatio apostolorum* (*CCL* 2;1351.36–37). It is typical of Prudentius' method that he substitutes a personal for the impersonal subject of the prose text, thus implying the literal, if dispersed, survival of the saint.

25. There are, of course, other reasons, including the manuscript tradition, for believing that *Pe.* 10 was not part of the original collection.

praesidet. Martyrs in the *Peristephanon* regularly provide protection (*praesidium*) for their communities, but the bishop "presides over" (*praesidet*) his congregation on his elevated throne in the apse of a basilica.[26] After his death, Cyprian through his writings becomes bishop and teacher of the whole western Christian world; by the manner of his death he qualifies as a martyr, but through the universal readership of his works he subverts the normal association of a martyr's cult with a particular place and makes his patronage and pastoral care directly available to all.

Two further points can be made about the biblical precedents for Cyprian as martyr/bishop. Bishop Fructuosus, it will be remembered, is likened to Moses. Petruccione is certainly right in arguing that Prudentius sees Cyprian as a second Paul.[27] To take just a few of the points he makes: Paul is described, conventionally enough, in *Pe.* 12.(24) as *gentium magistrum*; Cyprian (*Pe.* 13.2) as *orbis magistrum*. The African bishop's exegetical endeavors are said to concentrate particularly on the writings of Paul (*locuples* facundia *quae doceret orbem / quaeque* voluminibus Pauli famulata *disputaret, Pe.* 13.17–18). Like Paul, Cyprian undergoes a conversion after being a notorious opponent of Christianity—the comparison is already made by Gregory of Nazianzus.[28] The Carthaginian's writings on doctrinal matters are known in a large number of western churches; the apostle similarly directs his letters to a variety of churches and individuals. In a sermon of Maximus of Turin for the feast day of Peter and Paul the two chief apostles are said to complement each other; Paul uses the "key of knowledge" (*clavis scientiae*) "to open hard hearts to faith and lay bare the secret places of the mind"; Peter has the key to the kingdom of heaven, by which he can bestow immortality on those converted by his fellow apostles' teaching.[29] The

26. So Cyprian himself, *Cath. Eccl. unit.* 5, speaks of *episcopi qui in ecclesia praesidemus* (*CSEL* 3.1.213.15).

27. Petruccione, "Prudentius' Portrait."

28. *Orat.* 24.8 (*PG* 1177A–C). See Petruccione, "Prudentius' Portrait," 232–37, who draws other parallels between the biographies of Paul and Cyprian. The comparison is also made by Marianne Kah, *"Die Welt der Römer mit der Seele suchend . . .": Die Religiosität des Prudentius im Spannungsfeld zwischen 'pietas christiana' und 'pietas romana',* Hereditas 3 (Bonn, 1990), 66, n.302, who goes on (77–80) to compare Cyprian with Symmachus. Kah describes Cyprian as Prudentius' ideal of the Christian orator, one in whom the opposition between pagan form and Christian content has no place.

29. *Petro sicut bono dispensatori clavem regni caelestis [Dominus] dedit, Paulo tamquam idoneo doctori magisterium ecclesiasticae institutionis iniunxit. . . . Clavem ergo quodammodo a Christo scientiae et Paulus accepit; clavis enim dicenda est qua ad fidem*

bishop has both the duty of securing the salvation of souls by administering the sacraments and of preparing souls to receive this by instruction. In a sense he combines in one office the qualities preeminently associated by Maximus of Turin with the two apostolic martyrs of Rome. In Cyprian, however, the Pauline qualities predominate. The African bishop is, in Prudentius' account, a second Paul.

A second event in the history of the Christian mission is also relevant to Prudentius' Cyprian, the descent of the Holy Spirit to the disciples at Pentecost (Acts 2:1–13). Like the disciples, the Carthaginian bishop is inspired with eloquence by the Holy Spirit sent from heaven (*Pe.* 13.9–10).[30] In Acts an audience of different nationalities is able to understand preaching in tongues; in Cyprian's case the inspiration of the spirit gives him the power to instruct a variety of diverse nations, though in a single language. Prudentius goes on to compare the effect of such inspiration to that of an intoxicating drink.

> Ut liquor ambrosius cor mitigat, inbuit palatum,
> sedem animae penetrat, mentem fovet et pererrat artus,
> sic deus interius sentitur et inditur medullis.
>
> (12–14)

> [Just as a sweet draft[31] soothes the heart, steeps the palate, finds its way into the seat of the soul, warms the mind and courses through the limbs, so God is felt within and is introduced into our innermost being.]

The notion that the Holy Spirit intoxicates is not unique to Prudentius.[32]

---

pectorum dura reserantur mentium secreta panduntur.... Ambo igitur claves a domino perceperunt, scientiae iste ille potentiae; divitias inmortalitatis ille dispensat, scientiae thesauros iste largitur (*Serm.* 1.1; *CCL* 23.2.6–20). See also Charles Pietri, *Roma Christiana: Recherches sur l'Église de Rome, son organisation, sa politique, son idéologie, de Miltiade à Sixte III (331–440),* Bibliothèque des écoles françaises d'Athènes et de Rome 224 (Rome, 1976), 2: 1585–86.

30. Cf. Paulinus, *C.* 27.62–63, [*dies*] *qua sanctus quondam caelo demissus ab alto / spiritus ignito divisit lumine linguas.*

31. The phrase *liquor ambrosius* is used by Statius, *Theb.* 9.731 and in Prudentius, *C.* 3.23. Here Prudentius seems to have in mind an analogy with the intoxicating effect of a drink such as wine. Compare Augustine, *Conf.* 5.13.23, *veni Mediolanium ad Ambrosium episcopum ... cuius tunc eloquia strenue ministrabant ... sobriam vini ebrietatem populo tuo* (*CCL* 27; 70.6–9). There is, I think, a pun here on Ambrose's name, that depends on the association of the adjective *ambrosius* with intoxicating liquors.

32. E.g., Ambrose, *Hymn* 2.23-24 (Bulst) *laeti bibamus sobriam / ebrietatem spiritus,*

Ultimately it derives from the account of Pentecost in Acts, where skeptical members of the audience mock the Apostles and accuse them of being drunk (Acts 2:13). The comparison introduced by Prudentius reinforces the association with the biblical passage. Paulinus of Nola, in his poetic treatment of the biblical event, rings the changes on the theme of spiritual *ebrietas* (*C.* 27.103–6), suggesting that the association of such intoxication with Pentecost was well established.

The "new savor" (*novum saporem,* 11) described by Prudentius in lines 12–14 is normally taken of the effect Cyprian's teaching has on his readers/audience. So Thomson translates verse 14, "it makes *us* feel God within us entering into our marrows." The fact is, however, that there is no word corresponding to "us" in the Latin; the recipient of divine inspiration is left quite ambiguous. Up to this point I have preferred to take lines 12–14 as equivalent to 9–10, describing the effect on Cyprian. The "form of speech whiter than snow" (*nive candidius linguae genus*) apostrophized in line 11 would then be equivalent to the *fontibus eloquii* of the preceding verse. In practice, there is no reason why the two interpretations cannot coexist. So inspired are Cyprian's teachings that they are capable of communicating to his hearers/readers that feeling of possession by the divine that he himself experiences. Viewed in this light, the choice of the verb *inbuit* in verse 103 to describe the effect of the martyr's teaching on the Britons[33] takes on further significance. In my translation I treated the word as a functional synonym of *docet/ instruit.* But its proper meaning is to "drench" or "steep," used of a liquid. It is taken in this sense in the comparison of verse 12. The verb, then, is not idly chosen by Prudentius but is intended to recall the earlier description of the effect of the spirit. In this later passage the poet is unambiguously referring to the reception of Cyprian's writings by his readers, one of two possible interpretations of the earlier text. This association of the saint and his teachings with the Holy Spirit accounts also for the rather unlikely choice of the word *involitat* in line 100 to describe Cyprian's posthumous presence on earth. Flight is attributed to the Spirit in *A.* 667–68, where Prudentius paraphrases the reference

and *ThLL* 5.9.82–10.33. Malamud, *Poetics of Transformation,* 116–17 also observes the language of intoxication in this passage, but chooses rather to emphasize the passage's erotic content (see also 136–37); see this chapter, n.15.

33. I doubt, incidentally, that the verbs in lines 103–4 are chosen with particular reference to the nations in question. They complement each other to piece together a description of Cyprian's influence wherever he is read. That is, the verbs are interchangeable, at least as far as meaning is concerned.

in the Creation story to the Spirit of God passing over the waters (Gen. 1:2) as *spiritus . . . / . . .* **volitabat** *in undis*. Cyprian, by comparison, flies over the land (*involitat terris,* 100). He is here associated with the first involvement of the Holy Spirit in bringing order to the cosmos, just as in lines 8–14 he is associated with the events of Pentecost as a prefiguration of the spreading of the Christian message. At the same time, the image of flight recalls the pagan language of poetic inspiration.[34] Not for the first time in the poem has Prudentius created a distinctively Christian idiom for literary reflection that nevertheless betrays a continuity with the pre-Christian poetic tradition. In so doing, he draws attention to the degree to which such ideas have been transvalued in the new scheme of things.

Cyprian is a bishop and a martyr. But by his preeminence in the episcopal role of teacher he transcends the ordinary status of a bishop and aspires to the apostolic. By comparison, the teaching of the other bishops in the *Peristephanon* is oral and incorporated into the narrative of their passions, especially as they approach death. In particular, the last words of such martyrs, as they speak of punishment and salvation to a Christian audience, take on an exemplary function as models of a bishop's responsibility in post-persecution times to concern himself with the spiritual welfare of his flock. In this respect the poems in question reflect the public face of martyrdom and the hierarchical organization of the Church under episcopal supremacy. The blessings of episcopal martyrs, though, are available to all directly and without intermediary through prayer at their shrines. Prudentius himself is a devotee, and the next chapter will consider the nature of the poet's own response to the written and visual traces of the passion and to the spatio-temporal environment of the cult of the martyrs.

34. E.g., Horace, *Odes* 2.20.1–3, on which see R.G.M. Nisbet and Margaret Hubbard, *A Commentary on Horace: Odes, Book II* (Oxford, 1978), 332–33.

CHAPTER 5

Poet and Pilgrim

As observed in chapter 1, the majority of the poems in the *Peristephanon* have a tripartite structure. The bulk of each poem is taken up with the martyr narrative proper, but an introduction and conclusion locate a saint's shrine in the spiritual geography of late antiquity and give details of his or her cult. It is in these nonnarrative passages that the poet refers to himself in the first person.[1] Most often the reference is in the first person plural, associating the poet (confessionally) with his fellow Christians or (geographically) with Spain or a city or region within Spain.[2] In *Pe.* 1, 3, and 4 the poet is associated with a choir hymning the praises of the martyr, but the assimilation is incomplete as first person plural alternates with second-person apostrophe in which the poet instructs the chorus of worshippers.[3] In *Pe.* 2 Prudentius first speaks in the plural as a member of the Spanish Christian community, separated from Rome and the shrine of Lawrence. But the poem ends with a confession of the individual, the "sinner Prudentius" (*reum Prudentium* 2.582), and his prayer

1. The only exception in the conventionally structured poems (i.e., excluding *Pe.* 4 and 11) is *Pe.* 13.32, though this reference comes in a summarizing passage that is subordinate to the narrative proper.

2. Confessional: 1.16; 4.85, 190; 13.3, 32. Geographical: 1.115–16; 2.537, 547–50; 4.1, 3, 63, 97, 114, 141–42; 6.143, 146. The distinction between the two senses is often difficult to make, especially in the references to the cult of Vincent that conclude *Pe.* 5 (547–64).

3. 1.118–20, 3.206–10, 4.189–200, 6.145–53. Such choral passages frequently blend with or shade into metapoetic reflection (Isidoro Rodriguez-Herrera, *Poeta Christianus: Prudentius' Auffassung vom Wesen und von der Aufgabe des christlichen Dichters* [Speyer, 1936], 70–73). *Pe.* 10 is unusual in the collection since it does not relate the role of the poet to a larger context of Christian worship. For the literary affinities of these techniques, see Anne-Marie Palmer, *Prudentius on the Martyrs* (Oxford, 1989), 77–83.

for absolution.[4] Already in these more conventionally structured poems a number of tensions are at work: for instance, between poet and devotee, between individual and community, and between Spain and the wider Christian community. Prudentius, or at least the first person of the text, represents himself at various times as mouthpiece of all these points of view. In the pilgrimage poems, 9, 11, and 12, however, and particularly in the first two, narrator and devotee are most completely fused. For that reason they will be treated together in this chapter.

Pe. 9: The Poet as Petitioner

Poems 9, 11, and 12 form a triad of *itinerarium* or pilgrimage poems. They constitute a closely structured sequence in which *Pe.* 10 is clearly intrusive. The connections between them are very close—so close that it is difficult to avoid the impression that the poet himself intended these poems to be read as a self-contained group within the *Peristephanon.* All end with references to promoting the cult of the martyr in question in the author's homeland.[5] Although there is no unambiguous evidence in *Pe.* 12 that the person who speaks the first two lines and is addressed in the rest of the poem is to be identified with the author, it is a natural assumption, given the similar conclusions to all three poems and the fact that in *Pe.* 9 and 11 we have followed the poet to Rome, where *Pe.* 12, like 11, is set. Because it is dedicated to Cassian of Imola (ancient *Forum Cornelii*), *Pe.* 9 is an appropriate introduction to the triptych. Like *Pe.* 11 it contains martyr narrative, description of a work of art, and lyric of personal devotion (in the opening and concluding passages). *Pe.* 11 is the pivotal centerpiece of the triptych, combining these themes with descriptions of architecture and of communal observation at the annual festival of the saint that anticipate the subjects of *Pe.* 12. The whole group is united by the language of the journey, both inter- and intra-urban, and, in the case of Hippolytus' crypt, subterranean.

It is appropriate, then, that *Pe.* 9 begins with a topos from the verse

4. On the conclusion to *Pe.* 2, see Rodriguez-Herrera, *Poeta Christianus,* 71–72, Klaus Thraede, *Studien zu Sprache und Stil des Prudentius,* Hypomnemata 13 (Göttingen, 1965), 61–65, Reinhart Herzog, *Die allegorische Dichtkunst des Prudentius,* Zetemata 42 (Munich, 1966), 38–39. There is a similar movement, though without the local reference to Spain, at the end of *Pe.* 14 (124–33).

5. *Pe.* 9.106, 11.233–38, 12.65–66. Palmer, *Prudentius on the Martyrs,* 110–11 groups these three poems together as pilgrimage poems but does not explore the parallels among them further.

itinerarium: the circumstances of a city's founding and the etymology of its name.[6]

Sylla Forum statuit Cornelius; hoc Itali urbem
  vocitant ab ipso conditoris nomine.

(1–2)

[Cornelius Sulla established the town of Forum Cornelii; hence the name the Italians give it, after its founder.]

From the first couplet readers know that the Cassian poem is set in the context of a journey. By line 3 they know the traveller is the poet, and the end of the journey is Rome—hence the *iter* is not complete until *Pe.* 11. Verse 4 switches from the circumstances of the journey to the mental and emotional state of the author. The itinerary has a spiritual dimension. It is this that justifies the description of *Pe.* 9 and its companions as pilgrimage poems, although Prudentius' primary motives for travelling to Rome may have been secular.[7]

Hic mihi, cum peterem te, rerum maxima Roma,
  spes est oborta prosperum Christum fore.
Stratus humi tumulo advolvebar quem sacer ornat
  martyr dicato Cassianus corpore.
Dum lacrimans mecum reputo mea vulnera et omnes
  vitae labores ac dolorum acumina,
erexi ad caelum faciem, stetit obvia contra
  fucis colorum picta imago martyris,
plagas mille gerens, totos lacerata per artus,
  ruptam minutis praeferens punctis cutem.
Innumeri circum pueri (miserabile visu)
  confossa parvis membra figebant stilis,
unde pugillares soliti percurrere ceras
  scholare murmur adnotantes scripserant.

(3–16)

6. Compare, for instance, Rutilius Namatianus, *De reditu suo* 1.231–36, 249, 255–62, 571–74.

7. Italo Lana, *Due capitoli Prudenziani: La biografia, la cronologia delle opere, la poetica,* Verba Seniorum, Collana di testi e studi patristici, n.s. 2 (Rome, 1962), 26–29.

[It was here, when I was on my way to you, Rome, supreme city of the world, that I conceived the hope that Christ would be favorable. Prostrate on the ground I lay before the tomb that the holy martyr Cassian graces with his consecrated body. As I tearfully recalled my wounds and all the trials of my life and pin-pricks of sufferings, I raised my face to heaven, and opposite me stood the portrait of the martyr, depicted in brilliant colors, bearing a thousand wounds, his whole body torn, and displaying flesh ripped with tiny puncture marks. Around him, a pitiful sight, countless boys pierced his limbs with strokes from their small styli, with which they were accustomed to engrave their wax tablets and take down in dictation the schoolmaster's lesson.]

The passage falls into two halves: veneration at a martyr's shrine (3–8) and description of a work of art (11–16), with a fourth transitional couplet (9–10), moving from the poet's state of mind to the appearance of the painting before him. There is nothing particularly unusual in the manner of the poet's veneration at the martyr's shrine; as we have seen,[8] tears and prostration before the saint's tomb are standard elements in the syntax of petition and prayer. Paulinus of Nola similarly describes a countryman whose main means of livelihood, a pair of oxen, has been taken from him in the night, prostrating himself before the shrine of Felix and drenching the ground with his tears, as he seeks the saint's intercession.[9] The pattern is particularly clear in a generalized description of devotion at Lawrence's shrine in Rome, contained in *Pe.* 2. Prudentius there is praising the good fortune of the inhabitants of Rome:

cui propter advolvi licet,
qui fletibus spargit locum,
qui pectus in terram premit,
qui vota fundit murmure!

(*Pe.* 2.533–36)

[Who may throw himself before your tomb, who drenches the spot

8. See chapter 1, n.6 and context; for tears *Pe.* 1.14, 2.534, 4.193, 11.194.

9. *ingressusque sacram magnis cum fletibus aulam / sternitur ante fores et postibus oscula figit / et lacrimis rigat omne solum, pro limine sancto / fusus humi.* (*C.* 18.248–51.) The words *fores, postibus,* and *limine* seem to suggest an enclosed area or *aedicula* containing the saint's tomb, within the larger *aula.*

with tears, who presses his breast to the earth, who pours forth in soft tones his prayers.]

The polyptoton/anaphora, end-stopped lines, and high degree of syntactical parallelism reinforce the sense that the passage is exemplary of devotion to the martyrs. Returning to Prudentius in *Pe.* 9, we see the poet adopting the same physical posture as the suppliant of *Pe.* 2.533–35 (note the verbal parallelism *advolvebar* 9.5 / *advolvi* 2.533). But there is no equivalent in the introduction to the Cassian poem of the last line of the Lawrence passage, the address of the petitioner to the saint. Only at the end of the poem is the poet induced to address himself to the martyr, at the urging of the sacristan, who had told him the story of Cassian's passion: "if you have any righteous and acceptable prayer, any hope or inner distress, express it. The martyr, believe me, hears all prayers in his great goodness, and grants those that he finds worthy" (95–98).[10] At this point the interrupted syntax of a petition is resumed.

Pareo; conplector tumulum, lacrimas quoque fundo;
  altar tepescit ore, saxum pectore.
Tunc arcana mei percenseo cuncta laboris,
  tunc quod petebam, quod timebam murmuro,
et post terga domum dubia sub sorte relictam
  et spem futuri forte nutantem boni.
Audior, urbem adeo, dextris successibus utor,
  domum revertor, Cassianum praedico.

(99–106)

[I obey; I embrace the tomb, and shed tears; the altar is warmed by my lips, the stone floor by my chest. Then I run over all my hidden sufferings, and in a low tone utter my wishes and fears, my home left behind in perilous circumstances and my wavering expectation of future prosperity. I am heard, I travel to Rome, achieve success in my undertakings, return home and declare the name of Cassian.]

When the passage begins the poet is in the same position as he was in the first section of the poem: prostrate and weeping before the saint's

10. *Suggere si quod habes iustum vel amabile votum, / spes si qua tibi est, si quid intus aestuas. / Audit, crede, preces martyr prosperrimus omnes / ratasque reddit quas videt probabiles.*

shrine. Only the phrase *tepescit ore* suggests a further detail, that the petitioner is kissing the altar/tomb, a frequent feature of such *vota.*[11] Now the poet goes on not just mentally to review his sufferings and aspirations (*percenseo,* 101; cf. *reputo,* 7), but also to give expression in a soft tone (*murmuro,* 102; *murmure, Pe.* 2.536) to his hopes and fears. The petitioner must put his prayer into words; he must be "heard" (*audior,* 105; cf. *audit,* 97). Such verbal expression is the only stage in the petition that is absent from the introductory passage but not the concluding passage. From the perspective of the dramatic situation in Imola, conviction that the martyr has heard his devotee's prayer inspires confidence that the journey to Rome will be successful (3–4). From the perspective of the time of writing, when the poet is back in Spain, that confidence has been vindicated by the outcome of his journey. His vow to "declare the name of Cassian" (*Cassianum praedico,* 106) is an expression of gratitude; the poem itself is the fulfillment of that vow.

What, then, inspires Prudentius to utter his request to Cassian? The immediate cause, of course, is the urging of the sacristan. But Prudentius is receptive to that urging because of the immediacy of his response to the saint's martyrdom and particularly to his *poena* so vividly depicted in the shrine. Prudentius, it will be remembered, was thinking over the trials and sufferings of his life, when he raised his countenance to heaven and the picture of the martyr met his gaze (9–10): *stetit obvia . . . imago martyris.* The text continues with a mild hypallage; literally it is the picture, not the martyr, that is described as "bearing a thousand wounds" and "with all its limbs torn" (*plagas mille gerens, totos lacerata per artus,* 11). The transference is easily intelligible, but not accidental, for the devotee, in his emotionally excited state, cannot easily distinguish between martyr and image of martyr. Time of martyrdom and time of petition are merged, just as heaven and earth come together as the petitioner turns his countenance to heaven and sees the saint.

The worshipper's state of mind as he lies before the tomb prepares him to identify with the circumstances of the martyrdom. In *Pe.* 9 the suppliant is thinking of the trials and tribulations of his life, *vitae labores ac dolorum acumina,* to adopt Prudentius' terminology. Augustine's exegesis of martyr texts continually emphasizes that the martyrs present a model for the ordinary Christian to imitate in the everyday "passion"

11. Chapter 1, n.6, and this chapter, n.9. The paronomasia of *ore* and *pectore* to express devotion to a martyr or God is also found in *Pe.* 3.75 and 5.562. The combination is especially well chosen to communicate the coincidence of physical and spiritual posture.

of life in the world.[12] The trials and tribulations of terrestrial existence are the contemporary equivalents of the physical agonies that the martyrs endured. To that degree any representation of martyrdom, verbal or visual, can arouse a response in suffering humanity. In the present case, the correspondences are more specific. The poet thinks over not just "all the trials of his life" (*omnes / vitae labores,* 7–8), but also his "wounds" (*mea vulnera*); he writes not just of "sufferings" (*dolores*) but of "pin-pricks of sufferings" (*dolorum acumina*). His choice of language is significant: the mental wounds (*vulnera*) the poet feels find an equivalent in the "thousand wounds" (*plagas mille*) he sees on the saint's body; the "pin-pricks of sufferings" correspond to the puncture marks on the saint's flesh (*ruptam . . . punctis cutem*). The equivalence is established by synonymy rather than verbal repetition (*vulnera*: *plagas, acumina*: *punctis*; also *omnes*: *mille*), but is no less persuasive for that. Later in the poem the styli that inflict the wounds on Cassian are described as *acuti* (44), and finally *acumina* (51);[13] at this point, the language used for bodily and spiritual suffering coincides exactly. There is no ground, moreover, for distinguishing between metaphorical and literal usages, for the martyr text characteristically subverts such distinctions in its denial that body and spirit are separate realms. In this particular case, to which he chooses to give the authority of the first person, Prudentius emphasizes that the emotional force of veneration at a martyr's shrine depends on sympathetic identification between devotee and saint, an identification that is called forth by the vivid representation of the martyr's suffering depicted close by his tomb. Once the sacristan assures Prudentius that "in his great goodness" (*prosperrimus,* 97) Cassian hears and grants prayers, the poet leaves Imola confident (*spes est oborta,* 4) that the martyr can act as intermediary between devotee and heaven and that "Christ will be favorable" (*prosperum*).

Once again we return to the martyr narrative. As first constituted in *Pe.* 9, it takes the form of a "painted image of the martyr" that the poet sees as he raises his gaze to heaven. The image has all the garish qualities of the martyr text that so offend classical taste: bright colors (*fucis colorum picta,* 10; cf. 93) and special attention to the gruesome

12. Serm. 298.11 (*PL* 38.1364–65) is typical: *ergo, carissimi, festum sanctorum diem, qui adversus peccatum usque ad sanguinem certaverunt et Domino suo donante atque iuvante vicerunt, sic celebremus ut amemus, sic amemus ut imitemur, ut imitati ad eorum praemia pervenire mereamur.*

13. See also *Pe.* 9.62, *dolorum spiculis.*

details of the punishment. Synonymic repetition insists on the assault on the martyr's body; "all his frame is torn" (*totos lacerata per artus*), "his flesh ripped" (*ruptam . . . cutem*), "his limbs pierced and punctured" (*confossa . . . membra figebant*). Contributing to the effect on the observer is the play between quantity and magnitude; the body bears "a *thousand* wounds" over "*all* its limbs" inflicted by "*countless* boys" yet the weapons and puncture marks they leave are tiny (*minutis,* 12; *parvis,* 14). This conceptual tension intensifies the pathos; the reader/observer is all the more impressed by the large number of wounds/attackers that would be needed to cause such extensive physical injury with such small weapons. Criticism of such accentuation of the gruesome misses the point; the suppliant's response depends precisely on these qualities. They are emphasized because they are essential to the dynamics of the martyr-petitioner relationship. Once again, as we saw in chapter 2, though death on the orders of the persecutor is indispensable for the status of martyr, the *poena,* i.e., the physical details of suffering and spiritual transcendence, contributes most to belief in the efficacy of the cult.

The real historical existence of such a picture of the martyrdom of Cassian has been doubted. Similar skepticism has been expressed about the picture of Hippolytus' passion referred to in *Pe.* 11 (123–34). However, Testini[14] has been able to cite at least three parallel representations of martyrdom from the late fourth century, and Augustine refers to a representation of the stoning of Stephen, from a slightly later date, in the *memoria* of that proto-martyr near Hippo.[15] Under the circumstances the paintings of Cassian and Hippolytus may well have existed in reality. For our purposes it is more important that the poet shows himself fully aware of the powerful effect such iconography can have on the spiritually susceptible observer. Prudentius' contemporary, Paulinus, employs Christian painting for a rather different purpose at his basilica at Nola: to induce appropriately devout sentiments in the riotous celebrants of Felix' anniversary.[16]

Iconographic representation bridges the divide between time of martyrdom and time of devotional act. Observers before a picture of the

14. Pasquale Testini, "Di alcune testimonianze relative a Ippolito," in *Ricerche su Ippolito,* Studia Ephemeridis "Augustinianum" 13 (Rome, 1977), 56–58, with references to skeptical opinion.

15. Augustine, *Serm.* 316.5.5 (*PL* 38.1434).

16. Paulinus, *C.* 27.511–95. See especially 588–91: *atque ita se melior stupefactis inserat usus, / dum fallit pictura famem; sanctasque legenti / historias castorum operum subrepit honestas / exemplis inducta piis.* The paintings are biblical in subject matter.

suffering saint feel themselves observers of the event itself. The account of the martyrdom that the sacristan of Imola then gives, called forth as it is by the image, repeats this "representation" of the passion. Despite its fuller historical detail and greater chronological extent, the narration of the martyrdom and the picture of the same event are essentially equivalent. The latter, for the informed viewer, contains the whole narrative and evokes the same response in its observer. Only *Pe.* 9 of the conventionally structured poems in the *Peristephanon* sets the martyr narrative in the time of the devotional act not at the historical time of the passion. The device used is the reported narrative in direct speech; the account of the passion is put in the mouth of the sacristan. In so doing, Prudentius associates himself at Imola with the reader reading the poem and gives a model of the response his poetry is intended to evoke. By assimilating text with image, he further insists on the immediacy of reaction called forth by a martyr narrative. In ancient literary theory visual metaphors were employed for describing the illusion of presence. Successful description depended on making the impression that "an event was taking place or a subject appearing *before the very eyes* [*ante oculos*] of the reader."[17] The appeal of the martyr text to this "inner eye" parallels the effect of the image on the outer. To this extent such a text is quintessentially descriptive, for, like the classical description, it aims to make the events described present before the eyes of the reader. Augustine insists on this quality of the martyr narrative in the sermons he delivered shortly after the public reading of passages from *Passiones*: "The passion of the blessed Cyprian was just read," he says, "we heard with our ears, we watched with our mind, we saw his struggle, we felt fear for him in danger, we hoped for the assistance of God."[18] Augustine emphasizes his audience's emotional identification with the saint, the quality we have already noticed in Prudentius' response to the portrait of Cassian's martyrdom.[19] But the point I wish to emphasize now is the assimilation of sight and hearing. In describing the response

17. Rhet. ad Her. 4.55.68: *demonstratio est cum ita verbis res exprimitur ut geri negotium et res ante oculos esse videatur*; cf. Quintilian, 4.2.123, 6.2.32, 8.3.65, and 9.2.40, and the other passages collected by Heinrich Lausberg, *Handbuch der literarischen Rhetorik: eine Grundlegung der Literaturwissenschaft* (Munich, 1960), 1.400–401.

18. *Serm. Denis* 14.3: *Modo legebatur passio beati Cypriani: aure audiebamus, mente spectabamus, certantem videbamus, periclitanti quodammodo timebamus, sed dei adiutorium sperabamus* (*MA* 1.67.24–26).

19. For this quality, see also Augustine, *Serm. Denis* 14.3: *specto, delector, quantum valeo lacertis mentis amplector: video certatorem, gaudeo victorem* (*MA* 1.68.5–7).

of the inner eye to a passion, Augustine frequently echoes the technical language of rhetoric for the effect of visual immediacy that was the aim of literary description, the technical terms for which were *enargeia, evidentia, sub oculos subiectio* or *repraesentatio.*[20] Speaking of the passion of St. Vincent the preacher refers to a kind of "wonderful spectacle set up before our eyes" (*ante oculos nostros*);[21] in the same text are "plainly presented [*evidenter ostenditur*] a fierce judge, bloody torturer, and unconquered martyr."[22]

For informed viewers of the portrait of Cassian's martyrdom, the whole sequence of the martyr narrative would be present in shorthand in the image before them. Prudentius is a somewhat anomalous observer. Unlike the usual devotee, who would presumably be familiar with a favorite saint's passion, Prudentius is a nonnative who must seek explanation (*consultus,* 17) from a local informant. His exegete begins with a brief account of the relation between image and passion: "what you see," he says, "is no idle, old wives' tale. The picture tells a story; its burden is the true faith of former times" (17–20).[23] He mentions also a written version of the passion (*tradita libris,* 19), but whether painting or text has primacy is by no means clear. The story (*historia*) is recorded in both image and words; either could have come first. The Latin would bear the sense that the *libri* referred to followed, and were based on, the painting. This is certainly the sequence of the poet's own experience: image, followed by verbal narrative. As exegete, the sacristan derives his authority from his special relation to the shrine and its traditions, not primarily from an appeal to an authoritative literary text.

The actual account of the martyrdom depends for the most part on factual information that can either be inferred from the picture or is standard in martyr narratives. To the latter category belong the generalized description of persecution (29–30), the refusal to sacrifice (31–

20. For *repraesentatio,* see Augustine, *Serm.* 280.1: *Hodiernus dies anniversia replicatione nobis in memoriam revocat, et quodammodo* **repraesentat** *diem, quo sanctae famulae Dei Perpetua et Felicitas coronis martyrii decoratae, perpetua felicitate floruerunt* (*PL* 38.1281).

21. Augustine, *Serm. Caillou et St.-Yves* 1.1: *quodammodo ante oculos nostros mirandum spectaculum constitutum est* (*MA* 1.243.5–6); cf. *Serm. Denis* 16.4: *constituite iam vobis ante oculos agonem martyrum* (*MA* 1.77.21).

22. Augustine, *Serm.* 276.1: *In passione . . . evidenter ostenditur iudex ferox, tortor cruentus, martyr invictus* (*PL* 38.1255).

23. *Quod prospicis, hospes, / non est inanis aut anilis fabula. / Historiam pictura refert, quae tradita libris / veram vetusti temporis monstrat fidem.* There is an evident opposition here between *fabula* and *historia* in reliability and seriousness of purpose.

32), the immobilizing of the saint for the *poena* (43), and the liberation at death (85–92), the last amplified to meet the special circumstances of Cassian's passion. Closest to the content of the picture is the description of the pupils' assault on their teacher in verses 47–56.

Coniciunt alii fragiles inque ora tabellas
  frangunt; relisa fronte lignum dissilit,
buxa crepant cerata genis inpacta cruentis
  rubetque ab ictu curta et umens pagina.
Inde alii stimulos et acumina ferrea vibrant,
  qua parte aratis cera sulcis scribitur,
et qua secti apices abolentur et aequoris hirti
  rursus nitescens innovatur area.
Hinc foditur Christi confessor et inde secatur;
  pars viscus intrat molle, pars scindit cutem.

(47–56)

[Some hurl and break on his face their frail tablets; the wood splits as it crashes against his brow, the waxed boxwood rings out as it strikes against his bloody cheeks, and the surface is wet and maimed, and red from the blow. From another side others brandish as goads iron styli, both the end with which the wax is inscribed with the impression of furrows and that with which strokes already cut are erased and the gleaming level surface is again restored in place of the rough expanse. From this side and that the confessor of Christ is stabbed and slashed; some pierce his soft flesh, others tear his skin.]

Lines 10–14 describe the immediate effect a picture of Cassian's martyrdom has on the devotee. To achieve the same effect by verbal rather than visual means, rhetorical theory prescribed breaking up the scene to be described into its constituent parts, i.e., *leptologia,* or *enumeratio per partes.*[24] The abundance of bloody detail in the *Peristephanon* is in part attributable to this striving for the illusion of presence: such detailed visual description makes the martyrdom present to the mind's eye of the reader in a manner analogous to Prudentius' reaction to the painting of

24. The term *leptologia* derives from Aquila Romanus, *De Figuris Sententiarum et Elocutionis* 2 (23.12 Halm); for the principle, see Quintilian, 8.3.66–69 and 9.2.40 (Michael Roberts, *The Jeweled Style: Poetry and Poetics in Late Antiquity* [Ithaca, N.Y.,1989], 39–44).

Cassian's martyrdom in his shrine at Imola, and thereby achieves that breaking down of temporal distinctions that is characteristic of the cult of the martyrs.[25] In the present case the *innumeri pueri* of line 13 are enumerated as *alii* (47) . . . *alii* (51), *pars . . . pars* . . . (56), and with the relational terms *inde* (51) . . ., and *hinc . . . inde* . . . (55). Weapons include not just the *stili* of 14, but, by a process of metonymic elaboration, the indispensable concomitants of styli, wax tablets (*tabellas, lignum, buxa cerata, pagina*). Synecdochical analysis of *stilus* yields the double use to which it is put (52–54); similarly *tabellae* are analyzed as wax plus wood. The parts of Cassian's frame subjected to this assault (cf. *totos . . . per artus,* 11) receive some specification too: forehead (48), cheeks (49), and flesh and skin (56; cf. 12). With the exception of the verbs in the final couplet (*foditur, secatur, viscus intrat, scindit,* 55–56), however, the violent effect on the saint is not stressed. Instead, the "fragile tablets" suffer dissolution: they break, split, ring out, and are maimed and wet with blood. The blind fury of Cassian's pupils (45–46) is diverted from the intended object of the assault. Tablet's surface and martyr's skin are assimilated; both can be described as "maimed, wet, and red with blood" (50; cf. *genis . . . cruentis,* 49, of Cassian). The association prepares the way for the explicit comparison of writing and inflicting wounds in the speech of the anonymous pupil that precedes the saint's death (69–82). But for the moment it is the comparison between the frailty of literal writing surface and the integrity of the martyr's frame that impresses.[26]

The description ends with a summary of the situation (57–58). The language recalls that used of the portrait and reminds us that text and image are coextensive: all Cassian's limbs are transfixed (*omnia membra,* 57—*totos . . . artus,* 11), he is attacked by "two hundred hands" (*manus . . . ducentae,* 57, evidently the equivalent of *innumeri . . . pueri,* 13), and bears "as many dripping wounds" (*totidemque guttae vulnerum,* 58—*plagas mille gerens,* 11). The emphasis on the smallness of indi-

25. Cf. Quintilian, 9.2.40: *illa vero, ut ait Cicero, sub oculos subiectio tum fieri solet cum res non gesta indicatur sed ut sit gesta ostenditur, nec universa sed per partis.* For the immediacy and emotional force of such descriptions see the passages cited above, notes 17 and 24, and at the beginning of chapter 2.

26. The reference to the blunt end of the stylus, used for erasing (53–54), may be relevant here. While the surface (*area*) of the tablets can no longer be "renewed and made bright" (*nitescens innovatur*), once the frame is broken, the martyr can expect such a revivification as a consequence of the text, i.e., the wounds of martyrdom, with which he is inscribed.

vidual wounds, present in the earlier passage and implied by the locution *guttae vulnerum* here, is reinterpreted in terms of a contrast between superficiality and depth (*summa* : *profunda*), a distinction that would not be evident in visual representation and is consistent with a uniformly small point of entry. The fourfold schema of verses 55–56 is now reduced to a two-term antithesis, *ille levis* (61–62), i.e., those who only wound the surface, and those who penetrate to the internal vital organs (*hic quanto interius vitalia condita pulsat,* 63).[27] The situation is paradoxical, for the crueller his persecutors, the deeper their wounds penetrate and so the more merciful they are to the saint by bringing his death nearer. Prudentius repeats here, in a different register, the point made in describing the destruction of the writing tablets. Over-violent emotion actually defeats its own purpose.

The sacristan's version of Cassian's death opens out what is already present in the portrait, as described in verses 11–14. Metonymy, synecdoche, and metaphor (e.g., 53–54, the expanse of the tablets) elaborate the picture. The antitheses between flesh and skin, surface and depth, fatal and nonfatal are spun out from consideration of the kinds of wounds made by a long but thin pointed instrument. The rest of the narrative shows a similar process of lexical and logical inference from the content of the portrait. The poet already attributes to himself one interpretative comment on the picture: the styli are of the kind used in school to take dictation on wax tablets (15–16). This is enough to establish the profession of the martyr and his relationship to his pupils. The sacristan reports little that could not be inferred from the presence of boys with styli in the painting of the martyrdom. Much of the rest of the passion, when not dealing in the stock scenes of martyr texts, concerns the hostile relationship between pupil and teacher that fires the vindictiveness of Cassian's tormentors. It is, we are led to believe, universally true that the young find teacher and teaching irksome (27–28).[28] After the introductory lines establishing Cassian's profession (21–24) and

---

27. Looking back from the perspective of this clearly drawn antithesis we can see that verses 55–56 reduce themselves to two pairs of two terms each: *foditur* corresponds to *viscus intrat,* of deep wounds, *secatur* to *scindit cutem,* of less life-threatening injuries.

28. The influence of pagan and Christian authors is possible in this story of a schoolmaster's punishment by his pupils. Pio Franchi de' Cavalieri, "Di una probabile fonte della leggenda dei SS. Giovanni e Paolo," in *Nuove note agiografiche,* Studi e testi 9 (Rome, 1902), 57 and 68–69, compares the passion of Mark of Arethusa (= Sozomenus, *H.E.* 5.10.11) and, *Hagiographica,* Studi e testi 19 (Rome, 1908), 131-32, the story of the schoolmaster of Falerii in Livy 5.27.9.

his relation to his pupils (25–28) dialogue predominates, spoken by the prosecuting magistrate (37–42), *pueri* (35–36 and 69–82), and briefly the saint himself (65–66), and it is only interrupted by the central description of the assault. The expression of the conflict in dialogue form is highly dramatic and shares some of the qualities of the mime. In fact, Augustine compares the visual impact of martyr narratives to the similar effect of contemporary theatrical performances (*spectacula*), the mime and pantomime.[29] The passion of Cassian, with its lively speeches, abundance of physical business, and well-drawn lines of conflict accords well with the broad effects of mime.

Hitherto I have treated Cassian's profession of teacher as narrative extrapolation from the details of the picture in his shrine at Imola. There remains one point that is not a necessary inference from that portrait. Cassian is said to be "skilled in embodying all words in brief strokes [*notis brevibus*] and following what is rapidly spoken with quick points" (*punctis . . . praepetibus*); i.e., he is a teacher of shorthand.[30] The parallels with the description of Cassian's wounds immediately spring to the eye. The marks made by a *notarius* are small (*brevibus*) puncture marks (*punctis*), like the tiny puncture marks (*minutis . . . punctis,* 12) on the saint's body. In the final taunting address of an unnamed student (*quidam,* 69) to the martyr, this analogy between body and text becomes explicit: the pupils are performing a writing exercise with the saint's skin as their *pagina.* Why, then, shorthand rather than ordinary characters? In part, perhaps, because students of the *notarius* would be older and more physically capable of turning on their teacher. Physical strength, however, is not a necessary condition of the martyrdom; the very weak-

29. *Serm. Denis* 17.7: *Denique amo martyres, specto martyres: quando leguntur passiones martyrum, specto. Dic mihi, Talis sis, et laudasti. Tu specta mimum, specta pantomimum; dicam tibi, Talis sis, et noli irasci* (*MA* 1.87.13–15); cf. *Serm. Denis* 14.3 (*MA* 1.67.26–68.3). Rainer Henke, "Die Nutzung von Senecas (Ps.-Senecas) Tragödien in Romanus-hymnus des Prudentius," *WüJb* 11 (1985): 135–50, emphasizes the dramatic elements of *Pe.* 10; Walther Ludwig, "Die christliche Dichtung des Prudentius und die Transformation der klassischen Gattung," in *Christianisme et formes littéraires de l'antiquité tardive en occident,* Fondation Hardt, Entretiens 23 (Vandoeuvres, 1977), 333 describes *Pe.* 12 as a mime.

30. *Verba notis brevibus conprendere cuncta peritus / raptimque punctis dicta praepetibus sequi* (23–24). Compare Ausonius, *In Notarium* (*Ephem.* 7) 1–2, *puer,* **notarum praepetum** / *sollers minister*; and 4–5, *multa fandi copia, /* **punctis** *peracta singulis* (330 Prete = 12 Green); the parallels are noted by Jean-Louis Charlet, *L'influence d'Ausone sur la poésie de Prudence* (Aix-en-Provence, 1980), 69–70. For Cassian's profession, see also Robert A. Kaster, *Guardians of Language: The Grammarian and Society in Late Antiquity,* The Transformation of the Classical Heritage 11 (Berkeley, 1988), 252–53.

ness and frailty of their efforts (*conatus tener infirmusque,* 67) intensifies the saint's sufferings. Rather, shorthand notes have that synecdochical quality of embodying in small compass a larger whole (*verba . . . conprendere cuncta,* 23). The same is true of the "language" of martyrdom. Whether we speak of physical objects, a relic or drop of blood (cf. *sanguinis notis,* 1.3), a visual or verbal representation of *poenae,* a name or epigraphical formula for martyrdom, to the informed reader/viewer/devotee the whole course of the martyrdom is already present. This is the role of the *picta imago martyris* of Cassian's shrine; the representation shows the martyr's body as a page marked with a pattern of points, like a wax tablet marked with shorthand notes, from which the whole narrative can be read. "The picture tells/brings to mind [both senses of *refert*] a story" (19). In the case of the martyrdom of Cassian the distinction of reading/hearing and viewing is collapsed; both operations can be performed on the martyr's body. Subsequent versions of the martyr narrative, whether written, spoken, or depicted, reproduce the original martyr text that is the saint's lacerated flesh.[31] Written/spoken texts share the immediacy, the sense of presence and subversion of distinction between time of reading and time of martyrdom normally associated with the visual. Narratives, whether written or visual, may vary in length, but even the most abbreviated text or image, in its capacity to make actual or "re-present" the martyrdom to the informed reader or viewer, bears the fidelity of shorthand notes to its original: it encompasses in a few characters the whole passion.

Perhaps it would be wise to leave Cassian here. But I think it is at least possible that something more can be said about the saint's profession as a *doctor,* and its special relevance to the circumstances of Prudentius. Here, I recognize, I am venturing into the treacherous waters of a biographical reading of poetry, and a highly speculative one at that.[32] I can at least claim that by setting the martyr narrative in a first-person account of personal devotion and by associating *mea vulnera . . . ac dolorum*

31. The association between body of martyr and text is pervasive in the *Peristephanon.* There is much language common to the two subjects, notably the metaphor of plowing, on which see Thraede, *Studien,* 79–140. Eulalia (*Pe.* 3.136–40) reads her own body as a text; in heaven the angels have no need of stenography, taking down the actual words / wounds of Romanus, including the exact dimension of every gash (*Pe.* 10.1121–30).

32. The most thorough analysis of Prudentius' poetry for autobiographical information is Lana, *Due capitoli Prudenziani,* 1–60. While I would not want to follow the Italian scholar in all his speculations, some references can be pieced together with a certain degree of plausibility.

acumina (7–8) with the *vulnera* (58) and *dolorum spicula* (62) of the martyr, Prudentius provides some incentive for such a reading.

To begin with, of the martyrs in the *Peristephanon* only Hippolytus shares with Cassian a manner of death specially tailored to the circumstances of his biography. In both cases the persecutor hesitates, as he searches for a form of execution/punishment particularly appropriate to the figure before him (*Pe.* 9. 33–34; *Pe.* 11.83–84). In the case of Hippolytus, the saint's name is the immediate reason for the type of martyrdom chosen. But it is not difficult to recognize a further appropriateness to the saint's death: the former leader of a schismatic sect (*Pe.* 11.19–20) is pulled apart by a pair of horses. Just as he had formerly torn apart the Church, so now he himself is torn apart (*scissa,* 119). The manner of martyrdom absolves Hippolytus of the crime he had formerly committed against the Church. It conforms to the *lex talionis,* in that his own criminal action is now turned back upon himself.[33]

The comparison with Cassian suggests that he too, in being inscribed by his students' styli, is expiating a failing in his former life. That failing, I would suggest, is his chosen profession. As a teacher of a technical and, at best, ethically neutral *disciplina,* Cassian does nothing to promote the moral welfare and spiritual salvation of his charges. In the previous chapter we have already drawn the contrast with Cyprian, the bishop instructing his flock. It is worth remembering that in the *Preface* to his poems Prudentius expresses similar reservations about his own secular career and the literary education that launched it.

> Numquid talia proderunt
> carnis post obitum vel bona vel mala,
> cum iam quidquid id est quod fueram mors aboleverit?
> (*Pr.* 28–30)

> [Will such things, whether good or bad, be of any advantage after the death of the flesh, when death has already eliminated whatever it is that I once was?]

The poet will throw off his past *stultitia* (*Pr.* 35) and devote himself to celebrating God in his writing (*peccatrix anima . . . voce Deum conce-*

33. On this aspect of *Pe.* 11, see Martha Malamud, *A Poetics of Transformation: Prudentius and Classical Mythology* (Ithaca, N.Y., 1989), 93–101.

lebret, 35–36).[34] In the light of such sentiments it would be quite natural for Prudentius to view with disapproval Cassian's profession of *magister litterarum,* especially for a future martyr.

We have, then, a saint whose secular career involved imparting a literary education to his young charges, and a poet whose own career in the imperial administration depended on his literary capabilities. (Lana believes he was *proximus* in one of the imperial *scrinia,* possibly the *libellorum.*)[35] It would not be surprising, in the circumstances, if Prudentius' attitude to Cassian was influenced by his own discontent with secular learning. The parallel between poet and saint goes further, however. Both suffer wounds. Prudentius speaks of "the trials of my life and pin-pricks of sufferings" (*Pe.* 9.8). We later hear of a "home left behind in perilous circumstances and wavering expectations of future prosperity" (*Pe.* 9.103–4). The poet is, he tells us in *Pe.* 11, "sick in mind and body" (*corruptelis animique et corporis aeger, Pe.* 11.177). The clues are few enough. Lana concludes that "Prudentius' journey from Spain to Rome is caused by a serious question on which depend in large measure the fortunes of his family; at the same time, while suffering in body, he is also troubled by a secret concern of a spiritual nature."[36]

If we ask what the source of Prudentius' suffering is we can perhaps learn something from the case of Cassian. That saint, it will be remembered, has earned the hostility of his students by his strict *disciplina* (25–28); although he can be described, like a bishop, as "director of a flock of dependents" (*moderator alumni / gregis,* 31–32), he enjoys none of the affection that a congregation lavishes on its pastor. He experiences instead anger (26, 45), fear (26), and bitter scorn (*felle . . . libero,* 46, illustrated by the speech of the unnamed pupil, 69–82). This hostility is not just the misfortune of one particular teacher; it is *disciplina* itself, not just the individual *doctor,* that is universally abhorred by the young (28). This insistence on the enmity caused by literary education is surprisingly emphatic. If we remember the analogy between the wounds of saint and of poet, it is at least plausible that Prudentius himself had

34. These passages from the *Praefatio* have been extensively discussed; see, for instance, Lana, *Due capitoli Prudenziani,* 61–65. Similar sentiments are expressed in *C.* 2.33–56 (see Marianne Kah, *"Die Welt der Römer mit der Seele suchend . . . ". Die Religiosität des Prudentius im Spannungsfeld zwischen 'pietas christiana' und 'pietas romana',* Hereditas 3 [Bonn, 1990], 46–53).

35. Lana, *Due capitoli Prudenziani,* 10–23.

36. Ibid. 29; the entire discussion extends from 24 to 29.

experienced hostility aroused by his literary abilities, or rather by his conduct of office and opportunities for patronage as *proximus* of one of the imperial *scrinia,* a position secured by his literary attainments. I suggest that, like Cassian, Prudentius had aroused enmities through his career in letters, in his case in his native Spain (103), and that his journey to Rome was in some way occasioned by the need to circumvent the threats such opposition presented.

Whatever is thought of this construction, the identification of martyr and devotee in this poem is especially marked. Prudentius presents us here, in his own person, with a model of individual veneration at the martyr's shrine. Even writing poetry is incorporated into the syntax of such veneration: "I enjoy success, I return home, I proclaim Cassian" (*dextris successibus utor, / domum revertor, Cassianum praedico,* 105–6). As already noted, Prudentius' poem, with its speculation on the synecdochical and representational aspects of the martyr narrative, fulfils his vow to "proclaim Cassian." *Pe.* 9 is an appropriate vehicle for such speculation because it is devoted to a saint whose secular calling, the teaching of shorthand, provides an analogy with the veneration of the martyrs, both in its play with the inversion of magnitudes, to adopt a phrase from Peter Brown, and in the model of interpretation it offers. In gratitude for the favors received from the saint, Prudentius proclaims Cassian in his poem; in doing so he also teaches "the shorthand of martyrdom."

Pe. 11: Private Devotion and Public Festival

Like the Cassian poem, *Pe.* 11 was written after Prudentius' return to Spain, in part as an expression of gratitude, in this case, to the Roman martyr Hippolytus: "I know I owe to Hippolytus my joy in my return . . . and even that I am writing these words" (11.179-80).[37] But in addition to being an expression of Prudentius' personal devotion to the saint, the poem takes on an extra dimension in the address to Valerian, bishop of Calahorra,[38] with which it closes. Valerian is urged to include the annual festival of Hippolytus in the liturgical calendar of his con-

---

37. *Quod laetor reditu . . . / . . . scribo quod haec eadem, / Hippolyto scio me debere.*

38. For the see of Bishop Valerian, see Lana, *Due capitoli Prudenziani,* 7–8, and José Madoz, "Valerian, Bishop of Calahorra," in Joseph M.F. Marique, ed., *Leaders of Iberean Christianity* (Boston, 1962), 157–63.

gregation. The whole of the poem, with its epistolary introduction and conclusion, can be seen as an exhortation to the bishop of Calahorra to venerate the Roman martyr, Hippolytus. In providing such a framework for his narrative, Prudentius casts himself in a role analogous to that of the anonymous sacristan of *Pe.* 9, expounding the passion of and urging devotion to the martyr (*Pe.* 9.95–98).

In the case of the Cassian poem a work of art and the poet's reaction to it provide the impulse for exegesis. In *Pe.* 11 the starting point is Valerian's request for the names of the innumerable martyrs whose remains the poet has seen in Rome, and for the inscriptions recording their memory. In replying, the poet immediately hits a snag (*difficile est ut replicare queam,* 4); although many tombs do carry inscriptions and record the martyrs' names, there are others that are silent and only give a number (7–10). It is possible to know the number of bodies heaped in a tomb (*quanta virum iaceant congestis corpora acervis,* 11), even when no names can be read. The emphasis on number as the minimum datum supplied by martyrs' tombs is surprising, especially as the epigram of Damasus that Prudentius is apparently imitating does not supply any specific number itself, talking just of a "heaped crowd of the holy" (*congesta iacet . . . turba piorum, Epig.* 16.1) and "bodies of the saints" (*corpora sanctorum,* 16.2).[39] The puzzle is partly explained if we remember the first two lines of the first poem of the collection, dedicated to a pair of martyrs of Calahorra, Valerian's own see.

Scripta sunt caelo duorum martyrum vocabula,
aureis quae Christus illic adnotavit litteris.

(*Pe.* 1.1–2)

[Two martyrs' names are enrolled in heaven; there Christ registered them in letters of gold.]

The situation is analogous to that described in *Pe.* 11; a number, two, but no names, for despite the confident identification of the saints in

39. The Damasus epigram does contain the word *numerus* (*hic numerus procerum servat qui altaria Christi,* 16.5), but without specifying a figure. Ferrua takes the word in a quasi-military sense (122 *ad loc.*), following De Rossi, and glosses it as *cohors.* Could it be that a Roman informant had told Prudentius that the tomb bearing Damasus' epigram contained sixty bodies (cf. *sexaginta illic defossas mole sub una,* (13)? The poet's language, *nosse licet* (12) and *memini me didicisse* (14), is studiously ambiguous and could refer just as well to oral as to written information.

the manuscript superscription to the poem, the names of Chelidonius and Emeterius appear nowhere in the text. Instead they are recorded in golden letters in heaven by Christ—an assertion that is repeated in similar language of the nameless saints of *Pe.* 11: "only Christ has a record of their names" (*quorum solus habet conperta vocabula Christus,* 15).[40] The allusion to the first poem of the collection in the Hippolytus poem can hardly be accidental. *Pe.* 1 demonstrates that that number of martyrs, combined with a reliable tradition of the authenticity of martyrdom, is sufficient foundation for cult.

The total number of martyr relics in the city of Rome may be unspecifiable (*innumeros cineris sanctorum,* 1), but a number can be given for the bodies within a particular tomb. The relation of particular burial place to whole city is that of part to whole. Individual tombs and their numerable martyrs can stand by the principle of synecdoche for the incalculable multitude of which they form part, and supply the detail absent from the larger picture. The next step in the progression of diminishing quantity of bodies and increasing specificity of detail is the single inscription to an individual saint. In the present poem the saint is Hippolytus, the inscription that set up in the catacomb of that martyr by Pope Damasus. In two passages the Spanish poet has closely paraphrased the words Damasus had inscribed on the tomb (19–20 and 28–30).[41] The figure of Hippolytus, then, is exemplary of the countless martyrs whose remains are buried "in the city of Romulus" (*Romula in urbe,* 1).

Prudentius' narrative of the martyrdom of Hippolytus occupies the majority of the poem (17–152). It is introduced by a transitional couplet that presents Hippolytus as just one of the martyrs whose tombs have been furnished with inscriptions in Rome.

---

40. For this *liber vitae,* a sort of heavenly citizen list, see Leo Koep, *Das himmlische Buch in Antike und Christentum: eine religionsgeschichtliche Untersuchung zur altchristlichen Bildersprache,* Theophaneia 8 (Bonn, 1952), 68–79.

41. *Pe.* 11.19–20, *invenio Hippolytum, qui quondam scisma Novati / presbyter attigerat,* corresponds to *Hippolytus fertur . . . / presbyter in scisma semper mansisse Novati, Epigr.* 35.1–2, and 11.28–30, *consultus quaenam secta foret melior, / respondit*: "*Fugite, o miseri, execranda Novati / scismata, catholicis reddite vos populis*" to [*cum*] *quaesisset populus ubinam procedere posset, / catholicam dixisse fidem sequerentur ut omnes* [sc. *fertur*], *Epigr.* 35.5–6. The legends surrounding the name of Hippolytus are unusually complex, even by the standards of martyr literature. For the contribution of Damasus' epigram and its historical unreliability, see Agostino Amore, "Note su S. Ippolito martire," *RAC* 30 (1954): 85–88, and Testini, "Di alcune testimonianze," 52–54.

Haec dum lustro oculis et sicubi forte latentes
rerum apices veterum per monumenta sequor,
invenio Hippolytum.

(*Pe.* 11.17–19)

[As I range over these with my eyes and follow on the tombs the traces of ancient events wherever they are hidden, I find Hippolytus.]

As a hagiographer the poet combines the historian's concern for the past (*rerum veterum*) with a researcher's eagerness to track down and decipher material evidence for the saint. This act of historical research is also a duty of religious devotion, appropriate to a pilgrim who seeks to come into contact with all objects associated with the martyrs, the recipients of his veneration. In this regard the choice of the word *apices* is especially revealing. Both Lavarenne and Thomson understand it to mean "letter" in the present passage, which is certainly a possible translation.[42] But the word has a more specific sense: it refers to the strokes that make up an individual letter, rather than the fully formed and articulated letter. So Aulus Gellius writes of the technique for sending secret messages known as *scytale,* and attributed to the Spartans, whereby strips of parchment are wound round a rod and inscribed with a continuous text. When unwound the characters are mutilated and illegible; to read them the strips must be rolled round a stick once again. The unwound strip is described as follows:

resolutio autem lori litteras truncas atque mutilas reddebat *membraque earum et apices* in partis diversissimas spargebat. (*Noct. Att.* 17.9.12)

[Unwinding the strip rendered the letters mutilated and deformed, and scattered over various sections their limbs and constituent parts (*apices*).[43]]

42. Maurice Lavarenne, *Étude sur la langue du poète Prudence* (Paris, 1933), 444; Thomson translates "letters telling of the deeds of old."

43. See also Gellius, 13.31.10, with the note of J.C. Rolfe, *The Attic Nights of Aulus Gellius* (London, 1927–28) 2: 514, "*apices* here seems to refer to the strokes of which the letters were made up." Ausonius (*Epit.* 32.4 Prete = *Epigr.* 37.4 Green) uses the word *apex* in this sense, specifically of a mutilated letter M in an inscription.

By using *apices* rather than *litteras* of the inscriptions he is describing, Prudentius draws attention to the element of decipherment in making out the *ductus* of their texts. Even at the level of the individual letter of the alphabet, the unit is dissolved into its constituent parts. But the traces in question here are not just the incisions inscribed on tombs hidden underground (*latentes*) in the catacombs. They are also "traces of past events" (*rerum apices veterum*), the incomplete record of Christian history. There is an equivalence between, on the small scale, making out the inscription from the strokes drawn in stone, and making out past events (*res veteres*) from the traces left in the surviving historical record. Both involve decoding or decipherment, constructing a whole from some or all of its parts. They are in this respect akin to shorthand, which depends on "understanding a whole account from abbreviated characters" (*verba notis brevibus conprendere cuncta, Pe.* 9.23) or to the process the sacristan of Imola follows in reading the narrative of the martyr from its depiction in the shrine. This is the same "process" that Prudentius will be "following"—the metaphor of motion is worth insisting on here (cf. *lustro,* 17 and *sequor,* 18)—in reconstructing an account of the martyrdom of Hippolytus for Valerian.

In fact, the first sixteen lines of the martyrdom account (19–34) follow closely the content of Damasus' epigram, culminating in the injunction to the Christian populace to abandon schism and adopt the Catholic faith (29–34; Damasus, *Epigr.* 35.6). Martyr, Christian community, and persecutor together constitute the *dramatis personae* for the rest of Prudentius' narrative, which consists of two movements, confrontation between persecutor and the *populi* (35–76), and interrogation and death of Hippolytus (77–152). To that extent, the martyr narrative constitutes a reading of the inscription and teasing out of its implications, according to the norms of martyr literature. Although Prudentius may have had at his disposal a fuller version of the Passion—Testini believes he used a Latin version of a Greek Passion[44]—only two aspects of his narrative exceed the available data. These are the location of the martyrdom, a harbor town on the Tiber estuary (40, 42–48), and its manner, the saint's body is dragged behind a pair of unbroken horses (though the latter might be an inference from the name Hippolytus [86–88]). The location was presumably suggested by the fact that a martyr Hippolytus possessed a *memoria* at Porto as well as Rome; Prudentius' account has the merit

44. Testini, "Di alcune testimonianze," 55; but the evidence is far from conclusive. I am inclined to attribute to Prudentius a certain amount of hagiographical invention.

of explaining this duplication.[45] The evidence for the manner of death is different in nature, however, and specifically mentioned by Prudentius: it is a painting on the wall of Hippolytus' shrine (123–26). If giving an account of the martyrdom as a whole can be represented as analogous to the reading of an inscription—"following the obscure traces [*latentes/ . . . apices*] of past events" (17–18)—the details of Hippolytus' death derive from a similar decipherment of the painting in his tomb.

Image and inscription are complementary in Prudentius' poem, as they often were in late antique basilicas. Paulinus' basilica at Nola, Sulpicius Severus' at Primuliacum, the fifth-century church of St. Martin at Tours all illustrate this widespread phenomenon.[46] Walls became codices for the Christian congregation, from which it could read its history and derive lessons of Christian piety and salvation.[47] Although differing in rhetorical function—inscriptions were better suited to paraenetic purposes and their brevity made them readily memorable, while visual images were capable of arresting the attention and arousing the emotions[48]—the two media were employed as mutually reinforcing and semantically coextensive. In including both in his poem Prudentius is in accord with contemporary practice in the decoration of sacred buildings.

Unlike *Pe.* 9, in which painting and martyrdom are separately treated though equivalent in content, *Pe.* 11 fuses narrative with description of the work of art. This fusion reflects the fact that the two *personae* of the Cassian poem, devoted worshipper (the poet) and narrator/exegete (the sacristan), are combined into one in *Pe.* 11. It is, in fact, difficult

45. So Testini, "Di alcune testimonianze," 55–56. Hippolyte Delehaye, "Recherches sue le légendier romain," *AB* 51 (1933): 64, thinks the seaside location may have been suggested by the similar location of the mythical Hipppolytus' death, but this strikes me as improbable.

46. For the basilicas of Paulinus and Sulpicius Severus, see especially Paulinus, *Ep.* 32; for the church of Martin at Tours, see Raymond Van Dam, *Leadership and Community in Late Antique Gaul,* The Transformation of the Classical Heritage 8 (Berkeley, 1985), 230–55.

47. Augustine, *Serm.* 319.8.7 (*PL* 38.1442), of a four-verse inscription in the *memoria* of St. Stephen: *non opus est ut quaeratur codex: camera illa codex vester sit*; Paulinus of Périgueux, *Prol. ad Carm. Min.* (*CSEL* 16; 161.4), of inscriptions in Martin's church at Tours: *pagina in pariete reserata.*

48. For the paraenetic function of metrical inscriptions, see Gabriel Sanders, "Les chrétiens face à l'épigraphie funéraire latine," in D.M. Pippidi, ed., *Assimilation et résistance à la culture gréco-romaine dans le monde ancien,* Travaux du VIe Congrés international d'études classiques, Madrid, September 1974 (Bucharest and Paris, 1976), 297–99. Augustine recommends memorization of the inscription set up in the *memoria* of St. Stephen: *Legite quatuor versus quos in cella scripsimus; legite, tenete, in corde habete, Serm.* 319.8.7 (*PL* 38.1442). Presumably the illiterate could commit to memory what others had read to them.

to be certain where work of art ends and independent narrative begins, a difficulty that itself is an indication of the close relationship of verbal and visual.[49] The following lines are those that most unambiguously describe the painting.

> Exemplar sceleris paries habet inlitus, in quo
> multicolor fucus digerit omne nefas;
> picta super tumulum species liquidis viget umbris,
> effigians tracti membra cruenta viri.
> Rorantes saxorum apices vidi, optime papa,
> purpureasque notas vepribus inpositas.
> Docta manus virides imitando effingere dumos
> luserat et minio russeolam saniem.
> Cernere erat ruptis conpagibus ordine nullo
> membra per incertos sparsa iacere situs.
> Addiderat caros gressu lacrimisque sequentes,
> devia quo fractum semita monstrat iter.
>
> (*Pe.* 11.123–34)

> [A painted wall carries a representation of the crime, on which pigments of many colors set out the whole outrage, and above the tomb a likeness is depicted powerful in its clear images, delineating the bleeding limbs of the man dragged to his death. I have seen the moist points of the rocks, best of fathers, and the purple stains on the brambles. A hand skilled in imitating green vegetation had also portrayed the red blood with vermilion. You could see the torn frame and limbs scattered and lying randomly in unpredictable locations. The painter had included the saint's loyal friends following with tearful footsteps where his erratic course traced its fractured path.]

Prudentius depicts violent dismemberment in the world of uncultivated nature: the interaction of human violence with natural scenery dominates the description after the first two introductory couplets. Only

49. So Gabriel Bertonière, *The Cult Center of the Martyr Hippolytus on the Via Tiburtina,* BAR International Series 260 (Oxford, 1985), 42: "It is . . . curious that the description of the painting is not only mentioned in the context of the narration but serves as part of the narration itself. . . . In fact one is not sure where the description of the painting ends and the thread of the story is taken up again." Malamud, *Poetics of Transformation,* 86–87 and 110–13 makes this uncertainty central to her interpretation of *Pe.* 11.

the last two lines (133–34) go beyond this, introducing Hippolytus' followers and preparing the transition to the saint's burial and cult. The picture provides almost all that is needed to reconstitute the account of Hippolytus' death as given by Prudentius. The only exception is that there is no reference to the team of unbroken horses; it is tempting to suppose their presence somewhere in the background of the picture. As far as the role of landscape is concerned, the longer narrative, too, gives prominence to the natural setting of Hippolytus' mutilation. Metonymic enumeration of the constituent elements of the scenery (e.g., *scopulis . . . sentibus . . . frondes . . . humus,* 121–22) provides the dislocated, discontinuous framework for the martyr's minutely fragmented limbs (*scissa minutatim labefacto corpore frusta,* 119). While Virgil and Seneca have influenced Prudentius in his description of the traces left by the saint's lacerated body, the Christian poet goes beyond both of his models in the minuteness of his observation of the natural world.[50]

Finally, in describing the tracks left by Hippolytus' blood on the rocks and thornbushes over which he is dragged, Prudentius uses language employed of writing elsewhere in the collection: *apices* (127) and *notas* (128).[51] The notion that the blood of the martyr is the original text of his passion is familiar from *Pe.* 1 (1.3); in *Pe.* 3 (3.137) and 9 (9.53) the strokes inscribed by a torturer on his victim's body are called *apices.* In the present case the *ductus* of the martyrdom can be read in the landscape on which it is imprinted. The process of decipherment is analogous to that performed by Prudentius on the "obscure strokes" (*latentes / . . . apices,* 17–18) of the martyr inscriptions. But a closer parallel, this time situated at the time of martyrdom, can be detected in the activities of the group that collects together Hippolytus' bodily remains. The reader of the inscription "ranges over it with his eyes" (*lustro oculis,* 17) and "follows" (*sequor,* 18) its traces (*apices*); the devotees of the saint "follow" (*sequentes,* 133) where his track leads and "proceed with intent gaze" (*oculis rimantibus ibant,* 135) in their search for his limbs. Their problem is that body parts are scattered unpredictably

50. Virgil, *G.* 3.250–53 and 275–77 (Christian Schwen, *Vergil bei Prudentius* [Leipzig, 1937], 63–64), *Aen.* 8.642–45, especially 645 *sparsi rorabant sanguine vepres* (of the death of Mettus Fufetius); Seneca, *Ph.* 1102–7 (cf. G. Sixt, "Des Prudentius' Abhängigkeit von Seneca und Lucan," *Philologus* 51 [1892]: 502, and Thraede, *Studien,* 125–27). As Malamud, *Poetics of Transformation,* 87–93 suggests, Prudentius may have been influenced by a painting of the death of the mythical Hippolytus in the temple of Diana Trivia, which he refers to in *C. Symm.* 2.53–56.

51. Thraede, *Studien,* 126.

(*incertos,* 132) and "in no sequence" (*ordine nullo,* 131) over the course of his erratic career (134). They must gather together the saint's *membra* and reconstitute the body in its entirety (*corporis integri . . . numerus,* 148), if the martyr's cult and legend is to be secure.[52] Lines 139–40 depict this process of creating order from the inarticulate, intelligibility from what is unclear and hard to follow:

> hic umeros truncasque manus et bracchia et ulnas
> et genua et crurum fragmina nuda legit.

> [Another collects shoulders, mutilated hands, forearms and elbows, knees and bare fragments of legs.]

The previous couplet has described the discovery of Hippolytus' head, which receives special devotion.[53] Now his other limbs are enumerated, in metonymic detail, emphasizing the extreme fragmentation his frame has been subjected to, but in logical sequence—shoulders after head, then arms and hands, following naturally after shoulders, and finally the lower body. Order has been restored from disorder (*ordine nullo,* 131). The process is like that of reading inscriptions, in which an intelligible text must be pieced together from the constituent strokes (*apices*) of which the whole is made up, and that in isolation are incapable of communicating meaning. In fact, the verb *legere* is used (140) of the devotees' reassembling of the saint's body parts; the process might equally be described, adapting Prudentius' description of shorthand in *Pe.* 9.23–24, as *punctis brevibus conprendere cuncta.* Gellius, it will be remembered, in the account of the *scytale* quoted above (*Noct. Att.* 17.9.12), uses *membra* as synonymous with *apices.* Both are constituent members of a larger whole that depend for their sense on being viewed in that larger context. The reconstitution of the saint's body is simultaneously, then, an act of devotion and cult, and the restoration of meaning to the obscure traces of the martyrdom. Prudentius, in writing his poem, repeats this original de-

52. The piecing together of Hippolytus' body owes something to the ending of Seneca's *Phaedra,* in which Theseus similarly collates the scattered fragments of his son (1256–70), though it is significant that the mythical Hippolytus' body remains incomplete (*Ph.* 1261).

53. There is probably a reference here to the use earlier in the poem of *caput,* to express metaphorically Hippolytus' preeminence over his followers (79–80). The pagan's desire to eliminate "the head of the Christian populace" has failed. At the same time, the head is especially well suited to stand synecdochically for the martyr's person, and therefore it appropriately receives particular devotion.

votional and interpretative act. His poem both expresses his own gratitude to the saint and expounds the saint's legend to Bishop Valerian and subsequent readers.

The narrative of Hippolytus' martyrdom, though set in past time, has been repeatedly anchored in the traces of that saint's passion still visible in the Rome of Prudentius' own day: the inscription in the catacomb and the painting over his tomb. In each case the poet insists on his personal inspection of the monument in question (17–19, 127). His itinerary through the historical record of Christian Rome continues with a description of the catacomb where the saint is buried (153–70). Once again the poet speaks of personal experience in the first person (177–78).

Haud procul extremo culta ad pomeria vallo
  mersa latebrosis crypta patet foveis.
Huius in occultum gradibus via prona reflexis
  ire per anfractus luce latente docet.
Primas namque fores summo tenus intrat hiatu
  inlustratque dies limina vestibuli.
Inde ubi progressu facili nigrescere visa est
  nox obscura loci per specus ambiguum,
occurrunt celsis inmissa foramina tectis,
  quae iaciant claros antra super radios.
Quamlibet ancipites texant hinc inde recessus
  arta sub umbrosis atria porticibus,
at tamen excisi subter cava viscera montis
  crebra terebrato fornice lux penetrat.
Sic datur absentis per subterranea solis
  cernere fulgorem luminibusque frui.
Talibus Hippolyti corpus mandatur opertis,
  propter ubi adposita est ara dicata deo.

(*Pe.* 11.153–70)

[Not far from the outer rampart by the cultivated land of the pomerium a crypt opens up descending to hidden depths. Into its obscurity a path leads downward with curving steps and shows the way through the windings with fugitive light. For the brightness of day enters the first doorway as far as the top of the chamber's mouth and illuminates the threshold of the entrance chamber. From there it is an easy progression to where the dark night of the place seems to grow blacker in the indistinct cavern; where apertures let into the lofty ceiling shed bright rays over the cave. Though indeterminate alcoves swathe on either side the confined halls under shadowy galleries, yet within the hollow belly of the carved-out mountain frequent shafts of light penetrate from the openings in the vault. So it is possible to see and enjoy the radiancy of bright light even below the earth where there is no sun. Such was the chamber Hippolytus' body was entrusted to, and nearby was positioned an altar dedicated to God.]

The passage is an impressive evocation of the subterranean realm of Hippolytus' catacomb.[54] It begins, as such passages of literary description regularly do, with an indication of place (153); it ends with a reminder of the relevance of the site to the martyr narrative—this is where Hippolytus was buried (169)—as well as a detail, the "altar dedicated to God" (170), that anticipates the role of the shrine in contemporary Christian worship, the subject of the rest of the poem. The particular qualities of Prudentius' description emerge if it is compared with Jerome's account of Sunday visits to the catacombs.

Dum essem Romae puer et liberalibus studiis erudirer, solebam cum ceteris eiusdem aetatis et propositi, diebus Dominicis sepulcra apostolorum et martyrum circumire, crebroque cryptas ingredi quae, in terrarum profunda defossae, ex utraque parte ingredientium per parietes habent corpora sepultorum, et quia obscura sunt omnia, ut propemodum illud propheticum compleatur: "Descendant ad infernum viventes," et raro desuper lumen admissum, horrorem temperet tenebrarum, ut non tam fenestram quam foramen dimissi luminis putes, rursumque pedetemptim inceditur et caeca nocte circumdatis illud Vergilianum proponitur: "Horror ubique anima, simul ipsa silentia terrent." [*In Hiezechielem* 12.40. 5–13; *CCL* 75; 556.243–557.254]

[While I was a boy at Rome being educated in the liberal arts, on Sundays I used to tour the tombs of the apostles and martyrs with

54. Hippolytus' catacomb was excavated in the nineteenth century; for a recent archaeological report, see Bertonière, *Cult Center.* Avery R. Springer, "Prudentius, Pilgrim and Poet: The Catacombs and Their Paintings as Inspiration for the Liber Cathemerinon," (Ph.D. diss., University of Wisconsin, Madison, 1984), argues that the decoration of the Roman catacombs may have been influential on Prudentius' poetry.

> others of the same age and inclination and frequently to enter the crypts, dug deep into the earth, that sheltered—on the walls on either side of us as we entered—the bodies of those buried there. Because everything was so dark, so that the saying of the prophet was almost fulfilled, "Let them descend living to the dead" (Ps. 54:16), and the scanty illumination that penetrated from above to temper the oppressive gloom gave the impression of being admitted through a light shaft rather than a window, we made our way back step by step and were reminded by the darkness of night that surrounded us of that saying of Virgil: "Everywhere dread grips the mind, while even the silences terrify" (*Aen.* 2.755).]

Jerome was a young man when he explored the catacombs. His account, written later in life,[55] still vividly recalls the frisson communicated by those eerie underground chambers. Prudentius is writing after the construction, probably by Damasus, of an impressive underground shrine in the catacomb of Hippolytus, but his account communicates the same *horror* as Jerome describes.[56] Both writers emphasize the play of light and dark in the tunnels where the prevailing gloom is broken only by the constrained shafts of light provided by *lucernaria* in the ceiling. The opposition between light and dark is the leitmotif of Prudentius' account; it is miraculous that underground, out of the sunlight, the worshipper can finally enjoy radiant illumination (167–68). But that illumination is hard won. The traveller through the catacombs must experience a succession of disorienting impressions: he follows a winding, labyrinthine course (*gradibus . . . reflexis / ire per anfractus,* 155–56), moving from the bright light of day in the entranceway (157–58) to the darkness and indistinct outlines of the underground cavern (*specus ambiguum,* 160). As he passes through a narrow hallway, shadowy galleries (*umbrosis . . . porticibus,* 164) loom overhead and ill-defined alcoves (*ancipites . . . recessus,* 163) press in on either side. He has a sense of being confined (*arta,* 164); it is as though the traveller has passed below ground through a gaping mouth (*hiatu,* 157) and into the hollow belly of a mountain (*cava viscera montis,* 165)—or monster. The phrase *viscera montis* is

55. Jerome was eighty or so when he wrote the Commentary on Ezekiel. For his student years in Rome and visits to the catacombs, see J.N.D. Kelly, *Jerome: His Life, Writings, and Controversies* (New York, 1975), 21–23.

56. Bertonière, *Cult Center,* 136–37, 176, 184–85. The same comparison between Prudentius and Jerome is made by Malamud, *Poetics of Transformation,* 108–10.

Virgilian (*Aen.* 3.575). It might be nothing more than a faded metaphor—Claudian, too, uses the expression[57]—but with the word *hiatus* a few lines earlier, which includes among its meanings that of a "wide-open mouth," there is at least a suggestion that the catacomb "swallows" its visitor.

Jerome, it will be remembered, likens entering the catacombs to descending into Hell, quoting Ps. 54:16 (*descendant ad infernum viventes*). And indeed the burial place of Hippolytus has many of the qualities of Vincent's prison that we also described, in chapter 3, as an image of the underworld: it is a dark, subterranean cave.[58] And also like Vincent's prison it takes only a small source of light, in this case the *lucernaria* in the vaulted ceiling, to illuminate the infernal darkness with the light of salvation. In *Pe.* 5 the martyr reenacts Christ's triumphant *descensus ad inferos* after the Crucifixion; now the individual Christian, in his progress through the catacomb, experiences that contest of light and darkness in his own person, with its redemptive conclusion. The language of "swallowing," too, makes sense in this context, for the most common Old Testament type for Christ's *descensus ad inferos* is Jonah's three days in the belly of the whale; the interpretation is already found in the Gospel of Matthew (12:40). Prudentius gives his own version of this story in *Cathemerinon* 7. Some of the details are familiar. The whale's stomach is described as a "cavern" (*specu, C.* 7.115), and the prophet "wanders through the depths of its belly" (*per latebras viscerum, C.* 7.123) and "tours its twisting meanders" (*meandros circumibat tortiles, C.* 7.124). Confinement in the whale's belly in *C.* 7 takes on some of the properties of a journey, while journeying through the catacomb in *Pe.* 11 can seem like being swallowed alive. Both are allegories of the underworld; and both show the association of internal and infernal already observed in *Pe.* 5.

The poet's journey through the catacomb to the shrine of Hippolytus can stand synecdochically for the whole pilgrimage he takes from his native Spain to Rome and back again, his purpose successfully accom-

57. Claudian, *Rapt.*, 1.177.

58. It is relevant here that the word *hiatus,* which is regularly used of a cleft in the earth or entrance to a cave, frequently refers to the entrance to the underworld (*ThLL* 6.2682.40–46). It is also used metaphorically of *mors,* understood as a monster with gaping mouth (*ThLL* 6.2683.78–82); for example, from a Christian inscription: *mors quae perpetuo cunctos absorbet hiatu* (*ILCV* 173.1). For Hippolytus' catacomb as an underworld, see also Malamud, *Poetics of Transformation,* 106–8. Malamud also (104–6) compares the catacomb to a labyrinth.

plished. It is "to Hippolytus he owes this" (181). But it also has a larger soteriological connotation as a victory over the dark forces of the devil and Hell, which threaten the spiritual well-being of the individual Christian. In passing through Hippolytus' underground burial chamber Prudentius enacts in miniature the life of individual Christians as they pass through the darkness of this world, a world that is as death, to be rewarded at the end of their journey with a brilliant vision of light, a presentiment of their celestial reward. The poet's experience has something of the nature of rites of passage, rites that are often represented in tribal societies as a form of death.[59] It takes place on the boundary between city and countryside, "not far from the outer rampart by the cultivated land of the pomerium" (153), and involves crossing over the threshold (cf. *limina vestibuli,* 158) between upper and lower worlds, light and dark, and implicitly life and death. Not that the pilgrim decisively passes from one realm to the other. Rather, he remains "betwixt and between," in an existence where light and dark mysteriously coexist. The experience is one of initiation as a citizen of the heavenly city of God.

Up to this point the emphasis has been on the individual experience of the devotee, who is identified with the poet. This section ends with verses 177–82, the last occasion on which the poet speaks in the first person of his own experience until he addresses Valerian at the end of the poem. Despite the special contribution of the scene in Hippolytus' catacomb and the fact that worshipper and narrator of the martyrdom are the same person in *Pe.* 11, the poem up to this point follows in broad terms the sequence of *Pe.* 9. This is underlined by the echo of the ending of that poem; Prudentius attributes his happy return to his native land and the fact that he is writing the poem to the patronage of the saint, in this case Hippolytus (11.179–80; cf. 9.105–6). The rest of the poem then transfers attention from the individual and private to the communal and public and from relatively modest monuments to the saint—an inscription or painting in an underground shrine—to the large-scale architectural edifice.

When the description of Hippolytus' below-ground *aedicula* is picked

59. Victor Turner, *Process, Performance and Pilgrimage: A Study in Comparative Symbology,* Ranchi Anthropology Series 1 (Delhi, 1979), 125 (speaking of pilgrimage), "Ordinary, mundane life may be reinterpreted as the Terrene City; its abandonment as a first glimpse of the Heavenly City. The move into liminality is here, therefore, a death-birth or a birth-death." See also 128, "One might also see pilgrimage partly as a rehearsal of the pilgrim's own death."

up again after the interruption of 171–82, the change is already evident. Now Prudentius emphasizes the celestial glory of the shrine, in its visible earthly manifestation, the silver plaques (184) and Parian marble (187) that adorn it. Worshippers throng to the saint's tomb all day and every day (*mane . . . solis adusque obitum,* 189–90), religious devotion (*religionis amor,* 192) uniting Latin with pilgrim from more distant parts (*conglobat in cuneum Latios simul ac peregrinos / permixtim populos*). Although some of the elements of the standard syntax of devotion are present—kissing the shrine and weeping (193–94)—the whole is a far cry from the private experience of Prudentius at the tomb of Cassian or the ambiguous emotional state of the traveller through Hippolytus' catacomb. Here the regal splendor of the tomb is emphasized: kisses are pressed on shining metal plates (*oscula . . . inpressa metallo,* 193), i.e., the silver already referred to, and expensive balsam is poured as an offering (194). Such is the popularity of Hippolytus' shrine that ordinary days during the year take on the properties of the annual festival, with a promiscuous throng of native and foreign worshippers and the celebration of the saint in majesty.[60]

When Prudentius describes the annual celebration of Hippolytus' *dies natalis* (195–96), he strikes the same note as in his account of everyday devotion, but greatly intensified. A series of phrases draws attention to the sheer number of participants;[61] the crowd includes not only those from the city, but also Latins from Alba and worshippers from other regions and towns of Italy (199, 203–8). Hippolytus' festival unites the high and low in social rank (patrician and plebeian, 200–202), it attracts young children and their parents (209–10). The festival becomes an expression of *communitas,* in the sense in which Victor Turner uses this word,[62] a temporary release from the hierarchical and structural divisions of society in the experience of shared rejoicing. If the poet's journey through the catacomb to the martyr's shrine confers a sense of personal salvation, a change of individual status, participation in a saint's annual festival affirms the individual's membership in a single, undifferentiated Christian community. The distinction between the two experiences corresponds to the anthropological distinction between life-crisis rites and

60. Paulinus, *C.* 27.25–39 and 107–18, compares Felix of Nola's feast day with the devotion offered to him at other times of the year.

61. *Quanta putas . . . agmina* (197), *densa cohors* (212), *tantis . . . catervis* (213), *tanta frequentia* (215), *laborantes . . . undas* (227); cf. *conglobat in cuneum* (191).

62. Victor Turner, *The Ritual Process: Structure and Anti-Structure* (Chicago, 1969), 96–97, *Process, Performance and Pilgrimage,* 149–54.

seasonal or calendrical rites. The former occur at moments of transition and often "concern entry into a higher achieved status. . . . There is a tendency for them to be performed more frequently by individuals." The latter "almost always refer to large groups and quite often embrace whole societies," and as the name implies occur at fixed times during the year.[63] In Prudentius' poem the two rituals are complementary; the first confers or confirms the status of citizen of the Christian *civitas*; the second enacts the solidarity of the individual worshipper with the wider Christian community. Although Prudentius speaks in the first person of the catacomb of Hippolytus, his description of the saint's annual festival speaks only of groups and serried ranks.

The joyful community of celebrants packs tightly the wide plain upon which they are gathered (211–12). Unable, because of their numbers, to enter Hippolytus' underground shrine, they throng into a nearby basilica large enough to accommodate the crowds (213–16). As with the earlier description of the rich features of the *aedicula* of the saint, the poet once again emphasizes material splendor as an expression of divine majesty. The basilica is "distinguished by its regal decoration" (*cultu nobile regifico,* 216), "powerful in its proud majesty and enriched by offerings" (*superba / maiestate potens muneribusque opulens,* 217–18). As the last in a series of monuments to Hippolytus described in the poem, this splendid church, like its more humble predecessors, challenges the reader to elicit a message from its architectural and ornamental detail. The account is dominated by the language of height; it a lofty building with towering walls (*parietibus celsum sublimibus,* 217). The central nave with its soaring height overtops the lower side aisles.

> At medios aperit tractus via latior alti
>   culminis exsurgens editiore apice.
>
> (223–24)

> [A wider path extends along the intervening nave, soaring upwards with the pinnacle of its lofty roof elevated above the side aisles.]

As the worshippers progress along the central nave they see before them (*fronte sub adversa,* 225) the tribunal, raised on steps (*gradibus sublime tribunal / tollitur,* 225–26), whence the priest proclaims God (*antistes*

63. I quote here Turner, *Ritual Process,* 168–69.

praedicat unde deum, 226). If the traveller's journey into the catacomb of Hippolytus is a *descensus ad inferos,* the progression along the nave of the basilica is an *ascensus ad caelum,* with the soaring architecture, costly materials, and brilliant decoration evoking the celestial, and with the priest's elevation in the apse on his *sublime tribunal* replicating in the here and now that other heavenly tribunal. The central aisle of the church is a broad path for the worshipper's gaze to travel along, a path that leads to heaven.

This is the final journey of the poem. Initially the worshipper has followed the path of personal devotion and pursued the need for private reassurance. But at the last this has given way to and been absorbed in the intimations of celestial community evoked by celebration of the saint's annual festival in his splendid basilica. The building opens its arms to enfold its foster-children in a maternal embrace (*maternum pandens gremium quo condat alumnos,* 229). As we noticed in chapter 1, very similar language is used of the patron saint's relationship to the cities under his protection (e.g., 2.569–72). The company assembled in the basilica for the saint's festival embodies the new Christian *civitas,* brought together from various cities and stations in life, united by their common devotion to the saint, in whose presence they find themselves before a splendid heavenly tribunal. Some hierarchical division is now reintroduced into their number, most obviously in the status of the priest, the representative of God, on his high tribunal, but it also is suggested by the lower elevation of the side aisles in comparison with the central nave.[64] Yet if hierarchy is reintroduced into the Christian community with contemplation of the regal majesty of God, the organization of Christian society depends for its stability upon the sense of *communitas* that the celebrants of the saint's festival have experienced.

Prudentius' poem to Hippolytus has something of the nature of a charter for the Christian *civitas,* viewed vertically as hierarchically organized under God, but more particularly horizontally, as an undifferentiated community that transcends conventional social divisions of rank or geographical boundaries (city : country; Latin : non-Latin) and is conceived of as one with the martyr in an all-enveloping mutual embrace.

64. The use of side aisles in late antique basilicas to accommodate members of the congregation of distinct status has often been suggested; see Pasquale Testini, *Archeologia cristiana: Nozioni generali dalle origini alla fine del sec. VI,* 2d ed. (Bari, 1980), 598–99. For the role of sacred space in delineating distinctions of status, see Jonathan Z. Smith, *To Take Place: Toward Theory in Ritual* (Chicago, 1987), 47–73.

Lurking behind the final section of the poem, where this vision of the Christian community receives its fullest expression, is a text from the second book of Virgil's *Georgics* describing the happy life of the Italian farmer, as compared with the city-dweller who is compelled to dance attendance on his social superiors and contemplate the finery of their homes and possessions.

> O fortunatos nimium . . . / agricolas! . . .
> si non ingentem foribus domus alta superbis
> mane salutantum totis vomit aedibus undam,
> nec varios inhiant pulchra testudine postis
> inlusasque auro vestis Ephyreiaque aera.
>
> (*G.* 2.458–59, 461–64)

> [Oh, happy farmers, . . . if a lofty mansion does not pour forth from its haughty doorways a tide of morning well-wishers from every hall, and they do not gaze in wonder at a doorpost picked out with fine tortoiseshell, fabrics embroidered with gold or Corinthian bronzes.]

Prudentius twice incorporates reminiscences of this passage into his account of veneration at Hippolytus' shrine:

> *Mane salutatum* concurritur; omnis adorat
> pubis, eunt, redeunt solis adusque obitum.
>
> (*Pe.* 11.189–90)

> [There is a rush to pay respects in the morning; the whole populace offers veneration, tracing and retracing their steps till the setting of the sun.]

> Plena laborantes aegre *domus* accipit *undas*
> artaque confertis aestuat in *foribus.*
>
> (*Pe.* 11.227–28)

> [The house is full and can scarcely accommodate the surging tide of humanity; packed tight within its doors a seething mass occupies the space.]

Virgil disparages social obligations and discrepancies of wealth in first-century B.C. Rome. Prudentius in Christian Rome retains the Virgilian language and the attendant social forms, but they are now shorn of their negative implications because they are freed from their offensive association with distinctions of social status. The morning *salutatio* is now extended throughout the day; it is a voluntary activity undertaken by all the people (*omnis . . . / pubis,* 189–90), Roman and non-Roman. The *domus alta* now is not the proud mansion of the great, but a basilica; far from "vomiting forth" (*vomit*) a tide of humanity (*undam*—the metaphor is particularly distinctive) from its doors, it receives all, and is packed full with a surging tide of worshippers. The word *vomit,* glossed by *effundit,* is used earlier by Prudentius of the crowds pouring forth from the city of Rome to celebrate Hippolytus' festival: *Urbs augusta suos vomit effunditque Quirites,* "the venerable city spews out and pours forth its citizens" (199). Again Prudentius emphasizes that all leave the city together, regardless of social rank (200–202). The rituals of Roman social life are transferred from within the city to outside the walls, where a new community can be constituted that, though bearing a recognizable relationship to traditional patterns of Roman life, as Prudentius' language bears a recognizable relationship to that of Virgil, yet is animated by a new spirit of Christian community. In this new context material splendor, deprecated by Virgil as an offensive display of superior social status, is acceptable.[65] The architectural display of the Christian basilica is hospitable to all; not so the halls of the powerful magnate described by Virgil, which expel the humble well-wisher when the act of social obeisance has been performed. Prudentius does not contradict Virgil's low valuation of urban social forms. Instead, he describes a Christian *civitas* that by substituting *communitas* for social hierarchy achieves a transvaluation of the urban world Virgil presents.

Hippolytus is an appropriate martyr for such a poem because his legend involves the victory of unity over division and the transcendence of difference. Originally a schismatic, at the last he urges his followers to return to the orthodox faith (29–32), the faith of Peter and Paul. Though his body is torn into tiny fragments by unbroken horses, it can be restored

65. Schwen, *Vergil bei Prudentius,* 64–65, interestingly sees Dido's temple to Juno (*Aen.* 1.446–49) behind Prudentius' description of the Christian basilica (215–20); see especially *Aen.* 1.447, *donis opulentum,* and *Pe.* 11.218, *muneribusque opulens.* If so, it would be a case of contrast imitation; the legitimate use of rich materials in the service of the Christian God.

in its entirety (147–50), unlike the remains of the Hippolytus of mythology, of whom, according to Seneca (*Ph.* 1261), a part is never recovered. The later Hippolytus is a martyr of the city of Rome, whose passion takes place by the sea, but who is buried between city and harbor, outside the walls. His worship involves both a descent underground, into the catacomb, and an ascent to heaven, as experienced in the basilica where his annual festival is celebrated. In pursuing the traces of Hippolytus' martyrdom Christian pilgrims experience in their own persons something of that mystery of transcendence.

Pe. 12: A Model of Concordia

Pe. 12, on the apostles Peter and Paul, is the shortest of his pilgrimage poems and contains only brief accounts of the deaths of the two martyrs (11–20 Peter, 21–28 Paul). More space is devoted to buildings associated with the two saints: the baptistery, probably built by Pope Damasus,[66] at St. Peter's (31–44) and the new basilica of S. Paolo fuori le mura (45–56). The role of architectural description and the dramatic setting of the poem, the communal celebration of the saints' feast day, tie *Pe.* 12 to the preceding poem to Hippolytus, which also ends with a description of the saint's annual festival. However, *Pe.* 12 has in common with the Cassian poem that the bulk of the text is spoken by a secondary narrator, in this case in response to a question posed in the first two lines:

> Plus solito coeunt ad gaudia; dic, amice, quid sit;
>   Romam per omnem cursitant ovantque.
>
> (1–2)

> [The streets are more thronged than usual with celebrants; tell me why that is, my friend. All through Rome joyful crowds are on the move.]

66. Christine Smith, "Pope Damasus' Baptistery in St. Peter's Reconsidered," *RAC* 64 (1988): 257–86, argues that *Pe.* 12 describes a baptistery on the Janiculum and that the evidence is inconclusive for a baptistery built by Damasus at St. Peter's. I am unpersuaded. In Prudentius' martyr poetry *tumulus* (37) can refer only to Peter's tomb, not to a raised mound of earth as Smith maintains. Smith, in any case, exaggerates the difficulties of Prudentius' account.

Although the speaker of these lines is not unambiguously identified, there is every reason to believe he is identical with the speaker of *Pe.* 9 and 11, that is, with the poet or with the persona he adopts in the pilgrimage poems.[67] The instructions given to the questioner of lines 1 and 2 at the end of the poem to "return home and remember to celebrate the double saints' day" (*tu domum reversus / diem bifestum sic colas memento,* 65–66) are sufficiently like the ending of *Pe.* 9 (*domum revertor, Cassianum praedico,* 9.106) to make the association unavoidable.

The dialogue form given to the poem finds a parallel in some of the *Satires* of Horace: 2.4, for instance, which like *Pe.* 12 begins with a question, or 1.9. The latter also has in common with Prudentius' poem the importance of its setting in and around the city of Rome. The Christian poet's *ibimus ulterius qua fert via pontis Hadriani* (61—"we will walk on where the road leads over Hadrian's bridge") is a distant echo of *ibam forte via sacra* (*Sat.* 1.9.1—"I happened to be walking on the Sacred Way"). Both poems have probably been influenced by the mime in their use of dramatic setting and dialogue. Satire is one of the genres most closely related to that subliterary form. Moreover, religious festivals frequently provided the titles, and presumably the dramatic setting, for such compositions. We hear of a *Compitalia* and a *Saturnalia.*[68] Theocritus' *Idyll* 15, which is strongly influenced by mime and set at the festival of Adonis in Alexandria, gives an idea of the form such productions could take. Prudentius, too, is describing a religious festival. By casting his poem in the form of a dialogue with a recognizable urban setting, he adapts the pagan dramatic form, but he Christianizes it by giving it an unaccustomed elevation of tone and seriousness of content.

Like the first poem in the *Peristephanon, Pe.* 12 is devoted to a pair of martyrs. The Spanish martyrs who are the subject of *Pe.* 1 are treated as a virtually inseparable couple. They are without distinct features and are regularly associated together in undifferentiated plural forms; they act to all intents and purposes as a single entity.[69] Nothing could be more

67. We are not required to believe that the historical Prudentius was ignorant of the double saints' day before his trip to Rome.

68. Elaine Fantham, "Mime: The Missing Link in Roman Literary History," *CW* 82 (1989): 153–63, 156. For the influence of mime on the *Peristephanon,* see also n.28, above. Palmer, *Prudentius on the Martyrs,* 113–19, proposes Ovid's *Fasti* as a parallel to the question-answer format of *Pe.* 9 and 11.

69. The number two occurs only once in the poem apart from the first line, when the "faithful companionship" (*fida . . . sodalitas,* 53) and close affection of the "two brothers" (*duorum . . . fratrum,* 52) are referred to as they face death.

different from the situation of *Pe.* 12. Ten lines at the beginning of the poem are devoted to the pair of martyrs, balanced by ten lines at the end describing their joint festival. The bulk of the poem, however, describes separately the martyrdom of each apostle, Peter followed by Paul, and the religious edifices dedicated to each of them. The introductory and concluding sections emphasize the oneness of the two martyrs. The central sections, although treating the two figures symmetrically, differentiate them in manner and time of death and in the symbolic associations of the buildings that bear their names. The meaning of the poem depends on this interplay of separateness and identity. It is structured by the alternation of passsages that emphasize unity, the two in one theme,[70] with passages that distinguish the apostles in manner of death or place of cult.

It should come as no surprise that a poem dedicated to the festival of the apostles Peter and Paul, Rome's supreme martyrs, takes such a form. Augustine, in a sermon delivered before his African congregation, also emphasizes the theme of two in one: "One day for the passion of two apostles. But then these two were one" (*illi duo unum erant*).[71] The language finds a close analogy in *Pe.* 12: "A single day saw them both [*unus utrumque dies* . . . , 5] crowned with a proud death, though after the course of a full year."[72] In adopting, with Ambrose and Augustine against Damasus and Jerome, the version that the deaths of Peter and Paul took place a year apart, rather than on the same day of the same year, Prudentius gives more emphasis to the distinctness of the two martyrdoms than would be the case if they were represented as exactly coinciding.[73] The detail that the passions occurred on the same day, but one year apart, draws attention to the providential concord between historically distinct acts by insisting on the original duality from which unity is created. In this way a chronological principle, the calendar,

70. The most explicit formulation is *lux in duobus fervet una festis* (58), but see also 5–6.

71. The full quotation is: *Unus dies passionis duobus apostolis. Sed et illi duo unum erant; quanquam diversis diebus paterentur, unum erant* (*Serm.* 295. 7; *PL* 38.1352).

72. *Unus utrumque dies, pleno tamen innovatus anno, / vidit superba morte laureatum* (5–6).

73. For the various traditions about the date of the apostles' deaths, see Charles Pietri, *Roma Christiana: Recherches sur l'Église de Rome, son organisation, sa politique, son idéologie, de Miltade à Sixte III (331–440),* Bibliothèque des Écoles françaises d'Athènes et de Rome 224 (Rome, 1976), 2: 1540. I cannot be certain that Prudentius knew both versions represented in contemporary authors; the tradition he follows accords well with the thematic concerns of his poem.

unites separate events in the past. However, a feature of geography, the river Tiber, unites the shrines of the apostles spatially in the here and now. Their deaths are separated by "the course of a full year," their bones and memorials by the "holy Tiber."

> Dividit ossa duum Tybris sacer ex utraque ripa
>   inter sacrata dum fluit sepulcra.
>
> (29–30)

> [The holy Tiber divides the bones of the two on either bank, as it flows between their sacred tombs.]

The sacred geography of Christian Rome is represented in a schematic and symbolic form: the shrines of Peter and Paul hieratically arranged to the right and left of the Tiber (31, 45–46, 62).[74] The Tiber not only brings together the tombs of the saints geographically in the here and now; it is also the diachronic link with the past history of the passions.

> Scit Tiberina palus, quae flumine lambitur propinquo,
>   binis dicatum caespitem tropaeis,
> et crucis et gladii testis, quibus inrigans easdem
>   bis fluxit imber sanguinis per herbas.
>
> (7–10)

> [The Tiber marsh, washed by the nearby river, knows the earth was made sacred by a double trophy and is witness to cross and sword, by which a quickening shower of blood twice rained on the same grass.]

The river Tiber plays the role of authenticating witness to the martyrdom. Its marshes and meadows (*palus, caespitem, herbas*) have twice

---

74. Cf. Smith, "Pope Damasus' Baptistery," 278: "Spatially, the work receives its structure from the Tiber." The river Loire plays the same role at Tours, flowing between Martin's monastery at Marmoutier and his burial place: *fluvius testatur alumnus / mirandae virtutis opus, qui, moenibus urbis / iunctus, continuis adlambit saxa fluentis. / Hic medius cellam discriminat atque sepulchrum, / divisisque locis diffusum interserit aequor* (Paulinus of Périgueux, *Vita S. Martini* 6.71–75). For the Christian topography of Tours and the influence of Prudentius on this passage, see Luce Pietri, *La ville de Tours du IVe siècle au VIe siècle: Naissance d'une cité chrétienne,* Collection de l'École française de Rome (Paris, 1983), 429.

been watered by the blood of the apostles.[75] The main verb, *scit,* may be taken as a historical present, referring to the Tiber's past witnessing of the martyrdoms, but also as a genuine present. The Tiber continues to bear witness to the apostles' deaths. It is the line of transmission between past and present; rain still falls on its banks and vegetation still grows there (cf. *caespitem,* 46), recalling those "showers of blood" from the Neronian age. Prudentius' language is chosen to maintain the ambiguity between the past of the passion and the present of the reader. The word *tropaeis* (8) is often taken, following Lavarenne,[76] to refer by metonymy to the "triumphs" of the apostles, i.e., their historical martyrdoms. Certainly the word has this sense elsewhere in the *Peristephanon.* In that case the reader's mind would be taken back to the historical events of the reign of Nero. But the literal sense of *tropaeum* is "memorial to a victory." The memorial to a martyr's victory is the tomb, memoria, or other shrine where his remains are venerated, or by metonymy the relics themselves. Both senses of *tropaeum* are attested in Christian authors. It is difficult to believe that in choosing this word Prudentius did not intend to exploit this polysemy, especially as the earliest written evidence for the veneration of the apostles in Rome, the words of the early third-century priest Gaius (preserved in Eusebius, *H.E.* 2.25.7), calls the commemorative structures erected to the martyrs *tropaea.*[77] The word is appropriate to the succession of monuments built to honor the apostles in the city of their martyrdoms, up to and including the splendid basilicas of the poet's own day, which incorporated in a central location the earlier *tropaea.*

The careful symmetrical treatment of the apostles in Prudentius' poem and the emphasis on their harmonious accord in death and in cult reflect the propaganda of the Roman church in the second half of the fourth century. In iconography, homiletic, and the church calendar the two

75. The phrase *Tiberina palus* is especially appropriate to the site of S. Paolo fuori le mura, which, according to Richard Krautheimer, *Corpus Basilicarum Christianarum Romae: The Early Christian Basilicas of Rome (IV-IX Cent.)* (Vatican City, 1937–77), 5: 111, was subject to periodic flooding since antiquity. Some fourth-century sarcophagi depicting the beheading of Paul show reeds to indicate the place of execution (Pietri, *Roma Christiana,* 2: 1552).

76. Lavarenne, in his edition, 229; so too Christian Mohrmann, "À propos de deux mots controversés de la latinité chrétienne: *tropaeum-nomen,*" *VChr* 8 (1954): 158-61 (= *Études sur le latin des chrétiens II. Latin chrétien et liturgique* [Rome, 1965], 336–38). For the further Christian senses of the word, see Blaise (1967), 831.

77. Jocelyn Toynbee and John Ward Perkins, *The Shrine of St. Peter and the Vatican Excavations* (London, 1956), 128–29 and 154–62.

apostles were associated as *fundatores Ecclesiae,* whose common martyrdom at Rome assured the unity of the Church and the preeminence of the city of their deaths. The feast on June 29 was, in Pietri's words, "a festival of *concordia.*"[78] Gold-glass vessels, produced for purchase by pilgrims or to be given as gifts, in this period regularly depict the apostles in *concordia,* with a crown between them symbolizing their common victory in martyrdom. The iconography is imperial in inspiration. The small figure of Christ that is sometimes shown placing wreaths on the apostles' heads would in imperial imagery be a winged Victory.[79] Prudentius' poem breathes the same spirit as these objects of decorative art. Peter and Paul, or the shrines that represent them, are symmetrically disposed on either side of a symbol of their triumphant martyrdom, the river Tiber, image of their *concordia.* The features of the apostles are increasingly differentiated on such gold-glass vessels as the fourth century proceeds, especially in the representation of their hair and beards.[80] In homiletic Peter and Paul stand for distinct but complementary ecclesiastical functions: in Prudentius' words "one is the summoner of the nations, the other occupies the seat of ecclesiastical primacy" (*alter vocator gentium / alter cathedram possidens, Pe.* 2.461–62). Concord does not eliminate difference but transcends it. Similarly, in *Pe.* 12 Prudentius differentiates between the two apostles and what they stand for, marshalling under their names a variety of aspects of Roman Christianity that are united by the overarching harmony of apostolic *concordia.*

The two sections devoted to separate treatments of Peter and Paul, descriptions of their martyrdoms (11–20, 21–28) and of the buildings dedicated to them (31–44, 45–54), are formally homologous. In both cases Peter precedes Paul and in both cases the Petrine passages are slightly longer (10:8 and 14:10). Descriptions of the splendid edifices devoted to the apostles recapitulate in a different register the more sober accounts of the passions. The earlier section (11–28) emphasizes the

78. Charles Pietri, "Concordia Apostolorum et Renovatio Urbis (Culte des martyrs et propagande pontificale)," *MEFR* 73 (1961): 293. This article is fundamental for the theme of *concordia apostolorum*; see also Pietri, *Roma Christiana,* 2: 1537–1626 and, especially for the iconography of *concordia,* J.M. Huskinson, *Concordia Apostolorum, Christian Propaganda at Rome in the Fourth and Fifth Centuries: A Study in Early Christian Iconography and Iconology,* BAR International Series 148 (Oxford, 1982).

79. See, for instance, Pietri, *Roma Christiana,* 2: fig. r, and Huskinson, *Concordia Apostolorum,* 53. For a "crowning Victory" in imperial coinage, see Pietri, "Concordia Apostolorum," 287–88.

80. Huskinson, *Concordia Apostolorum,* 54.

moral and historical,[81] the later (31–54) the triumphal and salvific aspects of the martyrdoms. I shall concentrate on the later descriptions of the apostles' shrines, which carry a particularly heavy charge of metaphorical significance.

Dextra Petrum regio tectis tenet aureis receptum
  canens oliva, murmurans fluento:
namque supercilio saxi liquor ortus excitavit
  frondem[82] perennem chrismatis feracem.
Nunc pretiosa ruit per marmora lubricatque clivum,
  donec virenti fluctuet colymbo;
interior tumuli pars est ubi lapsibus sonoris
  stagnum nivali volvitur profundo.
Omnicolor vitreas pictura superne tinguit undas;
  musci relucent et virescit aurum
cyaneusque latex umbram trahit inminentis ostri;
  credas moveri fluctibus lacunar.
Pastor oves alit ipse illic gelidi rigore fontis,
  videt sitire quas fluenta Christi.

(31–44)

[The region to the right holds Peter in its care and shelters him under gilded roofs; a region of white olive trees and a murmuring stream, for water issuing from the brow of a rock has brought forth perennial foliage rich in unction. Now the stream runs through costly marbles and waters the hillside before it surges into a green basin; in an inner part of the shrine the pool is agitated in its snowy depths from the sounding rush of water. A multicolored image dyes the glassy waters from above; the mossy basin glows brilliantly and the ceiling-gold turns green. The liquid, deep blue, takes on the darkness of the purple suspended above it; you might think the ceiling was disturbed by

81. For the moral content of the passage, see the emphasis on Peter's humility (19–20) and Nero's *furor* (23). I use the word historical in the exegetical sense of the literal level of the narrative and mean to imply nothing about the historicity of the events described.

82. Jacques Fontaine, "La pélerinage de Prudence à Saint-Pierre et la spiritualité des eaux vives," *Orpheus* 11 (1964): 249–50 (=*Études sur la poésie latine tardive d'Ausone à Prudence* [Paris, 1980], 469–70), argues persuasively for the reading *frondem* against the variant *fontem* adopted by Bergman, Lavarenne, and Cunningham.

waves. There the shepherd himself feeds the sheep that he sees are athirst for the streams of Christ with the icy chill of the spring.]

The first surprise in reading this passage is that Prudentius chooses to describe not the magnificent Constantinian basilica—rather it is the basilica of Paul that is described—but a baptistery and the channeling of water that made it possible, the work, we know from a pair of inscriptions (3 and 4 Ferrua), of Pope Damasus. There can be little doubt that Prudentius knew of the pope's hand in the building of the baptistery. *Pe.* 11 shows his interest in the epigraphical contribution of Damasus to the Christian monuments of Rome. The *pastor* of line 43 has, in fact, been identified as Damasus.[83] But the reference is intentionally indeterminate. *Pastor* is intended generically, not just of Damasus but of all occupants of the see of Rome. By choosing a baptistery as the symbol of Peter's presence in Rome, Prudentius is both in accord with contemporary exegesis and iconography, and draws attention to the continuity between Peter and his successors in the see of Rome. In baptizing their flocks—and in Rome baptism was an episcopal duty[84]—the bishops were fulfilling the type represented by their illustrious predecessor Peter, who was three times instructed by Jesus to "feed my sheep" (*pasce oves meas,* John. 21: 15–17; *pastor oves alit, Pe.* 12.43). Baptism represented the entry of the individual into full membership in the Christian community on earth; Peter controlled entry to the celestial kingdom (cf. Damasus, *Epigr.* 4.3). Finally, as Fontaine notes, Peter came to be identified with the iconography of baptism on fourth-century sarcophagi, on which a scene originally representing Moses striking water from the rock, a type of baptism, was adapted to portray an apocryphal episode from the life of the apostle.[85] A baptistery was a suitable symbol of the pastoral role first performed by Peter to which successive bishops of Rome were heirs. The ideology of the Roman church is succinctly formulated by Damasus: there was "a single seat of Peter, a single true baptism" (*una Petri sedes, unum verumque lavacrum, Epigr.* 4.5).

---

83. José Ruysschaert, "Prudence l'espagnol, poéte des deux basiliques romaines de S. Pierre et de S. Paul," *RAC* 42 (1968): 281–82. I follow here the traditional interpretation of Damasus, *Epigr.* 3 and 4. Smith, "Pope Damasus' Baptistery," 257–61 questions whether the epigrams must refer to a Vatican baptistery, in accordance with her thesis that *Pe.* 12 describes a building on the Janiculum.

84.. Pietri, *Roma Christiana,* 1: 584–85.

85. Fontaine, "Le pélerinage de Prudence," 263–64 (=*Études,* 483–84). See also Pietri, *Roma Christiana,* 1: 332–41, and Huskinson, *Concordia Apostolorum,* 129–40.

Prudentius' account of the arrangements made by Damasus for channeling water to his new baptistery does not repeat the language of the pope's inscription, though it evidently refers to the same engineering works. Instead, the passage is influenced by Virgil's description of the irrigation of crop-lands in the first book of the *Georgics*.

> [quid dicam . . . qui . . .]
> . . . cum exustus ager morientibus aestuat herbis,
> ecce supercilio clivosi tramitis undam
> elicit? illa cadens raucum per levia murmur
> saxa ciet, scatebrisque arentia temperat arva.
>
> (*G.* 1.107–110)

> [(What shall I say of him who) when the parched field swelters and the plants are dying, lo he ekes out water from the brow of a sloping watercourse? Falling over the smooth rocks it sets up a harsh drone and relieves the dryness of the fields with its rivulets.]

The parallels with Virgil in the last few lines of the Prudentius passage are cumulative in their effect. The most distinctive is the use by both authors of *supercilio* in a similar context at the same place in the line.[86] Other equivalences are *clivosi* (*G.* 1.108) and *clivum* (*Pe.* 12.35), *murmur* (109) and *murmurans* (32), *elicit* (109) and *excitavit* (33), *per levia . . . / saxa* (109–10) and *pretiosa . . . per marmora* (35), and, perhaps, *scatebris . . . temperat* (110) and *lubricat* (35). In this way Prudentius adds the language of irrigation to the pastoral image of verses 43–44. The evocation of Virgil ensures that Damasus' activity will be seen also in terms of the raising of crops: Rome sown and watered by episcopal teaching and the sacrament of baptism will bring forth a fertile harvest of Christian souls.

Prudentius' substitution of *pretiosa . . . per marmora* for the Virgilian *per levia . . . saxa* strikes a key note for the description of the decoration of the baptistery that follows (39–42); architectural decoration is confused with and a substitute for the natural world. For instance, in line

86. The passage is cited as an example of possible imitation by Albertus Mahoney, *Vergil in the Works of Prudentius,* Catholic University of America, Patristic Studies 39 (Washington, D.C., 1934), 178. Smith's discussion, "Pope Damasus' Baptistery," 263–65, misses the significance of Virgilian influence in this passage.

39 the word *vitreas,* "glassy," is used of transparent water, as is often the case. But the word in its literal sense is appropriate to the tesserae of wall or ceiling mosaics, which were made of colored glass.[87] Word order—*vitreas* situated between *omnicolor* and *pictura*—suggests that such a polychrome mosaic decorated the baptistery of St. Peter's. By choosing a word to describe the natural appearance of water that can also be used of architectural decoration, the poet blurs the relationship between the realms of nature and art and the distinction between ceiling above and font below. The language enacts the situation it describes, the reflection of the mosaic in the water.

In the next line the effect of a mirror image is carefully reflected in the chiastic word order, with the second half of the line sending back a reversed image of the first. Again nature and art are confused. The "moss" (*musci*) referred to is unlikely to be real vegetation. The reference is rather to the green color of the baptismal basin mentioned previously (36—this is incidentally evidence that the *colymbus* of 36 and *stagnum* of 38 are identical, a point that has been a subject of contention among scholars).[88] Although the *Thesaurus Linguae Latinae* cites no parallel for *muscus* in a figurative sense, the metaphor is an easy one. Already Statius speaks of green marble as grass.[89] Under or near water such marble would naturally be described as moss.

The final stage in the confusion of art and nature, upper and lower, is reached in verse 42. What here is the perspective of the viewer/reader, that is, of the person addressed in the indefinite second-person singular *credas*? Are we to imagine ourselves looking up and seeing the reflection of the waves on the ceiling making the ceiling appear to move, or looking down and seeing the waters rippling over the reflection of the ceiling? Ultimately, at least in the terms of the poem, the two are indistinguish-

87. The same point is made by Paul Künzle, "Bemerkungen zum Lob auf Sankt Peter und Sankt Paul von Prudentius (Peristeph. XII)," *RSCI* 11 (1957): 347–48. I cannot agree with him, however, that we are to imagine the mosaic as decorating the apse of St. Peter's.

88. For instance, Fontaine, "La pélerinage de Prudence," 250–52 (= *Études,* 470–72), who believes in the identity of the two, as opposed to Ruysschaert, "Prudence l'espagnol," 273–74. Paul-Albert Février, "Baptistères, martyrs et reliques," *RAC* 62 (1986): 130–33 argues that the baptistery was outside the Vatican and, therefore, denies any reference to it in *Interior tumuli pars est,* and following.

89. Statius, *Silv.* 2.2.91; cf. *Pe.* 3.198–200, and Roberts, *Jeweled Style,* 76. Smith, "Pope Damasus' Baptistery," 265, had been unable to explain the presence of literal moss in the baptistery.

able. The reader can no more make a determination on the basis of Prudentius' language than viewers in the baptistery can sort out the confused impressions that the visual images make on them.

Such disorientation and fragmentation of focus are characteristic of much late antique poetry.[90] By blurring the real dimensions of a historical scene or situation the poet can transcend the particularity of the here and now and accommodate the representation of eternal values or the description of a spiritual landscape. In the present case landscape and edifice coincide. Damasus' baptistery is a *locus amoenus,* with spring of chill water, stream, shade, and grove. The site of the passion, we recall, was grassy, and well watered by the rain of the martyrs' blood (9–10); it too is a spiritual landscape, irrigated by fructifying liquid, a landscape that is reproduced in the building of the new baptistery. As the Tiber-bank provided the location for the martyrdom, that is, for baptism by blood (cf. *Pe.* 8), so in the new baptistery it provides a setting for baptism by water, available to all those in Rome who "thirst for the streams of Christ," and one that evokes both the original location of the passion and the beauty of Paradise to which candidates for baptism aspire.[91] The first leader of the Christian community in Rome, Peter, watered the grass of the Tiber-bank with his blood; a subsequent bishop of Rome reenacted that founding legend of *Roma Christiana* by channeling water to a new "ideal landscape," a new *luxuries* of vegetation produced from that original fructifying shower, on the site of the apostle's tomb.

In the case of the apostle Paul, Prudentius describes the basilica itself, a recent imperial foundation.

> Parte alia titulum Pauli via servat Ostiensis,
> qua stringit amnis caespitem sinistrum.
> Regia pompa loci est, princeps bonus has sacravit arces
> lusitque magnis ambitum talentis.
> Bratteolas trabibus sublevit, ut omnis aurulenta
> lux esset intus ceu iubar sub ortu.
> Subdidit et Parias fulvis laquearibus columnas,
> distinguit illic quas quaternus ordo.

90. Roberts, *Jeweled Style,* 73–76.
91. See also Fontaine, "Le pélerinage de Prudence," 257–59 (= *Études,* 477–79).

Tunc camiros hyalo insigni varie cucurrit arcus:
sic prata vernis floribus renident.

(45–54)

[In another region the Ostian road keeps watch over the memorial of Paul, where the river skirts the land to its left. The splendor of the site is regal; a good prince made this palace holy and decorated its structure at great expense. He coated beams with gold leaf, so that all the light in the interior was golden, like the blaze of the sun at dawn. He rested the burnished paneled ceiling on columns of Parian marble, arranged there in four rows. Then he spanned it with curving arches of brilliant multicolored glass, like meadows bright with springtime flowers.]

Again landscape and architectural decoration are merged. The mosaic, probably on the triumphal arch or apse of S. Paolo, is likened to a "meadow bright with springtime flowers";[92] the land (*caespes,* 46) on which the basilica is situated is identical with that (*caespes,* 8) made holy by the double *tropaea.* The geography of the passion is transfigured in the new foundation, but in such a way as to intensify the triumphal and celestial associations of the original event.

The phrase, *regia pompa loci est,* a variation on the formula for introducing ecphrases, *est locus,* gives prominence to the key themes of his description: the elaborate splendor of the basilica, and its appropriateness to or association with the regal. In the first instance the *rex* in question is likely to be identified as the *rex caelestis,* i.e., God. The magnificence of the basilica is appropriate to the divine majesty. Only as the reader reads on will the reference to the imperial patron of the basilica, the emperor Honorius, emerge.[93] Even the phrase *princeps bonus*

92. For this language, see Roberts, *Jeweled Style,* 51–52 and 75–76. Krautheimer, *Corpus Basilicarum,* 5: 162 believes the mosaic was probably on the triumphal arch or apse.

93. The identity of the *bonus princeps* is controversial. Construction was begun under Theodosius and completed under Honorius. Jill Harries, "Prudentius and Theodosius," *Latomus* 43 (1984): 72–73, among others, argues for Theodosius, and puts special weight on the meaning of the verb *sacravit,* "dedicated," which could only properly be used of that emperor. I have some doubt, however, whether Prudentius intends to be precise in his language here; the phrase *has sacravit arces* is in all probability explained by the following line (*lusitque magnis ambitum talentis*) in a manner characteristic of Latin poetry. For those reasons I follow Pietri, *Roma Christiana,* 1: 516–17, and Krautheimer, *Corpus Basilicarum,* 5: 98, in identifying the *princeps* as Honorius. I think it is likely that Pru-

is ambiguous, since Prudentius elsewhere uses the word *princeps* of God (e.g., *caelestis solii . . . principem, C.* 5.34). It is not until the second line of the couplet, with the greater specificity of the actions attributed to the *bonus princeps,* that the human ruler is clearly characterized. In associating divine and imperial majesty in this way, Prudentius is not only reflecting the historical role played by the Theodosian dynasty in the foundation of S. Paolo, but also giving verbal expression to a tendency long familiar to art historians of the fourth century for Christian architecture, iconography, and ceremony to appropriate forms that had evolved to celebrate the emperor. In comparing the brilliance of the basilica to the "the blaze of the sun at dawn" (*ceu iubar sub ortu,* 50) Prudentius again describes a splendor appropriate to the imperial and the divine.[94] The two apostles occupy an intermediate position in the divine and human hierarchy; they too are called *principes* by Prudentius, "who now reign here in Rome" (*hic nempe iam regnant duo / apostolorum principes,* 2.459–60).[95]

The basilica of S. Paolo is the work of one *princeps* to honor another, and through him to celebrate the supreme *princeps,* God. Is there, however, any particular reason for associating the emperor specifically with Paul, beyond the historical fact of the Theodosian dynasty's involvement in the building of the church dedicated to that apostle in Rome? Probably so. In the *Contra Symmachum* the emperor Theodosius is called "the master governing the scepter" (*magistro/ sceptra gubernanti, C. Symm.* 1.38–9). Prudentius does not have in mind here the technical sense of the word *magister* in the imperial administration of the late empire.[96]

dentius saw an inscription identical or similar to the first two lines of that set up after 440 on the triumphal arch by Galla Placidia: *Theodosius coepit, perfecit Honorius aulam / doctoris mundi sacratam corpore Pauli* (see Krautheimer). The phrase *bonus princeps* has a certain studied ambiguity, but its primary reference is to the reigning emperor, Honorius. (Danuta Shanzer, "The Date and Composition of Prudentius' *Contra Orationem Symmachi Libri,*" *RFIC* 117 [1989]: 461, n.1, argues for an Honorian date for the poem, but believes the *bonus princeps* would still be identified as Theodosius.)

94. Compare Claudian, *Ruf.* 2.144, *fratris regale iubar* (of Honorius) and Prudentius' description of the Nativity of Christ, *procedit et lux aurea* (*C.* 11.60).

95. See also Jerome (*In Ps.* 86.6 [*CCL* 78; 116.203–4]), who calls the apostles *principes Ecclesiae* and *principes Christi* (Pietri, *Roma Christiana,* 2: 463–66; Jacques Fontaine, "La figure du prince dans la poésie latine chretienne de Lactance à Prudence," in *La poesia tardoantica: Tra retorica, teologia, e politica,* Atti del V Corso della Scuola superiore di archeologia e civiltà medievali . . . , Erice 6–12 dicembre 1981 [Messina, 984], 119–20 and 130–32). The Prudentius passage quoted in the text is Lawrence's prophecy of conditions during the reign of Theodosius.

96. See Fontaine, "La figure du prince," 129. For the role of the emperor in the *Contra*

Rather, the role of the emperor in promoting Christianity in the Roman world makes him a secular equivalent of the *magister gentium,* Paul, and a positive antitype of the *tyrannus* Nero, who had persecuted the apostles (*Pe.* 12.11, 23). Earlier in the *Contra Symmachum,* Theodosius is described as the *moderator . . . orbis* (*C. Symm.* 1.9). Paul first brought the Christian message to the world of the Roman empire, and in so doing "subdued the fierce hearts of the nations [*gentium*] with his holy pen" (*C. Symm.* 1 pr. 1–2).[97] That world now finds itself united under the government of a Christian prince, master (*magister*) and protector of his people, a new, secular *magister gentium.*

The emperor, then, plays a providential role in Christian history as in some sense the successor of the apostle Paul. The basilica of S. Paolo is the visible expression of this relationship. Just as the two apostles are in *concordia* in fourth-century iconography, so baptistery and basilica are in *concordia* in Prudentius' poem. The former is the realm of Rome's *pastor,* where he sees to the spiritual welfare of his flock; it was also built by a bishop of Rome, though this never becomes explicit in Prudentius' poem. The latter is an imperial foundation and embodies the magnificence associated with the emperor's person. Together the two communicate an ideal concord between spiritual and secular powers, a concord that is prefigured by the harmony of the apostles at their martyrdom. The religious architecture of Rome, in Prudentius' description, becomes a model of the institutional foundations of the Christian Roman Empire.

The reader moves from the baptistery of St. Peter's to the basilica of St. Paul's. The sequence Peter to Paul is that followed by the bishop for the celebration of the saints' day (63–64), as it is by the pilgrim in Prudentius' poem.[98] But the sequence also reflects that followed by all candidates for baptism from the baptismal font to the altar. In an inscription that was intended to be set up in Sulpicius Severus' foundation at Primuliacum and that describes the relationship between double basilica and baptistery, Paulinus of Nola includes the following lines.

Symmachum, see also Remo Cacitti, "*Subdita Christo servit Roma Deo*: Osservazioni sulla teologia politica di Prudenzio," *Aevum* 46 (1972): 431–35.

97. *Paulus, praeco Dei, qui fera gentium / primus corda sacro perdomuit stilo.* Prudentius here intentionally describes Paul's teaching activities in language that evokes the military exploits of Rome's armies, generals, and emperors.

98. Unlike Smith, "Pope Damasus' Baptistery," 279–81, I do not believe that Prudentius' poem requires that baptisms were conducted at the feast of the apostles—he is describing the experience of all celebrants of the festival (*plebs Romula,* 57)—though, if that were the case, the poem would gain extra point.

Inde parens sacro ducit de fonte sacerdos
infantes niveos corpore, corde, habitu,
circumdansque rudes festis altaribus agnos
cruda salutiferis inbuit ora cibis.

(*Ep.* 32.5)

[Then their parent and priest leads the children snowy in body, heart, and dress from the holy font, and bringing the young lambs round the joyful altar gives their inexperienced mouths a taste of the food that brings salvation.[99]]

The progression from baptistery to basilica in Prudentius' poem traces the same course as was followed by a candidate for baptism at Primuliacum. The mosaic Prudentius describes in S. Paolo would either be on the triumphal arch leading into the transept where the altar was situated above the tomb of the apostle, or in the apse behind the altar, where it would provide a magnificent backdrop. In either case it furnished a visually impressive context for receiving the sacrament. The decoration of baptistery and basilica provides a foretaste of the joy to come for the newly baptised. The font and its surroundings evoke the ideal landscape of Paradise; the mosaic and its setting, with its affinities to the splendor of imperial reception halls, call up the transcendental radiance of the heavenly kingdom. Prudentius could preface this section of his poem with the words of Paulinus of Nola, set up above an entrance to his new basilica: "from here the deserving may pass to holy Paradise" (*unde sacrum meritis datur exitus in paradisum, Ep.* 32.12). Both poets share the sense that Christian architecture, its setting, and decoration can replicate the path to heaven.[100] Finally, baptism can also be represented as a *descensus ad inferos,* and a contest with the devil, from which the newly baptized emerge triumphant.[101] There is, then, a parallel with the

99. Ambrose, *Myst.* 8.43 (*CSEL* 73.107.1–2), *his abluta plebs dives insignibus* [i.e., white garments] *ad Christi contendit altaria,* describes the same ceremony in more straightforward language.

100. So Paulinus' poem begins **caelestes intrate vias** *per amoena virecta.* In Paulinus' case it is a natural setting—this entrance to the basilica must be approached through a garden—that provokes intimations of Paradise.

101. Rom. 6:3–4; Josef A. Jungmann, *The Early Liturgy to the Time of Gregory the Great,* trans. Francis A. Brunner (Notre Dame, 1959), 95 and 259. Baptism involved a triple immersion, corresponding to Christ's three days in the tomb (Geir Hellemo, *Adventus Domini: Eschatological Thought in 4th-Century Apses and Catecheses,* Vigiliae Christianae, suppl. 5 [Leiden, 1989], 182–83).

descensus—ascensus sequence of *Pe.* 11 in the baptistery-basilica arrangement of *Pe.* 12. The *descensus* theme, however, is transfigured by being situated in the institutional structure of the Roman church and represented from the point of view of a more detached observer than the devotee of *Pe.* 11.

Prudentius' text celebrates the experience of salvation available in the Church to Rome's devout. That Church is seen as the continuing expression of apostolic *concordia,* in which ecclesiastical and secular powers cooperate for the welfare of the community in this world and the next. *Concordia* is celebrated in the religious calendar on the feast day of June 29. Prudentius finds a further sign of *concordia* in the sacred geography of Christian Rome: the memorials to the two apostles, founded on opposite banks of the Tiber. The subject of *Roma Christiana* is especially dear to Prudentius. In the *Contra Symmachum* and *Pe.* 2 his Roman patriotism is strongly voiced. In *Pe.* 12 the ideology of Christian Rome finds particularly concentrated expression in the symbolic language of *concordia* and the descriptions of the apostles' festival and *memoriae,* embodiments of *concordia* in time and space.

The concept of *concordia* had long had political significance in Roman imperial propaganda. It represented the ideal harmony of the Roman Empire, a harmony that found its guarantee in the figure of the emperor and, when there was more than one such emperor, in their *concordia.* Its use as a catchword for the political system of the empire and its close association with the ideology and iconography of *urbs Roma* goes back to the second century. In Prudentius' own day coins were minted with the seated female figure of Rome and the legend *Concordia Augg.* (or *Auggg.*) on the reverse.[102] Prudentius speaks this language of Roman imperial *concordia* in the second book of the *Contra Symmachum.*

Discordes linguis populos et dissona cultu
regna volens sociare deus, subiungier uni
imperio quidquid tractabile moribus esset
concordique iugo retinacula mollia ferre
constituit, quo corda hominum coniuncta teneret

102. In my discussion of imperial *concordia,* I follow Pietri, "Concordia Apostolorum," 284–85 and 290–95. For coins bearing the figure of Rome and the legend *Concordia Augg(g),* see Jocelyn M.C. Toynbee, "*Roma* and *Constantinopolis* in Late-Antique Art from 365 to Justin II," in George E. Mylonas, ed., *Studies Presented to David Moore Robinson on His Seventieth Birthday* (Saint Louis, 1951–53), 2: 261–62.

religionis amor; nec enim fit copula Christo
digna, nisi inplicitas societ mens unica gentes.
Sola deum novit concordia, sola benignum
rite colit tranquilla patrem.

(*C. Symm.* 2.586–94)

[God, wishing to unite peoples of discordant language and kingdoms of different practices, determined to join in a single empire all whose manners were governable and to have them bear gentle reins in a yoke of concord in order that the love of religion should hold human hearts in unity; for no bond is worthy of Christ unless a single spirit unites nations in common ties. Concord alone knows God, it alone properly worships in peace the kindly Father.]

From the Christian perspective of Prudentius, Roman imperial *concordia* is the providential creation of God and provides the necessary precondition for the spread of Christianity among the *gentes* (cf. *C. Symm.* 2.634–36). The establishment of the Roman empire can be seen in historical terms as part of a process leading to the conversion of the civilized world, which for Prudentius is coextensive with the empire. But it is also possible to view pre-Constantinian Rome as a negative antitype of *Roma Christiana.* The structure of the Roman imperial system and its secular ideology can be taken over in the new scheme of things, but to achieve the necessary moral transvaluation two changes are required: a Christian emperor, and a state-recognized Christian church to replace pagan religious ritual and festivals with its own organization of liturgies, feast days, and the ceremonial space of Rome. As we have seen, these complementary aspects of *Roma Christiana* are celebrated by Prudentius under the names of the two apostles. It is no accident that the two books of the *Contra Symmachum* are introduced by prefaces describing episodes from the lives of Paul and Peter, and that the teaching and missionary activities of the former are described in terms appropriate to a Roman emperor: "he subdued the fierce hearts of the nations [*fera gentium / . . . corda . . . perdomuit*] with his holy pen" (*C. Symm.* 1 pr. 1–2).

The slogan of *concordia apostolorum* not only expresses the ideal unanimity of the Christian church but also, in adopting the imperial ideology of *concordia,* its coextension with the Roman Empire. The apostles Peter and Paul are both, in the words of Gaudentius of Brescia, "the two lights of the world and founders of the Church," and because they suffered martyrdom in Rome and are therefore its citizens, the guarantors of that city's status as *caput mundi*: "they laid their bodies to rest in the citadel of that city that had won preeminence [*principatus*] over the whole world, so that Christ, as a demonstration of his power, could put the leaders of his kingdom [*regni sui principes*] where the world had its head of empire" (*caput imperii*).[103] In a hymn attributed to Ambrose that, though of doubtful authenticity, is certainly a witness to the cult of the apostles in the late fourth century, Rome is said to be founded on the blood of the apostles.[104] Then, in the writings of Pope Leo, the first explicit comparison is made between the apostles and the legendary founders of the city, Romulus and Remus: "these are your holy fathers and true shepherds who founded you in a much better way and with a much happier omen than those by whose effort the first foundations of these walls were established. For the one who gave his name to you founded you with a brother's murder."[105] Although Prudentius never spells out the parallels between Romulus and Remus and Peter and Paul, it is often thought that the prefaces to *Contra Symmachum,* dedicated to the two apostles, are intended to suggest that connection.[106] Certainly the stories of the martyrdoms of the apostles provide a Christian alternative to the legends of early Roman history. When Prudentius describes the "senate-house of Evander" (*Evandria curia*) rushing to the "apostolic fonts" (*apostolicos . . . fontes, C. Symm.*

103. The passages quoted are Gaudentius of Brescia, *Sermo* 20, *duo vero mundi lumina, columnae fidei, Ecclesia fundatores* (*PL* 20.995A); Damasus, *Epigr.* 20.6, *Roma suos potius meruit defendere cives,* which was set up in the Basilica Apostolorum; and Maximus of Turin, *Hom.* 68, *Illi ergo sunt beatissimi Petri et Paulus qui . . . sua corpora in illius orbis arce reconderent, quae totius orbis obtinuerat principatum; quatenus potentiam virtutis suae Christus ostendens, ubi mundus caput habebat imperii, ibi regni sui principes collocaret* (*PL* 57.396B). These and the following references are collected by Pietri, "Concordia Apostolorum," 310–22, and *Roma Christiana,* 2: 1554–67.

104. *Hinc Roma celsum verticem / devotionis extulit, /* **fundata tali sanguine** */ et vate tanto nobilis,* 12.21–24 (Bulst). Rome is also described as *electa gentium caput / sedes magistri gentium,* 31-32. The reference in this hymn to the apostles being celebrated on three roads (*trinis viis*), i.e., the Via Ostiensis, the Vatican, and the Via Appia, guarantees an early date for the hymn since devotion to the apostles on the Via Appia does not survive the fourth century (Pietri, *Roma Christiana,* 2: 1567).

105. Leo, *Serm.* 82.1, *Isti sunt sancti patres tui verique pastores qui te . . . multo melius multoque felicius condiderunt quam illi quorum studio prima moenium tuorum fundamenta locata sunt, ex quibus is qui tibi nomen dedit fraterna te caede foedavit* (*PL* 54.422C-D).

106. E.g., V. Buchheit, "Christliche Romideologie im Laurentiushymnus des Prudentius," in Peter Wirth, ed., *Polychronion: Festschrift Franz Dölger zum 75. Geburtstag* (Heidelberg, 1966), 133; François Paschoud, *Roma Aeterna: Études sur le patriotisme romain dans l'occident latin à l'époque des grandes invasions,* Bibliotheca Helvetica Romana 7 (Rome, 1967), 227–28; Cacitti, "*Subdita Christo,*" 423–24.

1.550), the opposition between legendary past and the new Christian Rome under the protection of the apostles is especially pointed.

One further aspect of the ideology of Rome is relevant to Prudentius' conception of *Roma Christiana,* that the city is the *patria* not just of native Romans but of the whole Roman world.[107] The pagan poet Rutilius Namatianus gives voice to this belief in his *De reditu suo,* which describes a journey he took in A.D. 417. (He is offering a prayer to Rome.)

> Fecisti patriam diversis gentibus unam;
>   profuit iniustis te dominante capi,
> dumque offers victis proprii consortia iuris,
>   urbem fecisti, quod prius orbis erat.
>
> (*Red.* 1.63–66)

> [You created one native land for separate nations; the unjust benefited from being subjected to your rule, and while you were bestowing on the conquered a share in your justice, you made what previously was a world a city.]

The ideology of Rome in the late imperial period was that the whole empire was a single *patria,* the whole world (*orbis*) one city (*urbs*).[108] Prudentius expresses the same belief in the *Contra Symmachum.*

> Vivitur omnigenis in partibus haud secus ac si
> cives congenitos concludat moenibus unis
> urbs patria atque omnes lare conciliemur avito.
>
> (*C. Symm.* 2.610–12)

> [We live in every region no differently than if we were fellow citizens of the same family and our city and native land enclosed us in a single circuit of walls and we all came together at a single ancestral hearth.]

In Prudentius' vision of the Roman polity, the inhabitants of the empire

---

107. For the evolution in the sense of the word *patria* under the empire, see Paschoud, *Roma Aeterna,* 165–67 and 228–29; Wilhelm Gernentz, *Laudes Romae,* (Rostock, 1918), 134–36, cites parallels in rhetorical *Laudes Romae.*

108. For earlier examples of this theme, see Ernst Doblhofer, *Rutilius Claudius Namatianus, De Reditu Suo sive Iter Gallicum* (Heidelberg, 1972–77), 2: 48–50, ad loc.

are one family sharing common religious rites and a single *urbs patria,* defined by its circuit of walls, which in the Christian scheme of things are the tombs of the martyrs.[109] Rome is not just one city among many, however preeminent. It can stand by synecdoche for the whole Christian Roman world, the *patria* writ large. And that *patria* is but an imperfect approximation of the *Roma caelestis* where, we learn in the hymn to Lawrence, the martyrs already occupy a lofty status (*Pe.* 2.553–60). Fontaine has written of the epigrams of Damasus that they provide a new "foundation history" and an "exemplary image . . . of a Christian ancient Rome."[110] The same could be said with all the more truth of Prudentius' poems to the martyrs of Rome, especially *Pe.* 11 and 12. Together they constitute a new founding legend of Christian Rome, one that has its origins in the past but continues in the present to be part of the experience of individual Christians as they celebrate the saints' feast days and move about the city. Beyond that, however, a celebration of Rome is a celebration of the entire Christian Roman world: the new earthly *patria.* Rome is the model of the larger order; *urbs* is *orbis.* Viewed in this light, the Roman poems fit into the larger purposes of the *Peristephanon,* to celebrate the *concordia* of the Christian west, united in the veneration of the martyrs. The new Christian festivals take over from pagan ceremony the role of "articulating a corporate civic and municipal consensus."[111] In his account of Roman topography, Prudentius conforms with the character of sacred space as "marked-off space, in which . . . everything, at least potentially, demands attention."[112] In *Pe.* 12 the poet marks off certain features of Christian Rome and in so doing makes them sacred. In moving between the sites, the bishop and his congregation enact a ritual that has value beyond the immediate and contingent, since marking off and mapping a self-contained space in this way creates an area for the performance of ritual and ceremony that transforms the temporal here and now into the realm of sacrally sanc-

109. E.g., Paulinus, *C.* 19.337–42.

110. Jacques Fontaine, "Damase, poète théodosien: L'imaginaire poétique des epigrammata," in *Saecularia Damasiana: Atti del Convegno internazionale per il XVI centenario della morte di Papa Damaso I,* Studi di antichità cristiana 39 (Vatican City, 1986), 143–44.

111. Robert Markus, *The End of Ancient Christianity* (Cambridge, 1990), 103 (cf. 108–9).

112. Jonathan Z. Smith, *To Take Place: Toward Theory in Ritual* (Chicago, 1987), 103–4.

tioned values and cultural order. Prudentius, in *Pe.* 11 and 12, is "building a 'Holy City' with words."[113]

113. I adapt here Smith's description of Eusebius (*To Take Place,* 79) as "building a 'Holy Land' with words." My account of sacred space depends on Smith, especially 47–56 and 103–17. Prudentius' poems on Hippolytus and Peter and Paul make the experience of pilgrimage between the holy sites in Rome available to worshippers in Spain, where the spatial sequence of a real journey can be transposed into the temporal progression of the liturgy (see Smith 94–95 and 114–17).

Conclusion: Sacred Space and Time and the Poetics of Martyrdom

In writing his poems on the martyrs Prudentius does not primarily try to provide differentiated, historically detailed accounts of the period of the persecutions. He writes as a devotee of the cult of the martyrs at the end of the fourth century. Martyr narratives can be reduced to a simple two-stage scheme, combat and victory, a scheme capable of multiple repetition within the longer narrative, as in *Pe.* 5. The themes of the disassociation of body and spirit and of the movement to heaven that inform all levels of the narrative are vital guarantees of the efficacy of the martyr's bodily remains after death, and indeed of the ability of all objects connected with the passion to communicate a martyr's posthumous power. In martyrdom, as at the tomb, a martyr brings together heaven and earth through subduing body to spirit. The basic martyr text can also accommodate apologetics, homiletics, or polemics in the spaces opened by its simple narrative framework; it can include passages of direct speech, or descriptions, such as Eulalia's nighttime journey or Agnes' vision. As with Eulalia and Agnes, the martyrs can be presented as models of devotion to virginity, a powerful force in the world of late fourth-century spirituality, or as models for contemporary Christians in the daily martyrdom of earthly existence. The martyrs triumphantly demonstrate, in their supreme conflict between body and soul, that temptations of the flesh and the world can be overcome.

In the representation of the cult of the martyrs, as opposed to the narratives of the passions, space and time play a central role. The tomb of a martyr exists in a sacred milieu, set apart from the constraints of the profane world. It is as though Prudentius has redrawn the map of the Roman world and reinterpreted the course of Roman history. The outlines may, at first sight, be recognizably the same, but the organization of space and time has changed radically. The Roman empire—in Prudentius' case the western empire—has become sacred space, demarcated by the *monumenta piorum,* the shrines of the martyrs.[1] Mircea Eliade, in writing about the role played by city walls in delineating sacred space, uses language readily applicable to the memorials of the martyrs: "they [the walls] were a magic defence, for they marked out from the midst of a 'chaotic' space, peopled with demons and phantoms . . . an enclosure, a place that was organized [and] made cosmic."[2] Martyrs' shrines were regularly compared with defensive works, walls, or towers. Their role of delimiting sacred space finds eloquent expression in *Pe.* 4, where Saragossa is protected by its eighteen martyrs.

> Omnibus portis sacer immolatus
> sanguis exclusit genus invidorum
> daemonum et nigras pepulit tenebras
>   urbe piata.
> Nullus umbrarum latet intus horror,
> pulsa nam pestis populum refugit;
> Christus in totis habitat plateis,
>   Christus ubique est.
>
> (4.65–72)

> [At every gate the holy blood, shed in sacrifice, has shut out the tribe of envious demons and driven black darkness from the sanctified city. No dread of shadows lurks within, for their curse is routed and shuns the inhabitants; Christ dwells in every street, Christ is everywhere.]

Sanctified and protected by the martyrs, their blood, bodily remains, and shrine—all metonymic equivalents in Prudentius—each city becomes an *urbs piata,* sacred space, the domain of Christ, a junction between heaven and earth. In Eliade's terms all sacred space, including cities and

1. Cf. Paulinus, *C.* 19.18–19 (quoted, Introduction, n.1). Prudentius' own catalog of martyrs at the beginning of *Pe.* 4 is restricted to the western empire. In *Pe.* 13.102–4 Cyprian's influence extends to Africa, Gaul, Britain, Italy, and Spain.

2. Mircea Eliade, *Patterns in Comparative Religion,* trans. Rosemary Sheed (New York, 1958; reprint, Cleveland, 1963), 371. See also Paul Wheatley, *The Pivot of the Four Quarters* (Chicago, 1971), 416–18, and for some criticisms of Eliade's theories, especially of their aspirations to universality, Jonathan Z. Smith, *To Take Place: Toward Theory in Ritual* (Chicago, 1987), 14–23.

sacred buildings, is transformed into a "centre." They all are believed to stand in the self-same place, for "transcendent space [is] quite different in nature from profane space, and allows of the existence of a multiplicity and even an infinity of 'centres'."[3] And the "centre" is defined as the place through which the Axis Mundi passes, i.e., the point of junction between heaven, earth, and hell.[4] (The relationship between martyr shrine and heaven is unproblematic; for its special proximity to the underworld we should think of the importance of the *descensus ad inferos* theme in the martyr narrative and Prudentius' treatment of the crypt of Hippolytus.) The common presence of a single city with every other city under the protection of the martyrs helps explain the equivalence of the liturgical acts with which *Pe.* 4 begins and ends. The latter is performed by a single city, Saragossa, while a whole series of western Roman cities participates in the ceremony with which the poem begins. But the division between one and many, as well as the difference between the here and now and the eschatological future, is abolished by their co-presence in sacred space. Geographically disparate locations unite in the omnipresence of Christ (*Pe.* 4.71–72). Nor is it a question of distinct constituent parts being united into a whole. Each is full and complete in itself.[5] The principle is formulated by Victricius of Rouen, speaking of martyrs' passions:

> Sanctorum autem passio imitatio Christi est, et Christus est Deus. Ergo non est in plenitudine inserenda divisio, sed in ipsa divisione quae oculis subiacet plenitudinis est veritas adoranda.
>
> (*De laude sanctorum* 9; *PL* 20. 452A)

> [The passion of the saints is an imitation of Christ and Christ is God. Therefore division must not be introduced into fullness (*plenitudine*), but in the division that is perceptible to our eyes the truth of fullness should be worshipped.]

3. Eliade, *Patterns,* 379.

4. Ibid., 375.

5. Compare Robert Markus' characterization of post-Constantinian Christianity, *The End of Ancient Christianity* (Cambridge, 1990), 137: "Christians experienced their Church both as a single community spanning heaven and earth, past and present, and as a multiplicity of communities, each in its own way mirroring the one Community which, collectively, they constituted. The universal intersected with the particular in their own, local, groups."

From the point of view of the eyes of the heart (*cordis oculi*) and spiritual reason (*ratio spiritalis*), "the whole can be in the part."[6] For Victricius, writing on the occasion of the translations of relics of North Italian and Eastern saints to Rouen, the application of this principle to a martyr's bodily remains is of primary concern: "It is clear that the complete bodily form [*perfectionem membrorum*] is present in relics, because of their shared spiritual consecration [*spiritali sacratione consortium*]. In relics nothing can be not full."[7] For the *Peristephanon* the spatial consequences of equating part and whole are of particular interest. Every city is complete unto itself. When Prudentius describes the cult of Hippolytus in Rome in *Pe.* 11, he provides a model for the cult of the saints independent of the terrestrial status of a particular city. Any city can hope to match Rome in the worship of a native saint because the sacral plenitude conferred on cities by their martyrs admits no distinctions of degree. At a higher level of terrestrial magnitude, the whole western Roman world, united in the cult and under the protection of the martyrs, can be represented as sacred space coextensive with an individual city. *Pe.* 12, with its exploration of *concordia* under the protection of the apostles, presents a model of this larger *unanimitas*.

Prudentius himself extends the principle of the plenitude of relics to the text of the passion, and therefore to his own poetic endeavor. Whether it is the small puncture marks on the body of Cassian, traces of blood on the wounds torn on Eulalia's flesh, the inscriptions set up by Damasus, paintings of a martyr's death, or any other martyr text or its equivalent, each contains the fullness of the passion and corresponds to the heavenly texts, the names of the martyrs inscribed in letters of gold. The principle that each part of a martyr narrative is the equivalent of the whole is maintained in the construction of the text, in which constituent units repeat the combat-victory pattern of the whole. I have called this a synecdochical method of composition. But Victricius' account of the relation between part and whole in the cult of the martyrs suggests some qualification of this description. At least from the point of view of *ratio spiritalis,* the distinction between part and whole cannot be maintained. Synecdoche, in this case, expresses differences of magnitude not of plenitude.

6. Victricius, *De laude sanctorum* 10: *ostendimus itaque in parte totum esse posse* (*PL* 20.452C).

7. Victricus, *De laude sanctorum* 10: *Claret igitur in reliquiis perfectionem membrorum esse, quia inest in spiritali sacratione consortium* (*PL* 20.452D), and 9, *in reliquiis nihil esse* [*clamamus*] *non plenum* (*PL* 20.451C).

Sacred space not only admits the coexistence of distinct places, but also the common presence of discrete historical events. In the act of personal devotion at a martyr's shrine or in the liturgical act of celebration of a saint's feast day "the time of the event that the ritual commemorates or reenacts [i.e., of the passion of the martyr] is made present, 're-presented' so to speak, however far back it may have been in ordinary reckoning."[8] Central to this reenactment is a representation of the original passion, whether visual or verbal, written or oral. Prudentius shares this sense that in the sacred place of a martyr's shrine and in the "text" of a martyr's passion that passion is made present. His account in the *Peristephanon* of a Roman world devoted to the cult of the martyrs sets western Christians in sacred space and sacred time, where they have access to the time of the historic passions and through that to the Passion of Christ. In this way, the *Peristephanon* complements the *Cathemerinon*. Both are concerned with the sacralization of time. The *Cathemerinon* circumscribes the daily round of Christian devotion and marks it off as sacred time. The *Peristephanon* plots a calendar of saints' days that supplements the routine of the *Cathemerinon,* which also includes hymns for the major celebrations of the liturgical year, and brings sacred time into the civic context of the Roman world.[9] In so doing, Prudentius repeats in a literary form the project of Pope Damasus. The oratories dedicated to the martyrs of Rome that Damasus set up in the catacombs surrounding the city, oratories that he provided with finely drawn commemorative inscriptions, marked off Rome as sacred space. By including the feast days of the martyrs in the civic calendar as a supplement to the major Christian festivals of Christmas, Lent, and Easter, the pope spiritualized the traditional Roman calendar and realigned the civic year in accordance with sacred time.[10]

8. Eliade, *Patterns,* 392.

9. Jean-Louis Charlet, "Prière et poésie: La sanctification du temps dans le *Cathemerinon* de Prudence," in *Le temps chrétien de la fin de l'antiquité au moyen âge, IIIe-XIIIe siècles,* Colloques internationaux du Centre National de la Recherche Scientifique 604 (Paris, 1984), 391–97. Charlet assigns hymns 7 and 8 to Lent (fasting and penitence) and 9 and 10 to Easter (death and resurrection). Hymns 10 and 11 are devoted to Christmas and Epiphany. Jacques Fontaine, "Prose et poésie: L'interference des genres et des styles dans la création littéraire d'Ambroise de Milan," in G. Lazzati, ed., *Ambrosius Episcopus: Atti del Congresso internazionale di studi ambrosiani . . .,* Milano 2–7 dicembre 1974 (Milan, 1976), 1: 135 n.2, observes a similar pattern in the hymns of Ambrose. Hymns 1–4 (Bulst) are devoted to the hours of the day, 5, 7, and 9, to the major Christian festivals, and 6, 8, and 10–14 to the martyrs.

10. Charles Pietri, *Roma Christiana: Recherches sur l'Église de Rome, son organisation,*

In his representation of the cult of the martyrs in the *Peristephanon,* Prudentius reconceptualizes space and time. His poetic lexicon expresses new spatial and chronological concepts at the level of textual detail. We have frequently observed that metonymy and metaphor create uncertainty about the time and place of an action and suggest that events occur, for instance, simultaneously on earth and in heaven or in the past of the martyrdom and in the here and now. Heaven, when described in architectural terms, is assimilated to the earthly basilica; the raised seat or platform present at the martyr's examination, in the Christian basilica and in heaven at the Last Judgment, allows for lexical ambiguity and the productive collapse of temporal distinctions. Relations of similarity and analogy, for instance that between the earthly basilica and heaven, can be described as metaphors, but only if that concept is understood semiotically as a relationship between terms belonging to a common category of higher generality (hierarchical organization in space, perhaps) with no implications about the ontological relation between the terms.[11]

Polysemy is an important constituent of Prudentius' poetics of martyrdom. Language that can be understood at a variety of different levels is especially well suited to expressing the temporal and spatial indeterminacy associated with veneration of the martyrs. Attempts to impose a unitary meaning on Prudentius' Latin are likely to be misguided and run the risk of meeting an impasse. For example, Maurice Lavarenne, in his (brief) chapter on the stylistic faults of Prudentius cites the following passage from the *Peristephanon.*[12]

---

sa politique, son idéologie, de Miltiade à Sixte III (331–440), Bibliothèque des Écoles françaises d'Athènes et de Rome 224 (Rome, 1976) 1: 595–98, 603–5, 617–24.

11. For this definition of metaphor, see Umberto Eco, *Semiotics and the Philosophy of Language* (Bloomington, 1984), 87–129, especially 104–6. Christian Gnilka, "Die Natursymbolik in den Tagesliedern des Prudentius," in E. Dassmann and K. Suso Frank, edd., *Pietas: Festschrift für Bernhard Kötting, JbAC,* Erganzungsband 8 (Münster Westfalen, 1980), 413–46, criticizes the application of the terms metaphor and allegory to Prudentius' poetry, taking the specific case of nature symbolism in the *Cathemerinon.* In Gnilka's argument the natural world is rather a sign (*signum*) of spiritual reality, a sign that depends on an analogy created by God rather than on poetic invention, and to that degree it is not amenable to description in the language of poetic tropes. Eco's definition of metaphor, I hope, permits this objection to be circumvented. The basilica in the *Peristephanon* operates to some degree like nature symbolism in the *Cathemerinon* as a sign of the celestial realm, though it is often difficult in reading the *Peristephanon* to maintain the celestial : terrestrial opposition on which this account depends; categories become indistinguishably blurred.

12. Maurice Lavarenne, *Étude sur la langue du poète Prudence* (Paris, 1933), 552–53.

Subiecta nam sacrario
imamque ad aram condita
caelestis auram muneris
perfusa subter hauriunt.

(*Pe.* 5.517–20)

[Set in the shrine and buried beneath the altar [the bones] below are drenched and drink in the breath of heavenly bounty.]

The problem for Lavarenne is the meaning of the phrase *caelestis auram muneris.* He understands it of the Eucharist, celebrated on the altar above the saint's relics. The word *perfusa,* however, creates difficulties. Literally understood it means "drenched," and Lavarenne wonders whether Arevalo was right in understanding the phrase of perfumed oil offered by worshippers at the saint's tomb, which could be brought into contact with the remains through tubes specially inserted into the grave slab. The word *munus,* "gift" or "offering," is appropriate to the Eucharist, especially with the qualification *caeleste,* "heavenly," but it is also perfectly natural for the offerings of scented oil brought to the shrine by devotees.

Lavarenne's difficulties arise from an insistence that the passage in question must have a single, unitary meaning, that the two interpretations he gives cannot coexist. In fact, the situation is still more complicated than he allows. The *munus* can either be an offering made by worshippers to God or brought as a gift to the martyr's shrine, or a gift transmitted from heaven to earth in the Eucharist or to devotees of the martyrs through the intercession of the saints.[13] The ability of the saints to secure such bounty for their human devotees is central to their cult. From this point of view, too, their tombs are appropriately described as "saturated with the breath of heavenly bounty." Finally, the word *aura,* though it is not discussed by Lavarenne, contributes to the connotative density of the passage. Although naturally used of a scent wafted in the air, its original meaning is "a gentle breeze" and it is a standard constituent of descriptions of Paradise (cf. Gen. 3:8). The sweet scents that waft around Vincent's tomb evoke the blissful state of the martyr in heaven/Paradise; at the martyr's tomb/altar heaven and earth meet.[14]

13. For the Eucharistic use of *munus* of offerings made by the congregation or gifts transmitted from heaven by God, see Albert Blaise, *Le vocabulaire latin des principaux thèmes liturgiques* (Turnhout, 1966), 393–94 and 397–98.

14. The breezes and scents of Paradise, as described in the *locus amoenus* tradition, are frequently evoked in descriptions of martyr churches (e.g., *Pe.* 3.196–205 [cf. 10.361–63]; Paulinus, *C.* 27.403–5, *Ep.* 32.6; 281.5–7).

The passage, then, admits a variety of interpretations—more than Lavarenne acknowledges. Far from attempting to determine by philological methods a single correct meaning, the interpreter must respect the uncertainty Prudentius' language causes the reader. Such indeterminacy is not evidence of inadequate poetic facility, but rather a constitutive element of the poetics of the passage. In the terms of Stanley Fish's version of reader-response criticism, the reader's inability to determine a single unified sense in the text is the meaning of the passage, and should not be interpreted away.[15]

Such uncertainties are frequent in the *Peristephanon*. Many examples have been given in the course of this book. They frequently involve indeterminacies of time and place and communicate the sacral status of the martyr shrine. Readers of Prudentius often find themselves moving in a world where conventional semantic oppositions no longer apply and where differences we rely on to give meaning to the intelligible world are abolished in worship at a martyr's shrine. The uncertainties that readers feel in following the martyr text mirror those associated with the veneration of the martyrs and allow readers to experience through their reactions to the text the essential mysteries of the martyr cult. In the case quoted from *Pe.* 5, readers' uncertainty about the origin of "the breath of heavenly bounty"—whether it is transmitted from heaven to earth or from earth to heaven—is productive. In struggling with the passage readers are brought to appreciate in their own experiences the indistinguishability in the cult of the martyrs of heaven and earth and the close reciprocal relationship between martyr and worshipper.

Prudentius' martyr poems arise from a variety of different motives and serve a variety of purposes. Only in the address to Bishop Valerian at the end of *Pe.* 11, on Hippolytus, does Prudentius in his own person express a desire to promote the cult of the martyrs in Spain. But the collection as a whole, and the poems about Rome in particular, are certainly intended to serve as a model for the martyrs in the West. Although the poetic idiom Prudentius creates can be analyzed in terms of the lexical variation characteristic of pagan poetics, it is inspired by the changed realities and the new organization of experience in the cult of the martyrs. Prudentius forges a sacred poetics that involves the reader in the experience of worship at the martyrs' shrine or of the celebration

15. See, for instance, Stanley Fish, "Interpreting the *Variorum,*" *Critical Inquiry* 2 (1976): 465–70, reprinted in Jane P. Tompkins, ed., *Reader-Response Criticism: From Formalism to Post-Structuralism* (Baltimore, 1980), 164–69.

of their feast days, and that makes martyrs and their celestial home present in the here and now. The poems of the *Peristephanon* also, however, express the poet's own devotion. Whereas *Pe.* 11 ends with the promotion of the cult of Hippolytus in Prudentius' native Spain, the last lines of *Pe.* 9 represent that poem as a personal thank-offering for the consolation the poet received at the shrine of Cassian at Imola. The poems of the *Peristephanon* together give voice to Prudentius' Hispano-Roman Christian patriotism, a vision of the western Roman Empire united in veneration of the martyrs. They also, however, speak of and from the poet's own experience of the cult of the saints, and they thereby provide access for the reader to a central aspect of the spiritual experience and mental world of Christian late antiquity.

Bibliography

Amat, Jacqueline. *Songes et visions: L'au-delà dans la littérature latine tardive.* Paris, 1985.

Amore, Agostino. "Note su S. Ippolito martire." *RAC* 30 (1954): 63–97.

Barthes, Roland. "Introduction to the Structural Analysis of Narratives." In *Image—Music—Text,* trans. Stephen Heath, 79–124. London, 1977.

Bertonière, Gabriel. *The Cult Center of the Martyr Hippolytus on the Via Tiburtina.* BAR International Series 260. Oxford, 1985.

Blaise, Albert. *Le vocabulaire latin des principaux thèmes liturgiques.* Turnhout, [1966].

———. *Dictionnaire latin-français des auteurs chrétiens.* 2d ed. Turnhout, 1967.

Brown, Peter. *The Cult of the Saints: Its Rise and Function in Latin Christianity.* Haskell Lectures on History of Religions, n.s. 2. Chicago, 1981.

———. *The Body and Society: Men, Women, and Sexual Renunciation in Early Christianity.* New York, 1988.

Buchheit, V. "Christliche Romideologie im Laurentiushymnus des Prudentius." In *Polychronion: Festschrift Franz Dölger zum 75. Geburtstag,* ed. Peter Wirth, 121–44. Heidelberg, 1966.

Cacitti, Remo. "*Subdita Christo servit Roma Deo*: Osservazioni sulla teologia politica di Prudenzio." *Aevum* 46 (1972): 402–35.

Charlet, Jean-Louis. "L'apport de la poésie latine chrétienne à la mutation de l'épopée antique: Prudence précurseur de l'épopée médiévale." *BAGB* (1980): 207–17.

———. *L'influence d'Ausone sur la poésie de Prudence.* Aix-en-Provence, 1980.

———. *La création poétique dans le Cathemerinon de Prudence.* Paris, 1982.

———. "Prudence et la Bible." *RecAug* 18 (1983): 3–149.

———. "Prière et poésie: La sanctification du temps dans le *Cathemerinon* de Prudence." In *Le temps chrétien de la fin de l'antiquité au moyen âge, IIIe-XIIIe siècles,* Colloques internationaux du Centre National de la Recherche Scientifique 604, 391–97. Paris, 1984.

Costanza, Salvatore. "Rapporti letterari tra Paolino e Prudenzio." *Atti del Convegno, XXXI Cinquantenario della morte di S. Paolino di Nola (431–1981),* Nola 20–21 marzo 1982, 25–65. Rome, 1983.

Courcelle, Pierre. "Les pères de l'église devant les enfers virgiliens." *Archives d'histoire doctrinale et littéraire du moyen âge* 22 (1955): 5–74.

———. "Tradition platonicienne et traditions chrétiennes du corps-prison (*Phédon* 62b; *Cratyle* 400c)." *REL* 43 (1965): 406–43.

———. "*Mille Nocendi Artes* (Virgile, *Aen.*, VII, 338)." In *Mélanges de philosophie, de littérature et d'histoire ancienne offerts à Pierre Boyancé,* Collection de l'École française de Rome 22, 219–27. Rome, 1974.

Culler, Jonathan. *Structuralist Poetics: Structuralism, Linguistics, and the Study of Literature.* Ithaca, N.Y., 1975.

Cunningham, Maurice. "The Nature and Purpose of the *Peristephanon* of Prudentius." *Sacris Erudiri* 14 (1963): 40–45.

Curtius, Ernst Robert. *European Literature and the Latin Middle Ages.* Trans. Willard R. Trask. New York, 1953; reprint, New York, 1963.

Daniélou, Jean. *Sacramentum Futuri: Études sur les origines de la typologie biblique.* Paris, 1950.

Dassmann, Ernst. "Ambrosius und die Märtyrer." *JbAC* 18 (1975): 49–68.

Deléani-Nigoul, Simone. "Les *exempla* bibliques du martyre." In *Le monde latin antique et la Bible,* ed. Jacques Fontaine and Charles Pietri. Bible de tous les temps 2, 243–60. Paris, 1985.

———. "L'utilisation des modèles bibliques du martyre par les écrivains du IIIe siècle." In *Le monde latin antique et la Bible,* ed. Jacques Fontaine and Charles Pietri. Bible de tous les temps 2, 315–38. Paris, 1985.

Delehaye, Hippolyte. "Cyprien d'Antioche et Cyprien de Carthage." *AB* 39 (1921): 314–32.

———. *Les origines du culte des martyrs.* Subsidia Hagiographica 20. Brussels, 1933.

———. "Recherches sur le légendier romain." *AB* 51 (1933): 34–98.

———. *Les passions des martyrs et les genres littéraires.* Subsidia Hagiographica 13B. 2d ed. Brussels, 1966.

Doblhofer, Ernst. *Rutilius Claudius Namatianus, De Reditu Suo sive Iter Gallicum.* 2 vols. Heidelberg, 1972–77.

Doignon, Jean. "Perspectives ambrosiennes: SS. Gervais et Protais, génies de Milan." *REAug* 2 (1956): 313–34.

———. "'Procer', titre donné à Saint Martin dans une inscription Gallo-Romaine de Vienne." In *Saint Martin et son temps: Mémorial du XVIe centenaire des débuts du monachisme en Gaule, 361–1961,* Studia Anselmiana 46, 151–58. Rome, 1961.

Dudden, F. Homes. *The Life and Times of St. Ambrose.* 2 vols. Oxford, 1935.

Duval, Yvette. *Loca sanctorum Africae: Le culte des martyrs en Afrique du IVe au VIIe siècle.* Collection de l'École française de Rome 58. 2 vols. Rome, 1982.

Eco, Umberto. *Semiotics and the Philosophy of Language.* Bloomington, 1984.

Eliade, Mircea. *Patterns in Comparative Religion.* Trans. Rosemary Sheed. New York, 1958; reprint, Cleveland, 1963.

Elliott, Alison Goddard. *Roads to Paradise: Reading the Lives of the Early Saints.* Hanover, N.H., 1987.

Engemann, Josef. "Zu den Apsis-Tituli des Paulinus von Nola." *JbAC* 17 (1974): 21-46.

Ermini, Filippo. *Peristephanon: Studi Prudenziani.* Rome, 1914.

Evenepoel, Willy. *Zakelijke en literaire Onderzoekingen betreffende het Liber Cathemerinon van Aurelius Prudentius Clemens.* Verhandelingen van de k. Academie voor Wetenschappen, Letteren en schone Kunsten van België, Klasse der Letteren, Jaarg. 41, 1979, nr. 91. Brussels, 1979.

Fabre, Pierre. *Essai sur la chronologie de l'oeuvre de Saint Paulin de Nole.* Publications de la Faculté des lettres de l'Université de Strasbourg 109. Paris, 1948.

Fantham, Elaine. "Mime: The Missing Link in Roman Literary History." *CW* 82 (1989): 153-63.

Février, Paul-Albert. "Baptistères, martyrs et reliques." *RAC* 62 (1986): 109-38.

Fish, Stanley E. *Self-Consuming Artifacts: The Experience of Seventeenth-Century Literature.* Berkeley, 1972.

———. "Interpreting the *Variorum.*" *Critical Inquiry* 2 (1976): 465-85.

Fontaine, Jacques. "La pélerinage de Prudence à Saint-Pierre et la spiritualité des eaux vives." *Orpheus* 11 (1964): 243-66.

———. "Trois variations de Prudence sur le thème du Paradis." In *Forschungen zur römischen Literatur: Festschrift zum 60. Geburtstag von Karl Büchner,* ed. W. Wimmel, 96-115. Wiesbaden, 1970.

———. "Société et culture chrétiennes sur l'aire circumpyrénéenne au siècle de Théodose." *Bulletin de littérature ecclésiastique de Toulouse* (1974): 241-82.

———. "Prose et poésie: L'interférence des genres et des styles dans la création littéraire d' Ambroise de Milan." In *Ambrosius Episcopus: Atti del Congresso internazionale di studi ambrosiani . . . ,* ed. G. Lazzati, Milano 2-7 dicembre 1974, 2 vols. 1: 124-70. Milan, 1976.

———. "Romanité et hispanité dans la littérature hispano-romaine des IVe et Ve siècles." In *Travaux du VIe Congrés international d'études classiques,* ed. D. M. Pippidi, 301-22. Bucharest and Paris, 1976.

———. "La culte des martyrs militaires et son expression poétique au IVe siècle: L'idéal evangélique de la non-violence dans le christianisme théodosien." *Augustinanum* 20 (1980): 141-71.

———. *Études sur la poésie latine tardive d' Ausone à Prudence.* Paris, 1980.

———. *Naissance de la poésie dans l'occident chrétien: Esquisse d'une histoire de la poésie latine chrétienne du IIIe au VIe siècle.* Paris, 1981.

———. "Images virgiliennes de l'ascension céleste dans la poésie latine chrétienne." *JbAC,* Ergänzungsband 9: 55-67. Münster, 1982.

———. "La figure du prince dans la poésie latine chrétienne de Lactance à Prudence." In *La poesia tardoantica: Tra retorica, teologia, e politica,* Atti del V Corso della Scuola superiore di archeologia e civiltà medievali . . . , Erice 6-12 dicembre 1981, 103-32. Messina, 1984.

———. "Damase, poète théodosien: L'imaginaire poétique des epigrammata." In *Saecularia Damasiana: Atti del Convegno internazionale per il XVI centenario della morte di Papa Damaso I,* 113-45. Studi di antichità cristiana 39. Vatican City, 1986.

Franchi de' Cavalieri, Pio. "Di una probabile fonte della leggenda dei SS. Giovanni e Paolo." In *Nuove note agiografiche,* 53–65 and 68–69. Studi e testi 9. Rome, 1902.

———. "I martiri della massa candida." In *Nuove note agiografiche,* 37–51. Studi e testi 9. Rome, 1902.

———. *Hagiographica.* Studi e testi 19. Rome, 1908.

Gärtner, Hans Arnim. "Rome et les barbares dans la poésie latine au temps d'Augustin: Rutilius Namatianus et Prudence." *Ktema* 8 (1984): 113–21.

Gaudemet, Jean. *L'église dans l'empire romain (IVe-Ve siècles).* Histoire du droit et des institutions de l'église en occident 3. Paris, 1958.

Gernentz, Wilhelm. *Laudes Romae.* Rostock, 1918.

Gnilka, Christian. "Die Natursymbolik in den Tagesliedern des Prudentius." In *Pietas: Festschrift für Bernhard Kötting,* ed. E. Dassmann and K. Suso Frank, 413–46. *JbAC,* Erganzungsband 8. Münster Westfalen, 1980.

Grasso, Natale. "Prudenzio e la Bibbia." *Orpheus.* 19 (1972): 79–170.

Griffe, Élie. *La Gaule chrétienne à l'époque romaine.* 3 vols. 2d ed. (vols. 1 and 2). Paris, 1964–66.

Gussone, Nikolaus. "Adventus-Zeremoniell und Translation von Reliquien: Victricius von Rouen, De laude sanctorum." *Frühmittelalterliche Studien* 10 (1976): 125–33.

Harnack, Adolf. *Militia Christi: The Christian Religion and the Military in the First Three Centuries.* Trans. David McInnes Gracie. Philadelphia, 1981.

Harries, Jill. "Prudentius and Theodosius." *Latomus* 43 (1984): 69–84.

Haworth, Kenneth R. *Deified Virtues, Demonic Vices and Descriptive Allegory in Prudentius' Psychomachia.* Amsterdam, 1980.

Hellemo, Geir. *Adventus Domini: Eschatological Thought in 4th-Century Apses and Catecheses.* Vigiliae Christianae, suppl. 5. Leiden, 1989.

Henke, Rainer. *Studien zum Romanushymnus des Prudentius.* Europäische Hochschulschriften, Reihe 15, Klassische Sprachen und Literaturen 27. Frankfurt am Main, 1983.

———. "Die Nutzung von Senecas (Ps.-Senecas) Tragödien in Romanus-Hymnus des Prudentius." *WüJb* 11 (1985): 135–50.

Herzog, Reinhart. *Die allegorische Dichtkunst des Prudentius.* Zetemata 42. Munich, 1966.

Hoppenbrouwers, H.A.M. *Recherches sur la terminologie du martyre de Tertullien à Lactance.* Latinitas Christianorum Primaeva 15. Nijmegen, 1961.

Howell, Peter. *A Commentary on Book One of the Epigrams of Martial.* London, 1980.

Hummel, Edelhard L. *The Concept of Martyrdom According to St. Cyprian of Carthage.* Catholic University of America. Studies in Christian Antiquity 9. Washington, D.C., 1946.

Huskinson, J.M. *Concordia Apostolorum, Christian Propaganda at Rome in the Fourth and Fifth Centuries: A Study in Early Christian Iconography and Iconology.* BAR International Series 148. Oxford, 1982.

Jakobson, Roman. "Closing Statement: Linguistics and Poetics." In *Style in Language,* ed. Thomas A. Sebeok, 350–77. New York, 1960.

———. *Language in Literature.* Ed. Krystyna Pomorska and Stephen Rudy. Cambridge, MA, 1987.

Jungmann, Josef A. *The Early Liturgy to the Time of Gregory the Great.* Trans. Francis A. Brunner. Notre Dame, 1959.

Kah, Marianne. *"Die Welt der Römer mit der Seele suchend . . .": Die Religiosität des Prudentius im Spannungsfeld zwischen 'pietas christiana' und 'pietas romana.'* Hereditas 3. Bonn, 1990.

Kaster, Robert A. *Guardians of Language: The Grammarian and Society in Late Antiquity.* The Transformation of the Classical Heritage 11. Berkeley, 1988.

Keay, S.J. *Roman Spain.* Berkeley, 1988.

Kelly, J.N.D. *Jerome: His Life, Writings, and Controversies.* New York, 1975.

Kirsch, Wolfgang, *Die lateinische Versepik des 4. Jahrhunderts.* Schriften zur Geschichte und Kultur der Antike 28. Berlin, 1989.

Kitzinger, Ernst. *Byzantine Art in the Making: Main Lines of Stylistic Development in Mediterranean Art, 3rd–7th Century.* Cambridge, Mass., 1977.

Koep, Leo. *Das himmlische Buch in Antike und Christentum: eine religionsgeschichtliche Untersuchung zur altchristlichen Bildersprache.* Theophaneia 8. Bonn, 1952.

Krautheimer, Richard. *Rome: Profile of a City, 312–1308.* Princeton, 1980.

Krautheimer, Richard, Spencer Corbett, Alfred K. Frazer, and Wolfgang Frankl. *Corpus Basilicarum Christianarum Romae: The Early Christian Basilicas of Rome (IV–IX Cent.).* 5 vols. Vatican City, 1937–77.

Kroll, Josef. *Gott und Hölle: Der Mythos vom Descensuskampfe.* Studien der Bibliothek Warburg 20. Leipzig, 1932.

Kudlien, Fridoff. "Krankheitsmetaphorik im Laurentiushymnus des Prudentius." *Hermes* 90 (1962): 104–15.

Künzle, Paul. "Bemerkungen zum Lob auf Sankt Peter und Sankt Paul von Prudentius (Peristeph. XII)." *RSCI* 11 (1957): 309–70.

Lana, Italo. *Due capitoli Prudenziani: la biografia, la cronologia delle opere, la poetica.* Verba Seniorum. Collana di testi e studi patristici, n.s. 2. Rome, 1962.

Lausberg, Heinrich. *Handbuch der literarischen Rhetorik: eine Grundlegung der Literaturwissenschaft.* 2 vols. Munich, 1960.

Lavarenne, Maurice. *Étude sur la langue du poète Prudence.* Paris, 1933.

Lazzati, G. *Gli sviluppi della letteratura sui martiri nei primi quattro secoli.* Turin, 1956.

Ludwig, Walther. "Die christliche Dichtung des Prudentius und die Transformation der klassischen Gattung." In *Christianisme et formes littéraires de l'antiquité tardive en occident,* Fondation Hardt, Entretiens 23, 303–63. Vandoeuvres, 1977.

MacCormack, Sabine G. *Art and Ceremony in Late Antiquity.* The Transformation of the Classical Heritage 1. Berkeley, 1981.

———. "Loca Sancta: The Organization of Sacred Topography in Late Antiquity." In *The Blessings of Pilgrimage,* ed. Robert Ousterhout, 7–40. Urbana, Ill., 1990.

MacMullen, Ramsay. "Some Pictures in Ammianus Marcellinus." *ABull* 46 (1964): 435–55.

Madoz, José. "Valerian, Bishop of Calahorra." In *Leaders of Iberean Christianity, 50–650 A.D.*, ed. Joseph M.F. Marique, 157–63. Boston, 1962.

Mahoney, Albertus. *Vergil in the Works of Prudentius.* Catholic University of America. Patristic Studies 39. Washington, D.C., 1934.

Malamud, Martha. *A Poetics of Transformation: Prudentius and Classical Mythology.* Ithaca, N.Y., 1989.

———. "Making a Virtue of Perversity: The Poetry of Prudentius." *Ramus* 19 (1990): 64–88.

———. Review of *Prudentius on the Martyrs,* by Anne-Marie Palmer. *CPh* 86 (1991): 263–66.

Manitius, Max and Karl Manitius. *Antiker Autoren in mittelalterlichen Bibliothekskatalogen.* Beiheft zum Zentralblatt für Bibliothekswesen 67. Leipzig, 1935.

Markus, Robert. *The End of Ancient Christianity.* Cambridge, 1990.

Millar, Fergus. *The Emperor in the Roman World (31 B.C. to A.D. 337).* London, 1977.

Miscellanea Agostiniana. Testi e Studi pubblicati a cura dell'ordine eremitano di S. Agostino nel XV centenario dalla morte del santo dottore. 2 vols. Rome, 1930.

Mohrmann, Christine. "À propos de deux mots controversés de la latinité chrétienne: *tropaeum—nomen.*" *VChr* 8 (1954): 154–73 = *Études sur le latin des chrétiens. T. III Latin chrétien et liturgique,* 331–50. Rome, 1965.

Nash, Ernest. *Pictorial Dictionary of Ancient Rome.* 2 vols. New York, 1961–62.

Nauroy, Gérard. "Le martyre de Laurent dans l'hymnodie et la prédication des IVe et Ve siècles et l'authenticité ambrosienne de l'hymne 'Apostolorum supparem'." *REAug* 35 (1989): 44–82.

———. "Du combat de la piété à la confession du sang: Ambroise de Milan, lecteur critique du IVe Livre des Maccabées." *RHPhR* 70 (1990/91): 49–68.

Nielsen, Hanne Sigismund. "*Alumnus*: A Term of Relation Denoting Quasi-Adoption." *C&M* 38 (1987): 141–88.

Nisbet, R.G.M., and Margaret Hubbard. *A Commentary on Horace: Odes, Book II.* Oxford, 1978.

Nugent, S. Georgia. *Allegory and Poetics: The Structure and Imagery of Prudentius' Psychomachia.* Studien zur klassischen Philologie 14. Frankfurt am Main, 1985.

Opelt, Ilona. "Der Christenverfolger bei Prudentius." *Philologus* 111 (1967): 242–57.

———. "Prudentius und Horaz." In, *Forschungen zur römischen Literatur: Festschrift zum 60. Geburtstag Karl Büchner,* ed. W. Wimmel, 206–13. Wiesbaden, 1970.

Orselli, Alba Maria. *L'idea e il culto del santo patrono cittadino nella letteratura latina cristiana.* Università degli studi di Bologna, Facoltà di lettere e filosofia. Studi e ricerche, n.s. 12. Bologna, 1965.

Palmer, Anne-Marie. Review of *Studien zum Romanushymnus des Prudentius,* by Rainer Henke. *CR* 34 (1984): 327–28.

———. *Prudentius on the Martyrs.* Oxford, 1989.

Paschoud, François. *Roma Aeterna: Études sur le patriotisme romain dans l'occident Latin à l'époque des grandes invasions.* Bibliotheca Helvetica Romana 7. Rome, 1967.

Petruccione, John Francis. "Prudentius' Use of Martyrological Topoi in Peristephanon." Ph.D. diss., University of Michigan, 1985.

———. "The Portrait of St. Eulalia of Mérida in Prudentius' *Peristephanon* 3." *AB* 108 (1990): 81–104.

———. "Prudentius' Portrait of St. Cyprian: An Idealized Biography." *REAug* 36 (1990): 225–41.

———. "The Persecutor's Envy and the Rise of the Martyr Cult: *Peristephanon* Hymns 1 and 4." *VChr* 45 (1991): 327–46.

Pharr, Clyde. *The Theodosian Code and Novels and the Sirmondian Constitutions.* Princeton, 1952.

Pietri, Charles. "Concordia Apostolorum et Renovatio Urbis (Culte des martyrs et propagande pontificale)." *MEFR* 73 (1961): 275–322.

———. *Roma Christiana: Recherches sur l'Église de Rome, son organisation, sa politique, son idéologie, de Miltiade à Sixte III (331–440).* Bibliothèque des Écoles françaises d'Athènes et de Rome 224. 2 vols. Rome, 1976.

———. "La mort en Occident dans l'épigraphie latine: de l'épigraphie païenne à l'épitaphe chrétienne, 3e-6e siècles." *La Maison-Dieu* 144 (1980): 25–48.

———. "Les origines du culte des martyrs (d'après un ouvrage récent)." *RAC* 60 (1984): 293–319.

Pietri, Luce. *La ville de Tours du IVe siècle au VIe siècle: Naissance d'une cité chrétienne.* Collection de l'École française de Rome 69. Paris, 1983.

Puech, Aimé. *Prudence: Étude sur la poésie latine chrétienne au IVe siècle.* Paris, 1888.

Quilliet, H. "Descente de Jésus aux enfers." *DThC* 4 (1924): 565–619.

Richard, G. "L'apport de Virgile à la création épique de Prudence dans le Peristephanon liber." *Caesarodunum* 3 (1969): 187–93.

Roberts, Michael. "The Prologue to Avitus' 'De Spiritalis Historiae Gestis': Christian Poetry and Poetic License." *Traditio* 36 (1980): 399–407.

———. *Biblical Epic and Rhetorical Paraphrase in Late Antiquity.* ARCA. Classical and Medieval Texts, Papers and Monographs 16. Liverpool, 1985.

———. *The Jeweled Style: Poetry and Poetics in Late Antiquity.* Ithaca, N.Y., 1989.

———. "The Use of Myth in Latin Epithalamia from Statius to Venantius Fortunatus." *TAPA* 119 (1989): 321–48.

Rodriguez-Herrera, Isidoro. *Poeta Christianus: Prudentius' Auffassung vom Wesen und von der Aufgabe des christlichen Dichters.* Speyer, 1936.

Rolfe, J.C. *The Attic Nights of Aulus Gellius.* 3 vols. London, 1927–28.

Russell, D.A. and N.G. Wilson. *Menander Rhetor.* Oxford, 1981.

Ruysschaert, José. "Prudence l'espagnol, poète des deux basiliques romaines de S. Pierre et de S. Paul." *RAC* 42 (1968): 267–86.

Sabattini, P. Tino Alberto. "Storia e leggenda nei *Peristephanon* di Prudenzio I." *RSC* 20 (1972): 32–53.

———. "Storia e leggenda nei *Peristephanon* di Prudenzio II." *RSC* 20 (1972): 187–221.

———. "Storia e leggenda nei *Peristephanon* di Prudenzio III." *RSC* 21 (1973): 39–77.

Saller, Richard P. *Personal Patronage under the Early Empire.* Cambridge, 1982.

Sanders, Gabriel. *Licht en Duisternis in de christelijke Grafschriften: Bijdrage tot de Studie der latijnse metrische Epigrafie van de vroegchristelijke Tijd.* Verhandelingen van de k. vlaamse Academie voor Wetenschappen, Letteren en schone Kunsten von België, Klasse der Letteren, Jaarg. 27, nr. 56. 2 vols. Brussels, 1965.

———. "Les chrétiens face à l'épigraphie funéraire latine." In *Assimilation et résistance à la culture gréco-romaine dans le monde ancien,* ed. D.M. Pippidi, Travaux du VIe Congrès international d'études classiques, Madrid, September 1974, 283–99. Bucharest and Paris, 1976.

Saxer, Victor. *Morts, martyrs, reliques en Afrique chrétienne aux premiers siècles: Les témoignages de Tertullien, Cyprien, et Augustin à la lumière de l'archéologie africaine.* Théologie historique 55. Paris, 1980.

———. "Damase et le calendrier des fêtes de martyrs de l'église romaine." In *Saecularia Damasiana: Atti del Convegno internazionale per il XVI centenario della morte di Papa Damaso I,* 59–88. Studi di antichità cristiana, 39. Vatican City, 1986.

———. "La passion de S. Vincent diacre dans la première moitié du Ve siècle: Essai de reconstitution." *REAug* 35 (1989): 275–97.

Scarry, Elaine. *The Body in Pain: The Making and Unmaking of the World.* New York, 1985.

Schetter, Willy. "Prudentius, *Peristephanon* 8." *Hermes* 110 (1982): 110–17.

Schmid, J. "Brautschaft, heilige." *RlAC* 2 (1954): 528–64.

Schwen, Christian. *Vergil bei Prudentius.* Leipzig, 1937.

Shanzer, Danuta. "Allegory and Reality: Spes, Victoria and the Date of Prudentius' *Psychomachia.*" *ICS* 14 (1989): 347–63.

———. "The Date and Composition of Prudentius' *Contra Orationem Symmachi Libri.*" *RFIC* 117 (1989): 442–62.

Simonetti, Manlio. "Studi sull' innologia popolare cristiana dei primi secoli." *MAL* ser. 8a, 4, 6 (1952): 341–484.

Sixt, G. "Des Prudentius' Abhängigkeit von Seneca und Lucan." *Philologus* 51 (1892): 501–6.

Smith, Christine. "Pope Damasus' Baptistery in St. Peter's Reconsidered." *RAC* 64 (1988): 257–86.

Smith, Jonathan Z. *To Take Place: Toward Theory in Ritual.* Chicago, 1987.

Smith, Macklin. *Prudentius' Psychomachia: A Reexamination.* Princeton, 1976.

Springer, Avery R. "Prudentius, Pilgrim and Poet: The Catacombs and Their Paintings As Inspiration for the Liber Cathemerinon." Ph.D. diss., University of Wisconsin at Madison, 1984.

Ste. Croix, G.E.M. de. "Suffragium: From Vote to Patronage." *British Journal Of Sociology* 5 (1954): 33–48.

Syndikus, Hans Peter. *Die Lyrik des Horaz: Eine Interpretation der Oden.* Impulse der Forschung 7. 2 vols. Darmstadt, 1973.

Testini, Pasquale. "Di alcune testimonianze relative a Ippolito." In *Ricerche su Ippolito,* Studia Ephemeridis "Augustinianum" 13, 45–65. Rome, 1977.

———. *Archeologia cristiana: Nozioni generali dalle origini alla fine del sec. VI.* 2d ed. Bari, 1980.

———. "Note per servire allo studio del complesso paleocristiano di S. Felice a Cimitile (Nola)." *MEFR(A)* 97 (1985): 329–71.

Thraede, Klaus. "Untersuchungen zum Ursprung und zur Geschichte der christlichen Poesie II." *JbAC* 5 (1962): 125–57.

———. *Studien zu Sprache und Stil des Prudentius.* Hypomnemata 13. Göttingen, 1965.

———. "Rom und der Märtyrer in Prudentius, Peristephanon 2, 1–20." In *Romanitas et Christianitas: Studia Iano Henrico Waszink . . . oblata,* ed. W. den Boer, P.G. Van der Nat, C.M.J. Sicking, and J.C.M. van Winden, 317–27. Amsterdam, 1973.

Tompkins, Jane P., ed. *Reader-Response Criticism: From Formalism to Post-Structuralism.* Baltimore, 1980.

Toynbee, Jocelyn M.C. "*Roma* and *Constantinopolis* in Late-Antique Art from 365 to Justin II." In *Studies Presented to David Moore Robinson on His Seventieth Birthday,* ed. George E. Mylonas, 2 vols., 2: 261–77. Saint Louis, 1951–53.

Toynbee, Jocelyn, and John Ward Perkins. *The Shrine of St. Peter and the Vatican Excavations.* London, 1956.

Turner, Victor. *The Ritual Process: Structure and Anti-Structure.* Chicago, 1969.

———. *Process, Performance and Pilgrimage: A Study in Comparative Symbology.* Ranchi Anthropology Series 1. New Delhi, 1979.

Van Assendelft, Marion M. *Sol Ecce Surgit Igneus: A Commentary on the Morning and Evening Hymns of Prudentius (Cathemerinon 1,2,5, and 6).* Groningen, 1976.

Van Dam, Raymond. *Leadership and Community in Late Antique Gaul.* The Transformation of the Classical Heritage 8. Berkeley, 1985.

Van der Meer, F. *Augustine the Bishop: The Life and Work of a Father of the Church.* Trans. Brian Battershaw and G.R. Lamb. London, 1961.

Verbraken, Pierre-Patrick, *Études critiques sur les sermons authentiques de saint Augustin.* Instrumenta Patristica 12. Steenbrugge, 1976.

Vergote, J. "Folterwerkzeuge." *RlAC* 8 (1972): 112–41.

Vest, Eugene Bartlett. "Prudentius in the Middle Ages." Ph.D. diss., Harvard University, 1932.

Wheatley, Paul. *The Pivot of the Four Quarters.* Chicago, 1971.

Wiseman, T.P. "Practice and Theory in Roman Historiography." *History* 66 (1981): 375–93.

———. *Catullus and His World: A Reappraisal.* Cambridge, 1985.

Witke, Charles. *Numen Litterarum: The Old and the New in Latin Poetry from Constantine to Gregory the Great*. Mittellateinische Studien und Texte 5. Leiden, 1971.

Woodman, A.J. *Rhetoric in Classical Historiography: Four Studies*. London, 1988.

Text Editions Used

Ambrose. *De officiis ministrorum. PL* 16: 22–194.
———. *Les Devoirs,* ed. Maurice Testard. Paris, 1984– .
———. *Epistularum liber decimus,* ed. Michaela Zelzer. *CSEL* 82. Vienna, 1982.
———. *Hymni.* In *Hymni Latini Antiquissimi LXXV, Psalmi III,* ed. Walther Bulst, 37–52. Heidelberg, 1956.
Augustine. *De civitate dei,* ed. Emanuel Hoffmann. *CSEL* 40. 2 vols. Vienna, 1899–1900.
———. *Enarrationes in psalmos,* ed. E. Dekkers and J. Fraipont. *CCL* 38–40. Brepols, 1956.
———. *Sermones. PL* 38.
———. *Sermones post Maurinos reperti,* ed. G. Morin. *MA* 1. Rome, 1930.
Aulus Gellius. *Noctes Atticae,* ed. P.K. Marshall. 2 vols. Oxford, 1968.
Ausonius. *Opera,* ed. Sesto Prete. Leipzig, 1978.
———. *The Works,* ed. R.P.H. Green. Oxford, 1991.
Bible. See *Vetus Latina, Vulgate.*
Claudian. *Carmina,* ed. John Barrie Hall. Leipzig, 1985.
Cyprian. *Opera omnia,* ed. Wilhelm von Hartel. *CSEL* 3. 3 vols. Vienna, 1868–71.
Damasus. *Epigrammata Damasiana,* ed. Antonio Ferrua. Vatican City, 1942.
Gaudentius of Brescia. *Sermones. PL* 20: 791–1002.
Horace. *Opera,* ed. Friedrich Klingner. 3d ed. Leipzig, 1959.
Leo the Great, Pope. *Sermones. PL* 54.
Lucretius. *De rerum natura libri sex,* ed. Cyril Bailey. 3 vols. Oxford, 1947.
Menander Rhetor. Ed. D.A. Russell and N.G. Wilson. Oxford, 1981.
Ovid. *Metamorphoses,* ed. William S. Anderson. Leipzig, 1977.
Passio Sanctorum Martyrum Fructuosi Episcopi, Auguri et Eulogi Diaconorum. In *The Acts of the Christian Martyrs,* ed. Herbert Musurillo, 176–85. Oxford, 1972.
Paulinus of Nola. *Carmina,* ed. Wilhelm von Hartel. *CSEL* 30. Vienna, 1894.
———. *Epistulae,* ed. Wilhelm von Hartel. *CSEL* 29. Vienna, 1894.
Prudentius. Ed. F. Araévalo. *PL* 59: 567–60: 596.
———. *Carmina,* ed. J. Bergman. *CSEL* 61. Vienna, 1926.

———. *Carmina,* ed. Maurice P. Cunningham. *CCL* 126. Turnhout, 1966.

———. *Oeuvres,* ed. M. Lavarenne. 4 vols. 2d ed. Paris 1955–63.

Rutilius Namatianus. *De reditu suo sive iter Gallicum,* ed. Ernst Doblhofer. 2 vols. Heidelberg, 1972–77.

Sallust. *Catilina, Iugurtha, fragmenta ampliora,* ed. Alphonsus Kurfess. 3d ed. Leipzig, 1956.

Sidonius Apollinaris. *Opera,* ed. André Loyen. 3 vols. Paris, 1960–70.

Silius Italicus. *Punica,* ed. Joseph Delz. Stuttgart, 1987.

Vetus Latina. *Bibliorum sacrorum Latinae versiones antiquae seu vetus Italica . . . ,* ed. P. Sabatier. 3 vols. Reims, 1743.

———. *Itala: Das Neue Testament in altlateinischer Überlieferung,* ed. Adolf Jülicher. 4 vols. Berlin, 1938–63.

———. *Vetus Latina: Die Reste der altlateinischen Bibel. 2. Genesis,* ed. Bonifatius Fischer. Freiburg, 1951–54.

Victricius of Rouen. *De Laude Sanctorum. PL* 20: 437–58.

Virgil. *Opera,* ed. R.A.B. Mynors. Oxford, 1969.

Vulgate. *Biblia sacra iuxta vulgatam versionem,* ed. Robert Weber. 2 vols. 2d ed. Stuttgart, 1975.

Index

Index Locorum